PRAISE FOR KELLI BRONSKI AND PETER BRONSKI'S

[ARTISANAL GLUTEN-FREE COOKING]

"In this outstanding volume of 250 recipes, Kelli and Peter Bronski share tips, tricks, and favorite dishes . . . While recipes are uniformly excellent, Asian dishes are particularly toothsome . . . Gluten dodgers will also be pleased with the Bronskis' pizza recipes . . . The duo seem to have thought of every craving and indulgence, serving up crème brulée and cocktails, too; it's also worth noting that plenty of recipes don't call for special ingredients at all . . . This volume's impressive breadth and straightforward instructions make it an essential, horizon-broadening tool for those off gluten."
—*Publishers Weekly*, **starred review**

"*Artisanal Gluten-Free Cooking* by Kelli Bronski and Peter Bronski focuses on simple, from-scratch home cooking. Along with loads of easy-to-follow, family-friendly recipes, the Bronskis have also developed a gluten-free flour blend that truly tastes delicious (I can vouch for the apple pie!). A guide to navigating the supermarket, product recommendations, and gluten-free resources make this book a useful and informative addition to your cooking arsenal."
—*The Oregonian*

"An indispensable guide for the creation of tasty meals."
—*Long Island Pulse* **magazine**

"Treat yourself to a delicious gluten-free culinary excursion for any meal of the day with *Artisanal Gluten-Free Cooking*. Celebrating sweet and savory scratch-recipe traditions, Kelli and Peter Bronski feature a must-have treasury of recipes that anyone can savor. This book connects you with the true essence of artisanal gluten-free living. Enjoy!"
—**SUZANNE BOWLAND, founder and executive producer, GF Culinary Productions, Inc./ The Gluten-Free Culinary Summit™**

THE EXPERIMENT

BECAUSE EVERY BOOK IS A TEST OF NEW IDEAS

"Like no other gluten-free cookbook, Pete and Kelli's *Artisanal Gluten-Free Cooking* touches on the essential elements of why food, culinary culture, and family traditions are so important. What we eat is part of who we are. When a diagnosis of celiac disease or gluten sensitivity forces us to eliminate a key ingredient, preparing our favorite meals can become difficult and frustrating. This book reminds us that all we need are fresh, wholesome ingredients and a little creative guidance. Thank you, Pete and Kelli, for providing that guidance. The principles of good cooking, complete with mouth-watering recipes, are woven throughout the pages of this book. Oh, and they just happen to be deliciously gluten-free!"
—MELISSA MCLEAN JORY, MNT

"Kelli and Peter Bronski have made more than an amazing gluten-free cookbook.
They've made an amazing cookbook all the way around, gluten-free or not.
This cookbook is about more than great gluten-free food. It's about great food, period."
—ELISE WIGGINS, executive chef, Panzano, Denver, Colorado

"*Artisanal Gluten-Free Cooking* is a true delight. It's filled with uncomplicated recipes you'll want to make—whether you eat gluten-free or not. But, my favorite aspect is that the authors share their history with each dish . . . like homemade French fries using mom's method; a unique scallop dish first tasted when dining out, now improved and shared annually with college friends; or a lemon syrup–infused poppy seed bread inspired by a vendor from the local farmer's market. We all have those histories, don't we? Great food is about so much more than the food itself. You'll want this cookbook on your kitchen shelf, so you can create your own memories with these dishes."
—SHIRLEY BRADEN, author/owner, gfe—gluten free easily blog (http://glutenfreeeasily.com)
and leader, King George Gluten Intolerance and Celiac Group (KGGICG)

"Kudos to Kelli and Peter Bronski! I was impressed and, more importantly, genuinely entertained by *Artisanal Gluten-Free Cooking*. Peppered with great information throughout—from world food trivia to essential kitchen advice—this cookbook reads as if an old friend is talking you through a cherished family recipe over the phone. Filled with intuitive, straightforward, and delicious dishes, the recipes will empower any passionate cook to create seasonal, healthy, and 'from-scratch' dishes with the added bonus of avoiding gluten. This is a must-buy for anyone who hosts frequently, and certainly a no-brainer for those following a gluten-free diet."
—EDUARDO PORTO CARREIRO, sommelier/wine director, Grace restaurant, Los Angeles

"Whether you are new to the gluten-free diet or have been gluten-free for years, *Artisanal Gluten-Free Cooking* is a must-have guidebook. Kelli and Peter Bronski share an impressive compilation of mouthwatering gluten-free recipes, as well as sage advice on successfully navigating and maintaining the gluten-free diet."
—MAUREEN STANLEY, founder, Hold the Gluten blog and podcast

"Of the many cookbooks that I have received to add to our support group library, *Artisanal Gluten-Free Cooking* is the first one that I sat down with and went through, cover to cover. That is partly because I found the format and the presentation so appealing, and also because the recipes just sounded so darn good. Like you, I love cilantro, garlic, and many of the other ingredients that you use in your recipes—and I appreciate that you don't require too many exotic ingredients. I think you have a winner on your hands!"
—GLORIAN BEESON, Gluten Free in San Diego

"A whole book of doable, mostly simple recipes that anyone can cook. They have all kinds of familiar foods in here that I always want to make but need a good recipe . . . You can make all kinds of goodies with this quite extraordinary cookbook. It would be great for anyone, but especially for a newly diagnosed celiac who may be struggling with menu ideas and how to make them on their own. Trust me, you won't be disappointed in this cookbook. It's worth having on your shelf just for the pastry dough recipe."
—MARGO ANDERSEN, founder, Off the Wheaten Path blog

"This book is inspiring, personable, friendly, and makes you want to cook. You'll want to go to Peter and Kelli's for dinner, too. Recipes are easy, and not intimidating."
—STEVE ZEIDEN, Gluten Free Steve

"A cookbook with recipes that actually make me want to learn how to cook . . . The cookbook for those of us who might not know how to cook, but who want to learn."
—JENNIFER HARRIS, Examiner.com

"Your cookbook arrived yesterday and I must tell you, IT IS GREAT! I love to cook and have over 100 cookbooks, and probably 20 gluten-free cookbooks, but yours is the best! I'm impressed with the variety of everyday foods made with fresh ingredients and the pictures—beautiful!"
—ROSE CRUIKSHANK, RN, Augusta Gluten Intolerance Group

"I love how Kelli and Peter have taken international foods and shown how to make them gluten-free!"
—JANET HEITLER, Tampa Bay Celiacs

"Lots of good information—especially for new celiacs. Your recipes are outstanding!"
—JANE TREVETT, Greater New Haven Celiac Group

"The recipes that intrigue me most are the variety of pizza recipes . . . yes, I said variety!!! Get this . . . Deep Dish, Thin Crust, New York–Style, Chicago-Style . . . PIZZA!"
—Gluten Free Foodies blog

"The snickerdoodle recipe reminds me of the ones I used to make before I had to go gluten-free. Yum!"
—Gayle in Wyoming

"This is a seriously good book. I love it! The tacos were AWESOME! Last night I made the chicken cordon bleu. Very good. The sauce was delicious."
—Amanda in Hawaii

"I just made your mozzarella sticks. The kids loved them. [My husband] and I found them as good as any we had gotten at restaurants in our pre-gluten-free days."
—Cheryl in Maine

KELLI BRONSKI AND PETER BRONSKI

ARTISANAL
GLUTEN-FREE
COOKING

More than 250 Great-Tasting, From-Scratch Recipes from
Around the World, Perfect for Every Meal and for Anyone
on a Gluten-Free Diet—and Even Those Who Aren't

THE EXPERIMENT

NEW YORK

The Experiment, LLC
260 Fifth Avenue
New York, NY 10001–6408
www.theexperimentpublishing.com

Many of the designations used by manufacturers and sellers to distinguish their products are claimed as trademarks. Where those designations appear in this book and The Experiment was aware of a trademark claim, the designations have been printed in initial capital letters.

This book contains the opinions and ideas of its authors. It is intended to provide helpful and informative material on the subjects addressed in the book. It is sold with the understanding that the author and the publisher are not engaged in rendering medical, health, or any other kind of personal professional services in the book. The reader should consult his or her medical, health, or other competent professional before adopting any of the suggestions in this book or drawing inferences from it. The authors and publisher specifically disclaim all responsibility for any liability, loss, or risk—personal or otherwise—which is incurred as a consequence, directly or indirectly, of the use and application of any of the contents of this book.

Library of Congress Control Number: 2009927865
ISBN 978-1-61519-003-4
Ebook ISBN 978-1-61519-107-9

Cover design by Susi Oberhelman
Cover photograph by Stock Food / Janne Peters, photographer

Design by Pauline Neuwirth, Neuwirth & Associates, Inc.

Manufactured in the United States of America
First printing October 2009
10 9 8 7 6

To our daughter, Marin

CONTENTS

ARTISANAL

GLUTEN-FREE

COOKING

THE GLUTEN-FREE JOURNEY

GLUTEN, A FAMILY of proteins found in wheat, barley, and rye, is pervasive in American cooking and eating. At first glance, it's everywhere we look: bread, pasta, cake, beer, cereal, pizza . . . and the list goes on. If cells are the building blocks of life, then gluten might rightly (and unfortunately) be called the building block of the average American diet.

Maybe it's for that reason that, for many people, the shift to a gluten-free diet can be an abrupt and jarring one. One moment you're enjoying every food under the sun, and the next moment your gastronomic world has shrunk considerably as many of those foods suddenly become off-limits. The supermarket looks a lot smaller when 90 percent of the aisles are a no-buy zone.

People adopt a gluten-free diet for a variety of reasons—to mitigate the symptoms of autism, attention deficit hyperactivity disorder, and multiple sclerosis, for example. But most find their way to gluten-free living through a diagnosis of celiac disease (an autoimmune disorder of the small intestine), gluten intolerance, or a wheat allergy.

So it was for me. Though I was diagnosed with lactose intolerance at birth, and have remained so since, merely avoiding lactose never solved all my problems with food. However, over a two-year period from 2005 until early 2007, my condition grew dramatically worse. Desperate for answers, I began seeing a new doctor, a holistic practitioner who combined Eastern and Western medicine. After explaining my symptoms and frustrations during my first visit, he looked me squarely in the eye: "Your problem is gluten," he said.

Subsequent visits confirmed his initial suspicion. I was immediately placed on a lifelong gluten-free diet. Not that I knew what that meant, exactly. Admittedly, gluten was a new word in my vocabulary. But once I understood what gluten was and how to avoid it, and then modified my diet accordingly, the shift was nothing short of remarkable.

Within two weeks of going gluten-free, I felt healthier than I had in literally ten years. I hadn't even realized that I had recalibrated what "normal" meant. For far too long, normal equated to being sick. Now, I was healthy. I remember sitting on the couch in the living room with my wife, Kelli. "You know when it's so quiet that your ears feel like it's loud?" I asked. "That's how my body feels." I was so absent of symptoms that it was conspicuous and noticeable. And wonderful.

In this sense, a diagnosis with celiac disease or gluten intolerance can be a relief. A diagnosis is an answer. Finally, we are empowered to do something about our own health. We know the cause of the problem, have the capability to control what we eat, and in the process, can make food work for our body, instead of against it.

Not that it's always as simple as that. The gluten-free diet can have a steep learning curve, and it's a lesson that Kelli and I learned firsthand, particularly in the beginning. We had some successes, for sure, but also some spectacular failures.

An early experiment with gluten-free pizza immediately comes to mind. Often on Sunday nights, Kelli and I would make homemade pizza for dinner. Thinking that a gluten-free pizza dough box mix from the grocery store would be a good entry into the gluten-free cooking world, we bought a box at random and took it home. In our typical division of labor in the kitchen, Kelli would make the pizza dough, and I'd make my pizza sauce, shape the dough, and pop the pizza in the oven. As I prepared the sauce, Kelli made the dough in our mixer. "The pizza dough is ready for you," she called over to me.

Peering into the mixing bowl of our KitchenAid, I saw a batter that had the look and consistency of cake frosting. "How am I supposed to shape that into a pizza?" I asked.

"You're not. You plop it into a pan and spread it with a spatula."

The Sicilian part of my heritage recoiled in horror. Using a spatula to make a pizza felt so . . . wrong. But determined, we persevered, dutifully par-baking the crust, adding the sauce, mozzarella cheese, and toppings, and finishing the pizza in the oven. The result was . . . interesting. The crust had puffed up to twice the height of a slice of Sicilian pizza, and had the texture of sponge cake. The flavor, meanwhile, was so undesirable that Kelli couldn't finish her first slice of pizza, and I couldn't finish my second.

There had to be a better way, we thought. And finding a better way was important. Not only for the sake of taste and texture. There was much more at stake. For one, I'm a Long Island boy; a New York native born into a Sicilian, Belgian, and Polish family.

From a culinary perspective, that means I love certain foods. Things like beer, pasta, bagels, thin-crust pizza, cannoli . . . you get the idea. These foods are in part how I form my personal identity—they are a connection to place, to family, to heritage. Losing such foods would necessarily also mean a loss of part of me.

Such a sense of loss is common among people who have abruptly—even unexpectedly—switched to a gluten-free diet. And it's not uncommon, or unreasonable, for us to go through a period of mourning. I remember talking with a couple—friends of my mother- and father-in law—at a family party shortly after my diagnosis. "Our daughter-in-law was diagnosed with celiac disease," they explained. "She got so depressed she's seeing a psychiatrist." Really? Is this what I had to look forward to? A life of sacrifice? Of giving up the foods that have meant so much to me? A life of one-hour sessions spent on the couch of a psychotherapist explaining the emotional trauma and lamentations of my dietary hardships?

The hardship and sense of loss weren't mine alone. They also affected Kelli. Though she has no problems ingesting gluten, she willingly and voluntarily adopted a gluten-free diet as well. Part of her reasoning was romantic—as a young married couple, we wanted to cook and eat dinners together, rather than prepare separate meals for her and me. But part of Kelli's reasoning was also pragmatic—by taking the gluten out of our kitchen at home, we basically eliminated the potential for cross-contamination that would make me sick. Kelli going gluten-free was an act of love, and I recognized how difficult it must have been in the beginning. One of her great passions in life is baking, and any baker will tell you that one of their single most powerful tools in the kitchen is gluten. Without gluten, baking becomes an unbelievably difficult and frustrating endeavor (or so we once thought).

Even with Kelli by my side, there were times when being gluten-free felt lonely, isolating. Some people have described feeling like a social outcast, unable to join friends in a round of beers at the local pub.

Others feel awkwardly conspicuous trying to explain their dietary restrictions when invited to a friend's house for dinner. Still others understandably agonize over meals eaten at restaurants, waiting to see whether or not they get sick in the wake of eating.

It's been infinitely helpful to realize, though, that I'm not—and you're not—alone. Psychotherapy and counseling sessions are not needed. An estimated 1 in 133 Americans have celiac disease, whether they're formally diagnosed or not. Many more have gluten intolerance. And still more adhere to a gluten-free diet. There are support groups, restaurants with gluten-free menus, gluten-free sections of supermarkets, and gluten-free cookbooks like this one. Indeed, it's a better time than ever to be gluten-free.

And in this twenty-first-century world of citizen journalism and the Internet, we also have a community of gluten-free blogs and bloggers. They are people who share their experiences with gluten-free living, everything from restaurant and product reviews to recipes, photos, and stories. Kelli and I became a part of that blogging community in July, 2008, when we unveiled No Gluten, No Problem (http://noglutennoproblem.blogspot.com). In nine short months, we went from no readers to roughly 1,000 readers per month.

Motivated by a deeply held conviction to eat well and gluten-free and to maintain a culinary connection to my heritage, and also bolstered by the motivational support of the community of people who regularly read our blog, we determined to overcome the challenges of gluten-free cooking. Gluten-free living didn't have to be difficult, or isolating, or a second-rate experience of food and culture. We wanted not only to survive gluten-free, but to thrive gluten-free. We wanted to enjoy gluten-free versions of our beloved foods . . . things like lasagna and waffles and other foods that in their traditional forms would be off-limits. And we wanted to do it well. We wanted the food to taste delicious, to have good texture, and to be indistinguishable (or nearly so) from the gluten versions.

Now, nearly three years after first switching to a gluten-free diet, I can happily report that we've succeeded. Cooking and eating with no gluten is no problem.

As we've traveled along this culinary journey, we've also found unexpected joys in the gluten-free diet.

For one, as we have had to reacquaint ourselves with the kitchen and to learn anew how to develop recipes and utilize ingredients, the gluten-free diet has deepened our passion for cooking and baking.

Second, we're much healthier thanks to the gluten-free diet. By eliminating almost all of the processed (and often, gluten-containing) foods so prevalent in the American diet, and by sticking mostly to fresh fruits and vegetables and whole meats and fish, we've improved our health in ways that reach beyond merely avoiding the symptoms and consequences of ingesting gluten.

Third, through gluten-free cooking, we've more tangibly touched our family roots, in a sense memorializing our grandparents and great-grandparents by bringing them into the kitchen with us. You see, for us, gluten-free cooking also means from-scratch cooking, and scratch cooking is nostalgic. It's a return to an earlier way of cooking and eating. It's a return to our grandparents' and great-grandparents' way. It's an approach to food defined more by culture and family tradition than by diets and medical research and prepared foods and the science of eating and the science of making processed food.

Fourth, we've gained power. A scratch-cooking approach to the gluten-free lifestyle gives you absolute control over what is in your food. This is significant not only for ensuring that meals are gluten-free but also in terms of being able to decide whether or not they are filled with preservatives or loaded with sodium or sugar, and in terms of deciding about the foods' origins and quality.

Perhaps the simplest way to say all this is to say that gluten-free cooking has given us a more intimate relationship with our food. We are more directly connected to the issues of what we eat and why.

The questions of what we eat and why are important ones to Kelli and me. Long before we switched to the gluten-free lifestyle, the answers to such questions informed our decisions in the kitchen. We cooked then—and continue to cook now—using fresh, local, seasonal ingredients whenever possible. For produce, that means trips to our local farmers' market starting in spring and continuing through summer and into fall, and opting for Colorado Proud produce (locally grown fruits and vegetables) at our supermarket when it's available. For meat, it means buying our steaks from a local rancher and, when it comes to other meats, choosing a supplier based not only on the quality of the meat but also on the natural, humane conditions in which the animals are raised and ultimately slaughtered. (For further reading on the topic, we recommend the eloquent, detailed and well-informed *The Omnivore's Dilemma*, by Michael Pollan, who—like me—coincidentally hails from the town of Farmingdale, New York, on Long Island.)

Based on the preceding paragraph, some people would rightly put us into the locavore category of eaters. But that's only part of our story. Each person's gastronomic identity is like a fingerprint—no two are alike. And the collective identity of Kelli and me is multilayered. Importantly, it is a reflection of who we are, and it informs the collection of recipes you'll find within these pages. It of course includes a central gluten-free component, and a strong locavore tendency. But it also includes our combined cultural heritage, and the heirloom recipes of our families. As a result, you'll find dishes ranging from a Flemish beer roast (Carbonnade) to an Italian lasagna to a Polish pastry (Mock cake). It also reflects our American upbringing. Thanks to that element, you'll also find recipes like apple and pumpkin pie, and roasted turkey, along with mashed potatoes, gravy, and stuffing. And it also reflects our passion for travel, which yields culinary creations ranging from Asian to Indian to Mexican to Andean. And, it must be said, it reflects my lifelong lactose intolerance. As a result, you won't find many dishes that are heavy on the cheese or

milk, and when they are used they tend to be mild, as with the mozzarella cheese on pizza (although Kelli's love of dairy does shine through in recipes such as crème brûlée, flan, and pastry cream on a fruit tart).

For the vegetarians out there, we do admittedly cook with meat in many of our entrées—but we also include meat-free variations for many of these recipes. We tell you how you can easily make the dishes vegetarian by simply omitting the meat (as with the Meat Lovers' Lasagna), by substituting suitable veggies (such as portobello mushroom in lieu of a beefsteak, or eggplant in lieu of chicken for the Chicken Parmesan), by using tofu in many of the Asian dishes, or by combining chickpeas with rice for a complete protein (as in the Indian Red Curry).

As varied as the recipes in this book are, they all do share a common thread, beyond their being gluten-free. They are *artisanal*. They are from-scratch, delicious recipes made with fresh, quality ingredients. But they're more than that, too. They are acts of love—love of cooking, love of food, love of life and culture, and love of sharing with others . . . sharing with you.

At this point, I feel compelled to offer a disclaimer of sorts. *Artisanal* may have one meaning for one person, and quite another meaning for a different person. We think that's okay. As with the locavore movement, there are many shades of gray. If your goal as a locavore is to drink a glass of homemade apple cider, is it enough to buy cider made from local apples, or should you use raw apples and make the cider yourself? And if you use raw apples, should you grow them yourself, or buy local apples? And if you buy local apples, how local is local enough? Ten miles? One hundred miles? More?

There isn't a right or wrong answer, I think. Artisanal gluten-free cooking is the same way. This book represents *our* version of artisanal gluten-free cooking, but you can make the recipes more or less so, according to your preferences. (And, in fact, throughout the book we offer shortcuts for how to use store-bought, premade ingredients to expedite some of the recipes.) We sincerely hope, though, that you'll discover—as we did—the pleasures of cooking artisanally. And please . . . while we describe our cooking as artisanal, it's definitely not pretentious. Cooking should be fun—we don't take ourselves, or our recipes, too seriously.

To use a well-worn phrase, we're big advocates of "the joy of cooking" (which is also the title of a classic cookbook). Too often, though, that joy is lost for people on a gluten-free diet. Quite frankly, they often lose both the joy of cooking *and* the joy of eating. Our ultimate goal is for readers like you to regain both. The best compliment I think we ever received was in the days following a cooking demonstration we did at a Whole Foods near Denver where we demonstrated our Belgian waffle recipe. One of the attendees sent an e-mail that simply said, "You've made me love breakfast again." If this cookbook exists for no other reason, it exists for that one—to help people on a gluten-free diet love the food they cook and eat.

And so, on behalf of Kelli and me—and in the words of my Belgian grandmother and Sicilian grandfather, respectively—we say to you, *bon appetit* and *mangia*!

—*Peter Bronski, 2009*

SAFELY NAVIGATING THE SUPERMARKET

By SOME ESTIMATES, there are more than 3,000 products on the market today that make gluten-free claims. That number doesn't begin to capture the many more that are naturally gluten-free but aren't specifically labeled as such. Then consider that, according to the Food Marketing Institute, the average supermarket in the United States carried some 45,000 products in 2006. How are you to know what is and is not safe to buy? The supermarket can be a gluten gauntlet, and navigating those waters can get murky at times.

First, remember that **fresh fruits and vegetables, whole meats and fish, as well as corn, rice, and potatoes are all naturally gluten-free.** Hence, **Rule #1: Avoid the center aisles of the supermarket, and instead focus your shopping on the periphery of the store, where you usually find the produce and meat sections.**

Second, remember that **wheat, barley, and rye are the offending grains.** They are strictly off-limits. So are products made from them—**the traditional forms of bread, pasta, cake, pizza, flour, pastries, cookies, cereal, etc.** (There are, however, a number of alternative, gluten-free grains worth trying. The most widely available may be buckwheat, which is unfortunately named, because it has no relation to wheat. There's also quinoa, a high-protein grain from the Andes that we are particularly fond of, and a long list of others . . . sorghum, millet, rice, etc.) Beyond the traditional products listed above, gluten also has a way of hiding in an astonishing number of processed foods, and where you might not normally assume you'd find it. Start reading ingredient labels, and you'll often find gluten—in one form or another—in everything ranging from hot dogs to malt vinegar to chicken broth to yogurt to imitation crab meat. Thus, **Rule #2: Always read the ingredients label on any products you buy to ensure they are free of gluten.**

Which brings us to the vitally important topic of product labeling. At present, food labeling is regulated by the United States Food and Drug Administration (FDA), and ingredient labels have been required for many years. If you look past all the complicated and very "chemistry kit" sounding names of ingredients found in most processed foods, then reading ingredient labels is straightforward: ingredients are listed in descending order according to their presence in the product, as measured by their weight.

In recent years, as awareness about food allergies has grown, new regulations have expanded the requirements of food labeling. Most significant is the Food Allergen Labeling and Consumer Protection Act of 2004 (FALCPA). The legislation identified eight major allergens, one of which is wheat, and requires foods containing any of those allergens to declare them in a statement following the ingredients label (for example, "Contains: wheat"). Knowing if wheat is and isn't in a particular food has proven very useful in answering the "does this have gluten?" question. But since gluten also comes from barley and rye, which aren't included in the list of main allergens, it's not a foolproof method.

In addition, while FALCPA requires manufacturers to declare what *is* in their products, it doesn't require manufacturers to declare what *might* be in their products. This is known as advisory labeling, and some companies voluntarily make such declarations when there's a concern about cross-contamination with a major allergen (for example, "May contain: wheat," or "Processed in a facility [or on machinery] that also processes wheat"). While very helpful, it's not as reliable as a hard and fast labeling regulation since advisory labeling is voluntary.

And what about those 3,000-plus products that are labeled "gluten-free?" As of this writing, *gluten-free* is an unregulated term in the United States. This means that all those companies labeling their products as such are doing so voluntarily, and they're applying their own varying standards in terms of what it means for a food to be gluten-free. For consumers, this is troubling. For example, we've seen more than a few products that are labeled "gluten-free," but that also contain an advisory statement—"May contain: wheat"—following the ingredient list. To many people on a gluten-free diet, these two statements are contradictory. A food could be one or the other, but not both.

The reality is that foods labeled "gluten-free" are not all created equal, and have differing levels of risk for gluten cross-contamination, ranging from extremely unlikely to quite possible. There are three basic scenarios that we like to call Possible Gluten Contamination Threat Levels: Green, Yellow, and Red. First, a product could be made in a dedicated gluten-free facility. This is the best-case scenario, Code Green.

Second, a product could be made on a dedicated gluten-free production line, but in a facility that also processes wheat or other gluten cross-contaminants. This is less desirable, Code Yellow. Lastly, a gluten-free product could be made on a shared production line that is also used for wheat or other gluten cross-contaminants (in theory with the production line appropriately cleaned in between each product). This is the least desirable scenario, Code Red. However, this type of information is not always available on product labels, and getting to the bottom of things might require a few inquiries to a company's Web site or customer service department.

It's been said that knowledge is power, and having greater transparency about the production of a gluten-free product would allow consumers to individually decide how much risk is acceptable in terms of possible cross-contamination of a product labeled as "gluten-free." Until "gluten-free" is defined, standardized, and regulated, to a degree we're at the mercy of the companies and their individual labeling policies.

Thankfully, change in that regard is coming. The same FALCPA that mandated allergen labeling also charged the FDA with establishing a gluten-free labeling protocol for the United States. Although that process should have been concluded in August, 2008, delays have pushed back the date. However, a gluten-free labeling standard is coming. As with many countries that already have such standards—including Canada, Italy, Australia, and New Zealand—the U.S. standard will be largely based on the recommendations of the Codex Alimentarius Commission, a joint effort of the Food and Agriculture Organization of the United Nations and the World Health Organization to set international food standards in the interest of protecting the health of consumers.

But while the U.S. standard, and other countries' standards, share a common background in the Codex Alimentarius recommendations, they also all differ from one another, sometimes in small ways, sometimes big. This complicates the importing of gluten-free products from one country to another, not to mention understanding gluten-free labeling when traveling abroad. Even so, a U.S. standard is a welcome and overdue development. Until that standard becomes official, though, it's best to abide **by Rule #3: Gluten-free and allergen labeling are helpful, but be your own best advocate. Remember that, for now, both advisory labeling and gluten-free labeling are voluntary and unregulated in the United States.** *If concerned about possible gluten cross-contamination, never hesitate to contact a company to inquire.*

In the absence of a U.S. standard for gluten-free labeling (and even when that standard is finally approved and becomes official), you can also look to an independent, third-party gluten-free certification program when seeking out reliably gluten-free products. The Gluten-Free Certification Organization (GFCO)—a Washington-based nonprofit and outgrowth of the Gluten Intolerance Group—operates the only such certification program in the world. Many companies have pursued their certification, which is very stringent. GFCO sets a maximum threshold of 10ppm (parts per million) of gluten in tested products. This far exceeds any international standard, including Codex, which range anywhere from 20ppm to 200ppm. If you see the GFCO certification logo on an item in the supermarket, you can be confident that it will indeed be gluten-free.

But where to find these gluten-free products when you're shopping? With improved product labeling—both for allergens and for gluten-free specifically—supermarket managers are left with having to decide where to stock items on store shelves. There are basically two schools of thought: integration and segregation. They're exactly what they sound like. Integration advocates locating gluten-free foods alongside other similar foods: For example, placing gluten-free cereals in the cereal aisle. Conversely, segregation advocates establishing a designated section of the store where a consumer can go to find all specialty gluten-free products.

In practice, we find that most stores employ a

combination of the integration and segregation schools of thought. For example, at our local supermarket in Colorado, General Mills' Rice Chex (which was recently reformulated to be gluten-free by removing the barley malt extract from the recipe) can be found in the regular cereal aisle, but other gluten-free cereals are located in the gluten-free subsection of the natural foods section of the store. Similarly, all gluten-free Asian sauces and condiments (such as red curry paste and ground fresh chili paste) can be found in the Asian aisle, but the tamari wheat-free soy sauce is located in the gluten-free section of the store. Which gives us **Rule #4: Seek, and you shall find . . . even if it takes some hard looking, or in the worst-case scenario, ordering specialty gluten-free products through the Internet.**

Armed with the four rules outlined above (and the rationale behind them), you can safely navigate your typical supermarket. We do, however, want to offer several words of caution.

First, **beware of buying from bulk bins.** One reality of the gluten-free diet is that certain foods are more expensive. This is especially true of specialty products such as gluten-free flours (like flours and starches made from sorghum, brown rice, tapioca, and a host of others). In an effort to cut costs and reduce the grocery bill, it can be tempting to buy these products from the bulk section of the store. Be aware that doing so carries risks. For one, we find that bulk versions of gluten-free flours often include advisory labeling warning of the possibility for cross-contamination with wheat. For another, you're taking it on faith that other supermarket shoppers haven't unintentionally cross-contaminated the different bulk bins by using the wrong scoop for the wrong bin. From our perspective, you're much better off (and safer) paying a little bit more and buying products that you know are gluten-free *and* free of cross contaminants. The consequences of gluten cross-contamination simply aren't worth the risk. (If you can find a reliably gluten-free bulk item, such as brown rice flour, by all means, purchase it to save money. In our experience, however, such items are typically found online, or direct from the manufacturer, and the cost savings of buying a 50-pound bag of flour, for example, is offset by the cost of shipping it to your home.)

Second, there are several foods and ingredients that have been widely debated within the gluten-free community as to whether they are safe for people adhering to a gluten-free diet. Chiefly, these foods are oatmeal (or oats, more generally), vinegar, and modified food starch.

The debate about oatmeal has two parts. First, there's the question of whether or not the proteins in oats mimic gluten proteins closely enough to cause a gluten-like response in people with celiac disease. Scientific consensus seems to be settling in favor of pure, untainted oats being safe for people on a gluten-free diet, although the most sensitive individuals may still have a reaction. Please consult your health care provider for advice on whether or not you could introduce oats into your gluten-free diet. Second, there's the issue of cross-contamination. Oats are often grown in fields alongside wheat, or crop-rotated in fields that also grow wheat. In addition, oats are often processed on the same machinery. Some companies are now offering gluten-free oats, so that might be an option.

The debate regarding vinegar is thankfully much easier to clear up. Almost all vinegars are made from red or white wine, apple cider, or rice wine. These "vinegar foundations" are inherently gluten-free, and therefore, so is the vinegar made from them. Plus, the distillation process for making vinegar would theoretically render it free of gluten anyway. (For a detailed discussion of distillation and vinegar, please see the box on page 81.) There is one glaring exception to the safety of vinegar, however. Malt vinegar is NOT gluten-free. Malt vinegar contains barley and is typically not distilled. Thus, it is not safe for people adhering to a strict gluten-free diet.

Finally, there's the debate centered around modified food starch (MFS). MFS is a complex carbohy-drate whose physical or chemical properties have been altered in order to make it perform better as a thickening agent, emulsifier, or stabilizer. Historically, MFS has also been a hidden source of gluten in food. That's because MFS can be made from any variety of starches, including corn, potato, and . . . wheat. In the past, if an ingredient label didn't specify the source of the starch, gluten-free foodies were forced to err on the side of caution and assume the MFS was based on wheat. Now, with mandatory allergen labeling, an ingredients label would have to be followed by a "Contains: wheat" statement if the MFS was sourced from that grain. If a label shows MFS, but no allergen statement, in theory you can safely conclude that the MFS is made from corn or another gluten-free source. However, also remember that this line of logic applies only for MFS in the United States. For MFS from another country, approach with more caution.

In the final analysis, we find it simpler to divide the grocery store into three distinct categories: a) naturally gluten-free foods, b) buyer-beware foods, and c) specialty foods. (These distinctions apply to whole classes of foods. This is different from our codes Green, Yellow, and Red for individual products, which refer to the potential for gluten cross-contamination based on the manufacturing methods for each product.)

Naturally gluten-free foods are exactly what they sound like, and for the most part, you'll find them in the periphery of the supermarket in the produce, meat, and fish sections. Here you'll find your fresh fruit and veggies, whole meats and fish, and so on. This category would also include things like rice, but please keep in mind that only raw, basic rice is naturally gluten-free. All boxed, flavored rice dinners fall into the next category of buyer beware.

Buyer-beware foods are those where you should exercise caution and carefully scrutinize the ingredient labels. Some companies will make gluten-free versions of these foods, but many will not. The only way to know is to check the labels. Good examples of buyer-beware foods would include chicken broth, yogurt, baking soda or baking powder, and extracts.

Finally, the specialty foods are those whose traditional versions contain gluten. Gluten-free versions of these foods would be considered specialty items. Good examples of specialty foods would include pasta (normally made from wheat, gluten-free versions might be made from rice, corn, or quinoa), as well as soy sauce (normally contains wheat, while tamari wheat-free soy sauce would be the gluten-free option).

Of course, when you cook artisanally—from scratch, with wholesome, fresh ingredients (and largely free of premade, processed food products)—much of this becomes a moot point. You'll know exactly what goes into your food, and how it is made. You'll know that it's free of modified food starch, and the "manufacturing facility" and "production line" are the same place . . . your own kitchen. Which is where we firmly believe the best gluten-free meals are made anyway!

The result is not just gluten-free food, but food that is both healthier and tastier. Admittedly, we do make the occasional exception to our "healthy" approach to cooking and eating. For example, we still use Heinz ketchup, which has high fructose corn syrup. And we can have a pretty fierce sweet tooth at times and use refined sugar in many of our desserts. Consider them guilty pleasures—they're vices, we admit, but don't we all have at least one or two? But by and large, cooking healthy artisanal gluten-free food is where our heart is. We're happier for it, and we think you will be, too.

THE ESSENTIAL
GLUTEN-FREE KITCHEN

*T*HE PREVIOUS SECTION spent a lot of time talking about safely navigating the supermarket. In essence, it was a discussion about how to shop for food, but it was much less about what exactly you should buy. That's what we'll cover here. But before we start talking about food and ingredients, it's worth spending some time to talk about tools.

TOOLS

As long as you understand how to execute the techniques used in the recipes in this book, there's no reason you can't use any tool that will get the job done. For example, when squeezing lemons or limes, you could use a fancy countertop juicer, or a handheld citrus juicer, or a lemon reamer (this is what we use), or simply a fork and a firm squeeze with the opposite hand.

But there are times when using the right tool for the job will make your life infinitely easier. We remember some years ago, when Kelli was working at the Waldorf=Astoria Hotel in New York City. She often brought in homemade cookies for her coworkers, who marveled at the cookies' consistent size and uniformly perfect shape. How did Kelli do it? Simple. In-

stead of using a spoon to plop random-sized balls of cookie dough onto the cookie sheet, she used a cookie scoop. The result was a perfect dough ball every time. The right tool for the job.

The following tools—which, unlike things such as a rolling pin, measuring cups, and mixing bowls, might not be found in every kitchen—will be invaluable in helping you make the recipes in this book. They aren't strictly needed, but they *will* make your life easier—and cooking should be fun, not tedious, don't you think?

- ▶ **Stand mixer:** Stand mixers are motorized, countertop mixers invaluable for making doughs and batters. Most come with three standard attachments: a paddle, a dough hook (in our experience, this is not used in gluten-free baking), and a whip (also known as a whisk). More elaborate models may also have optional accessories, such as for making ice cream.
- ▶ **Handheld mixer:** Handheld mixers are electric mixers, typically with twin beaters. They are very useful for whipping egg whites into peaks and for mixing small batches of batter in small bowls. Strictly speaking, a handheld mixer overlaps with a whisk (for beating egg whites) on one end, and with the stand mixer

(for mixing batter) on the other end. However, the convenience of a handheld mixer can't be overstated. It will save you tons of time (and arm energy) compared to beating egg whites or heavy cream by hand with a whisk, and it's perfect for mixing jobs you want to do directly in the mixing bowl, when using the stand mixer would simply be overkill.

▶ **Immersion blender:** Immersion blenders are handheld blenders that can be used directly in your pots and pans to blend or mix sauces, soups, and other liquids. We could never have anticipated how much we'd use (and love) our immersion blender until we received one as a gift. Now it's one of the most-used tools in our kitchen. More elaborate immersion blenders may also come with attachments, such as a whisk or a small-scale food processor.

▶ **Blender:** A classic blender is great for making smoothies and shakes. Enough said.

▶ **Food processor:** A standard food processor can be invaluable for preparing certain marinades and wet rubs, pulsing gluten-free breads to make bread crumbs, and even for making your own ground meat from whole cuts.

▶ **Chef's knife:** Every kitchen should have at least one good, sharp chef's knife, an all-purpose knife that can be used for chopping, cutting, etc. These come in a variety of blade lengths, typically from 6 to 12 inches. If you own only one knife, consider making it a high-grade, eight-inch, hollow-ground chef's knife. Hollow-ground knives have small concavities on each side of the blade that allow whatever you're cutting to release off the knife more easily. We also recommend you invest in a second knife with a serrated blade, which is essential for cutting things such as tomato and loaves of bread.

▶ **Pepper grinder:** There's no comparison between the intense flavor of fresh-cracked pepper from a pepper grinder and the comparatively mild flavor of store-bought ground pepper.

▶ **Lemon reamer:** When juicing lemons, limes, or oranges, we think a lemon reamer is the way to go. They're inexpensive and very effective.

In addition to the tools listed above, throughout this cookbook you'll also find information on a variety of other specialty tools (such as a pizza stone or tortilla press). They'll be located on the same page as the recipe for which they're used. We've chosen to locate them there, rather than in this list, because if you don't make that particular recipe, you're unlikely to need that specific tool. And if you don't have (and don't want to invest in) a particular tool, not to worry. We also provide an alternative technique using other implements you're likely to find in the kitchen.

INGREDIENTS

A solid foundation of ingredients—in addition to having the right tools for the job—is the other half of the Essential Gluten-Free Kitchen. In the sections that follow, we'll help you build that foundation, beginning with a gluten-free flour blend, and followed by a list of the most-used ingredients in this book that will leave you well-prepared and well-stocked for making most any recipe.

Gluten-Free Flour Mix

Gluten-free cooking, and especially gluten-free baking, is heavily reliant upon a good gluten-free flour mix. From premade store-bought blends, to gluten-free flour blends sold by specialty gluten-free bakeries, to custom blends you make yourself at home, it seems everyone has their favorite mix. We're no different—after spending innumerable hours baking in the kitchen, playing with blends and fussing with ratios, we arrived at our Artisan Gluten-Free Flour Mix. It's a great all-purpose blend you can use to make everything from cakes and cookies, to pancakes and waffles. But before we share the recipe (below), it's worthwhile to spend a little time talking about how gluten-free flours differ from "regular" wheat flour, and why using a good gluten-free flour blend is so important.

MUCH ADO ABOUT GLUTEN

Why all the to-do about gluten? What's so great about it, anyway? And why does it make a difference in baking? The short answer is that gluten is what makes dough "doughy." Gluten gives dough stretch and elasticity, and it also gives dough viscosity (thickness and stickiness). These are important traits in a dough. They're what give the final product its delightful, chewy texture. They're also what prevent a cookie from spreading paper-thin on the cookie sheet while it bakes. And for yeast breads and baking powder–activated cakes, gluten is what allows the dough or batter to rise but not fall during the baking process. During baking, air bubbles form in dough, and those bubbles then expand, causing the rise. However, the dough needs to be viscous enough to hold on to those bubbles. If the bubbles are able to escape from the dough, whatever you're baking collapses back on itself. Gluten provides the magic amount of viscosity, making baking possible.

Gluten-free flour mixes, though, obviously lack gluten. But without it, how are they able to replicate the effect of gluten? The answer is . . . xanthan gum.

X IS FOR XANTHAN GUM

Xanthan gum is one of the secrets of successful gluten-free baking. It is named for the bacteria Xanthomonas campestris. Technically speaking, xanthan gum is a polysaccharide, which is just a fancy way to say "a string of multiple sugars." (Starch, in its myriad forms, is a polysaccharide.) To create xanthan gum, the Xanthomonas campestris bacterium is allowed to

ferment on a sugar. In the United States, corn sugar is typically used as the base for the fermentation. The result is a "slime" (there's no other way to put it) that is then dried and milled to create the powdered xanthan gum you buy at the store. It's expensive, but thankfully, a very little bit goes a long way!

Importantly, xanthan gum has a number of powerful properties. First, it works as an emulsifier, encouraging liquids that normally don't like one another to mix together. For this reason, xanthan gum is often used in salad dressings to prevent the oil and vinegar from separating. Second, it works as a thickener, increasing the viscosity of liquids and batters. Third, it can create a creamy texture. For this reason, it's sometimes added to ice creams and dairy-free recipes that want to emulate the creaminess of milk.

Interestingly, xanthan gum first gained wide use not in the realm of gluten-free baking, but rather in the realm of molecular gastronomy, a field of cooking in which chefs do unconventional things with conventional ingredients. For example, a chef might use xanthan gum to increase the viscosity of a mango puree so that it resembles an egg yolk. Or a chef may make a flavored foam, enlisting the help of xanthan gum so that the flavored liquid has enough "holding power" to retain the gas bubbles that comprise the foam.

Within the world of gluten-free baking, xanthan gum does a wondrous job of mimicking gluten. For that reason, you'll find it in almost every gluten-free flour blend, including ours. The artisan gluten-free flour blend includes a baseline level of xanthan gum that works for all-around baking, but depending on the application, a recipe may call for adding an additional quantity of xanthan gum to get the job done.

ALTERNATIVE FLOURS—THE PATH TO A GLUTEN-FREE BLEND

Once you look beyond the narrow confines (but omnipresence) of wheat flour, you suddenly realize that there is an entire world of alternative, gluten-free flours and starches out there. Sorghum, brown rice, tapioca, corn, potato, garbanzo bean, almond . . . and the list goes on.

Each flour or starch will have different characteristics that impact the final product . . . chiefly in the areas of taste and texture, which will vary. What's more, no single alternative, gluten-free flour works as a good substitute for wheat flour. For the best results, multiple alternative flours and starches are typically blended together. The trick, then, is to figure out which ones to blend together, and in what ratios.

We've done that work for you, so don't fret. After benchmarking other flour blends, and looking at the ingredients labels on tasty foods, and experimenting on our own with mixing flours, and finally tweaking the ratios of those flours, we arrived at our Artisan Gluten-Free Flour Mix. We think it's the best blend for all-around gluten-free baking and cooking (we're biased, we know), and the flour blend recipe is used throughout the book. It has six components: brown rice flour, sorghum flour, cornstarch, potato starch, potato flour, and xanthan gum. The brown rice flour serves as an excellent base whose flavor and texture are influenced by the remaining ingredients. The sorghum flour adds more of a "whole grain" taste to the blend, while the potato flour, potato starch, and cornstarch help to ensure a bread-like, moist, chewy texture (rather than the dry and crumbly baked goods often synonymous with gluten-free baking). The potato flour and starch also enables baked goods to brown nicely. The xanthan gum, as you've already read, mimics gluten.

Store-bought, all-purpose, gluten-free flour blends also typically include a baseline level of xanthan gum, and they're similarly comprised of a blend of different flours, though the actual ingredients and their ratios differ from ours. There's an incredible variability from blend to blend, and, for our money, the Artisan Gluten-Free Flour Mix can't be beat. Gluten-free recipes are built upon a certain blend, and so for the recipes in this cookbook, we urge you to stick to the Artisan Gluten-Free Flour Mix—it'll give you the best results!

artisan gluten-free flour mix

[MAKES ABOUT 3 CUPS]

1¼ cups brown rice flour

¾ cup sorghum flour

⅔ cup cornstarch

¼ cup potato starch

1 tablespoon + 1 teaspoon potato flour

1 teaspoon xanthan gum

Combine all the ingredients and store in an air-tight container in the refrigerator.

For convenience, we recommend making a quadruple batch of the flour mix and storing it in the fridge. The flour will stay fresh and usable for several months, though we bake often enough that we've never come close to having to toss out a batch of old flour. In fact, our biggest problem is having to constantly mix up a new batch!

When making a quadruple batch (which makes about 12 cups), the measurements are easy:

5 cups brown rice flour

3 cups sorghum flour

2⅔ cups cornstarch

1 cup potato starch

¼ cup + 4 teaspoons
   potato flour

1 tablespoon +
   1 teaspoon xanthan gum

NOTE: When measuring out flour in recipes throughout this book, do not densely pack the measuring cup. Instead, stir your master batch of flour with a spoon to aerate, then spoon flour from your master batch into the measuring cup, and use a knife or other straight object to level off the scoop.

In addition to preparing a batch (or several) of the flour blend, we also recommend keeping several individual flours and starches on hand: cornstarch, sorghum flour, brown rice flour, and xanthan gum. Some recipes in the book will call for supplementing the base flour blend, or for using these individual flours and starches exclusively.

Lastly, a final note about gluten-free flours: They have a finer texture than wheat flour, and as a result, gluten-free flours absorb moisture more readily. Thus, when adding gluten-free flours to a dough or batter to achieve a desired consistency or moisture content, do so sparingly, a little at a time, so as not to suddenly make your dough overly dry.

The Complete Essentials

With a storage container of the Artisan Gluten-Free Flour Mix happily living in your refrigerator, it's time to stock up on a few essentials for the pantry. The following compilation of Complete Essentials is a list of ingredients that will leave you well-prepared and well-stocked for making most any recipe in the book. If you were to drop by our house unannounced on any given day and swing the pantry doors open, the items in this list are what you would find. Please note that this list excludes perishables and other fresh ingredients that you would buy the "week of" when menu planning (produce, cheese, meat, etc.). It includes only long-term pantry items, as well as a few refrigerated staples.

HERBS AND SPICES
- Allspice, ground
- Basil, dried
- Chili powder
- Cinnamon, ground
- Cocoa powder
- Coriander, ground
- Cumin, ground
- Garam masala
- Garlic powder
- Ginger, ground
- Nutmeg, ground
- Oregano, dried
- Paprika
- Pepper, cayenne
- Peppercorns, whole black
- Poppy seeds
- Salt
- Thyme, dried
- Turmeric, ground

BAKING INGREDIENTS
- Almond extract, pure, gluten-free
- Baking powder, gluten-free
- Baking soda, gluten-free
- Chocolate, semisweet (chips and squares)
- Corn syrup, light
- Cream of tartar
- Milk, evaporated (12-ounce cans)
- Milk, sweetened condensed (14-ounce cans)
- Molasses
- Sugar, brown
- Sugar, granulated
- Sugar, confectioners' (powdered)
- Vanilla extract, pure, gluten-free

COOKING INGREDIENTS
- Agave nectar
- Broth, chicken, gluten-free
- Pasta, brown rice, gluten-free
- Cornmeal
- Sherry, dry
- Honey
- Masa (instant corn masa flour)
- Noodles, rice, Asian-style, straight-cut
- Olive oil, extra light
- Rice, jasmine
- Tomatoes, canned, diced, no-salt-added (14.5-ounce cans)
- Vinegar, apple cider

- ▶ Vinegar, balsamic
- ▶ Vinegar, red wine
- ▶ Vinegar, rice
- ▶ Wine, Marsala

IN THE FRIDGE

- ▶ Butter, salted
- ▶ Chili paste, ground fresh
- ▶ Maple syrup, 100 percent pure
- ▶ Curry paste, red, gluten-free
- ▶ Soy sauce, tamari wheat-free

NOTES ABOUT USING
THIS BOOK

*T*HROUGHOUT THIS COOKBOOK, we will regularly use certain terms to refer to different pots and pans. The important distinctions are:

▶ **Skillet:** A pan with a flat bottom and sloped sides. For our purposes, a skillet is interchangeable with a frying pan, and in Asian recipes, also interchangeable with a wok. Throughout the book we use the term *skillet,* but feel free to use the pan you have on hand.

▶ **Sauté pan:** A pan with a flat bottom and vertical sides, usually with a lid. The flat bottom has a larger surface area than a skillet, making it a good choice for cooking larger quantities and making sauces. The lid also makes it good for braising. However, unless a recipe specifically calls for a sauté pan, feel free to use a skillet (or frying pan, or wok).

▶ **Saucepan:** Refers to smaller single-handed pots ranging in capacity from 1 quart to 4 quarts. Throughout the book, we simply refer to small, medium, or large saucepans. Use whatever size will get the job done.

▶ **Pot:** Refers to larger two-handled pots over 4 quarts in capacity.

For fruits, vegetables, and fresh herbs, we typically express the quantity in terms of the whole ingredient (unless there's a specific need for a more exact measurement). For example, a recipe may call for "1 medium onion, chopped," or "4 garlic cloves, minced," or "1/2 lime, juiced." We think that's easier than expressing the quantities in terms of cups and teaspoons. What does 3/4 cup chopped onion look like, anyway? On the other hand, "1 medium onion, chopped" is something we can relate to.

Also throughout the book, you'll see the term *gluten-free* abbreviated as *GF.* Strictly speaking, the entire book is gluten-free, so reiterating that fact is redundant. However, we've opted to use the "GF" abbreviation as a reminder for ingredients that are not normally gluten-free (specialty items such as tamari wheat-free soy sauce), and for ingredients that might not be gluten-free (such as baking powder and vanilla extract).

Finally, throughout the cookbook you'll find boxes alongside many of the recipes. These offer different kinds of valuable information:

▶ **Tools:** Information about specialty tools you'll use to execute the recipe (for example, a tortilla press)

► **Tips:** Information about techniques, ingredients, and recipe recommendations

► **Shortcuts:** Information about store-bought, premade ingredients you can use to expedite a recipe (for example, store-bought GF pasta, in lieu of pasta from scratch)

► **Facts:** Information about the origins of ingredients and recipes

Happy cooking!

BREAKFASTS
AND
BREADS

blueberry muffins with streusel topping

[MAKES 16 MUFFINS]

When we lived in New York, and later New Jersey, we often went rock climbing at the Gunks, popular cliffs near New Paltz in the mid-Hudson valley. Bushes of wild blueberries grew along the tops of the cliffs, set back into the forest just a few steps from the edge. The blueberries stayed cool enough in the shade that when we nibbled on a few at the top of a climb on a warm summer afternoon they seemed to be naturally refrigerated! Whether you use wild blueberries or not, you'll love them in these muffins with a streusel topping. The muffins have a wonderfully moist texture, and anyone we've served them to hasn't been able to tell they're gluten-free. If you have only one muffin tin, or would like to make just 12 muffins, you can put the extra batter in a small loaf pan and bake at the same time for 20 to 25 minutes.

> 4 cups Artisan GF Flour Mix (page 15), plus additional for tossing
> with the blueberries
> 2 teaspoons xanthan gum
> 2 cups sugar
> 1 tablespoon GF baking powder
> 1/2 pound (2 sticks) salted butter, melted
> 1 cup half-and-half
> 4 eggs
> 1 teaspoon GF vanilla extract
> 2 cups blueberries (fresh or frozen)

1. Preheat the oven to 375°F. Spray 16 cups of two 12-cup muffin tins with nonstick cooking spray. Place paper liners in the greased cups if desired. (Liners are not strictly needed—the muffins should pop out of the tin, but the liners make it easier.)

2. Mix together the 4 cups flour, xanthan gum, sugar, and baking powder.

3. Add the melted butter and stir to form a crumbled mixture. Set aside 1 cup of the mixture for the topping.

4. Mix together the half-and-half, eggs, and vanilla in a separate bowl. Add to the remaining crumble mixture, stirring just until moist to make a batter.

5. Lightly toss the blueberries in a little flour, then fold into the batter. (The flour coating prevents the fruit from sinking to the bottom of the muffins.)

6. Scoop the batter into the prepared muffin cups, filling each three-quarters full. (A cookie scoop or ice cream scoop works very well to transfer the batter.) Sprinkle the top of the muffins with the reserved crumbled mixture.

7. Bake for 20 to 25 minutes, until the muffins spring back when lightly pressed. The muffins should be slightly golden brown on top.

8. Let the muffins cool in the tins for 10 minutes. Remove and serve.

Variations

- **Cranberry Muffins:** For the blueberries, substitute an equal quantity of dried cranberries and add 1 teaspoon grated orange zest to the batter.
- **Cherry-Almond Muffins:** For the blueberries and vanilla, substitute equal quantities of cherries (fresh or frozen) and GF almond extract.

banana nut muffins

[MAKES 16 MUFFINS]

We would often buy large bunches of bananas at the supermarket, but once we got home, we wouldn't be able to eat them fast enough. The remainder of the bunch would sit on the kitchen counter, slowly developing brown spots as the bananas overripened. We first began making these muffins as a way to use up those bananas before they went too far over the hill, but have come to love the recipe for its own sake, too. The banana flavor infuses the muffins, while small chunks of banana offer extra bursts of goodness. If you have only one muffin tin, or would like to make just 12 muffins, you can put the extra batter in a small loaf pan and bake at the same time for 20 to 25 minutes.

4 bananas, peeled

1 egg

2/3 cup sugar

4 tablespoons (1/2 stick) salted butter, melted

1 teaspoon GF vanilla extract

1 1/2 cups Artisan GF Flour Mix (page 15)

1 teaspoon xanthan gum

1 1/2 teaspoons GF baking powder

1/4 teaspoon baking soda

1 teaspoon ground cinnamon

1/2 cup walnuts or pecans

1. Preheat the oven to 350°F. Spray 16 cups of two 12-cup muffin tins with nonstick cooking spray. Place paper liners in the greased muffin cups, if desired. (Liners are not strictly needed—the muffins should pop out of the tin, but the liners make it easier.)

2. Mash the bananas in a large mixing bowl until mostly smooth with a few large lumps. (A stand mixer is ideal for this job, using the paddle attachment.)

3. Mix in the egg, sugar, melted butter, and vanilla. Add the flour, xanthan gum, baking powder, baking soda, and cinnamon and mix until incorporated. Make sure to scrape down the side of the mixing bowl while mixing to ensure that the batter is thoroughly mixed. Fold in the nuts.

4. Scoop the batter into the muffin cups, filling each three-quarters full. (A cookie scoop or ice cream scoop works very well to transfer the batter.)

5. Bake for 20 to 25 minutes, until the muffins spring back when lightly pressed. The muffins should be golden brown on top.

6. Let the muffins cool in the tins for 10 minutes. Remove and serve.

Variations

For a banana-only, nut-free version, simply omit the walnuts or pecans.

This recipe can also be used to make banana nut bread. Grease a 8 x 4 x 2-inch loaf pan, add all the batter, and bake for 50 to 55 minutes, until the bread is golden brown and springs back when lightly pressed.

pumpkin spice muffins

[MAKES 12 MUFFINS]

One thing we love about our style of artisanal cooking is how it is often intimately connected to the variations of the seasons. And when it comes to fall, few foods are as evocative of that season as the pumpkin. When the leaves have fallen off the trees and the mornings are crisp and cool, a pumpkin spice muffin is a perfect way to start the day. The cinnamon, nutmeg, ginger, and cloves really come through, in combination with the more subtle flavor of the pumpkin.

1 cup cooked pumpkin (canned or home roasted)

$1/2$ cup milk

2 eggs

$1/3$ cup ($2/3$ stick) salted butter, melted

2 cups Artisan GF Flour Mix (page 15)

1 teaspoon xanthan gum

$1/4$ teaspoon baking soda

1 cup packed brown sugar

2 teaspoons ground cinnamon

$1/2$ teaspoon ground nutmeg

$1/4$ teaspoon ground ginger

$1/8$ teaspoon ground cloves

$1/4$ teaspoon salt

1. Preheat the oven to 350°F. Spray the cups of a 12-cup muffin tin with nonstick cooking spray. Place paper liners in the greased cups, if desired. (Liners are not strictly needed—the muffins should pop out of the tin, but the liners make it easier.)

2. Mix the pumpkin, milk, eggs, and melted butter until blended well. Add the flour, xanthan gum, baking soda, brown sugar, cinnamon, nutmeg, ginger, cloves, and salt and mix just until incorporated.

3. Scoop the batter into the muffin cups, filling each three-quarters full. (A cookie scoop or ice cream scoop works very well to transfer the batter.)

4. Bake for 15 to 20 minutes, until the muffins spring back when lightly pressed. The muffins should be slightly golden brown on top.

5. Let the muffins cool in the tin for 10 minutes. Remove and serve.

Variation

This recipe can also be used to make pumpkin spice bread. Grease an 8 x 4 x 2-inch loaf pan, add all the batter, and bake for 50 to 55 minutes, until the bread is golden brown and springs back when lightly pressed.

chocolate chip scones

[MAKES 12 SCONES]

About ten years ago—before our gluten-free days—Pete visited some of his family in Belgium, just outside the city of Antwerp. When his great aunt, Tante Georgette, realized that he loved chocolate, he woke up the next morning to an entire tray of freshly made croissants literally oozing with chocolate. While that amount of chocolate was a bit overwhelming, these chocolate chip scones provide just the right amount of sweet to start the day. The scones keep very well and can be stored up to 1 week in an airtight container. In fact, we prefer our scones about 3 days old. Over that period of time, they lose just enough of their moisture to become flakier.

$3\frac{1}{2}$ cups Artisan GF Flour Mix (page 15)

2 teaspoons xanthan gum

2 tablespoons GF baking powder

$\frac{1}{4}$ cup sugar

$\frac{3}{4}$ cup ($1\frac{1}{2}$ sticks) cold salted butter

1 cup heavy cream

1 egg

1 teaspoon GF vanilla extract

$\frac{1}{2}$ cup mini chocolate chips

1. Preheat the oven to 375°F.
2. Mix the flour, xanthan gum, baking powder, and sugar in a large bowl.
3. Cut the butter into the flour mixture until the mixture resembles pea-sized crumbles. (To cut butter into a flour mixture, use a pastry blender, two knives, or your hands.)
4. Mix together the cream, egg, and vanilla in a separate bowl. Add to the flour mixture and work together until a dough forms. (Using your hands is the best way to combine the ingredients.)
5. Gently knead in the chocolate chips.
6. Form the dough into a flat rectangle about 15 inches long, $2\frac{1}{2}$ inches wide, and $\frac{3}{4}$ inch thick. Cut the dough into triangles to form 12 scones: Start by cutting the dough crosswise in half, then divide each half into three $2\frac{1}{2}$-inch squares. Then cut each square diagonally to form triangles.
7. Place the scones on an ungreased cookie sheet 1 inch apart. Bake for 20 minutes, or until light golden brown.
8. Allow the scones to cool on the cookie sheet. Serve warm or at room temperature.

Variations

- **Vanilla-Raisin:** Substitute raisins for the chocolate chips.
- **Cherry-Almond:** Substitute almond extract for the vanilla and dried cherries for the chocolate chips.
- **Pecan-Bourbon:** Substitute 1 tablespoon bourbon for the vanilla and chopped pecans or walnuts for the chocolate chips.

bread

[MAKES 1 LOAF, ABOUT 12 SERVINGS]

Many gluten-free breads can be dry and crumbly, and a little bland on the taste side of things. By comparison, this bread is moist and flavorful, and is great fresh out of the oven, served with butter or jam, toasted for breakfast, or used to dip in soups.

2 1/4 cups milk
2 tablespoons sugar
1 tablespoon salted butter
1 1/2 teaspoons salt
3 1/4 cups Artisan GF Flour Mix (page 15)
1 teaspoon xanthan gum
2 1/4 teaspoons (1 package) active dry yeast

1. Grease a 9 x 5-inch loaf pan.
2. Heat the milk, sugar, butter, and salt in a small saucepan over medium heat until warmed and the butter is fully melted (about 120°F). If the milk heats too quickly before the butter fully melts, remove the saucepan from the heat and finish melting the butter.
3. Mix the GF flour, xanthan gum, and yeast in a large bowl. Add the warm milk mixture, mixing to combine. The dough will be very sticky.
4. Spread the dough into the prepared loaf pan. Cover and let rise in a warm location free from drafts for 30–60 minutes, or until the dough doubles in size.
5. Preheat the oven to 375°F.
6. Bake the loaf for 40 minutes, or until firm to the touch.

To MAKE GARLIC toast that's great for dipping in soups, slice the bread loaf, spread the slices with butter, and sprinkle with salt and garlic powder. (Even better, add chopped fresh garlic to melted butter and use a pastry brush to coat one side of the bread.) Toast flat in a toaster oven or under the broiler in your oven until golden brown.

lemon poppy seed bread

[MAKES 1 LOAF, ABOUT 12 SERVINGS]

We've both been longtime fans of lemon poppy seed bread, but had largely forgotten about it since going gluten-free. A trip to our local farmers' market in Boulder, Colorado, changed all that. A local gluten-free bakery was offering samples of lemon poppy seed cake, and we felt inspired to make our own version. It's very moist, with an intense lemon flavor thanks to the lemon syrup that permeates the bread.

Lemon Loaf

1³/₄ cups Artisan GF Flour Mix (page 15)

1 teaspoon xanthan gum

2 teaspoons GF baking powder

³/₄ cup sugar

¹/₄ cup poppy seeds

¹/₄ teaspoon salt

1 egg

1 cup milk

1 teaspoon GF vanilla extract

Zest of 1 lemon

2 tablespoons freshly squeezed lemon juice

4 tablespoons (¹/₂ stick) salted butter, melted

Lemon Syrup

2 tablespoons freshly squeezed lemon juice

1 tablespoon sugar

WHEN ZESTING CITRUS fruits such as a lemon, we recommend using a Microplane grater. It's the perfect tool for the job, end of story. Make sure you're zesting only the yellow rind (in the case of a lemon), and not the white pith behind the rind, which is very bitter. The same rule applies for the green rind of a lime and the orange rind of an orange. In lieu of a Microplane grater, you can use the small grate on a cheese grater.

1. Preheat the oven to 350°F. Grease a 9 x 5-inch loaf pan.

2. To make the lemon loaf: Using a stand mixer, mix together the flour, xanthan gum, baking powder, sugar, poppy seeds, and salt in a mixing bowl. Add the egg, milk, vanilla, and lemon zest and juice and mix for 30 seconds. Add the melted butter, scrape down the side of the bowl, and mix on medium speed for 30 seconds.

3. Pour the batter into the prepared loaf pan. Bake for 50 to 55 minutes, until a wooden toothpick inserted in the center of the loaf comes out clean.

4. While the bread is baking, make the glaze: Mix together the lemon juice and sugar. Heat for 30 seconds in the microwave and stir until the sugar fully dissolves.

5. Brush the top of the loaf with the syrup and let the bread rest in the pan for 10 minutes. Remove the bread from the pan and allow it to cool completely on a wire rack.

6. When cool, wrap the bread in plastic wrap and let set for at least 8 hours to allow the syrup to spread throughout the bread.

corn bread

[MAKES ONE 9 X 9-INCH PAN, ABOUT 9 SERVINGS]

Corn bread is one of those foods that's seldom gluten-free in the outside world, but very easy to make gluten-free at home. Our version is slightly sweet and chewy and works especially well with savory dishes. We particularly love it when paired with Chili (page 116), or used to make Corn Bread Stuffing (page 102).

1 cup Artisan GF Flour Mix (page 15)

1 tablespoon GF baking powder

1 cup cornmeal

3 tablespoons sugar

1 teaspoon salt

2 eggs

1 cup milk

4 tablespoons (½ stick) salted butter, melted

1. Preheat the oven to 425°F. Grease a 9-inch square baking pan.
2. Mix together the flour, baking powder, cornmeal, sugar, and salt.
3. Add the eggs and milk and mix. Stir in the melted butter and mix until all the dry ingredients are incorporated.
4. Pour the batter into the prepared pan. Bake for 20 minutes, or until a wooden toothpick inserted into the center comes out clean.

garlic naan

[MAKES 12 PIECES]

We admit, we've never been to India. But that doesn't stop us from loving Indian food. From the aromatic basmati rice, to the meats, to the spicy sauces that bring it all together, we can't get enough Indian. One of the real pleasures, though, is using the naan—a leavened flat bread—to scoop up all the extra sauce that's often left over.

1 cup warm water (about 115°F)

3 tablespoons honey

2¼ teaspoons (1 package) active dry yeast

3 tablespoons milk

2 eggs

3½ cups Artisan GF Flour Mix (page 15)

2 teaspoons xanthan gum

8 garlic cloves, minced

2 teaspoons salt

4 tablespoons (½ stick) salted butter, melted

1. Preheat the oven to 400°F with a pizza stone inside. (It's important for the pizza stone to fully preheat.)

2. Combine the warm water, honey, and yeast in a medium bowl and let stand until the mixture bubbles, about 5 minutes. The bubbles mean your yeast is alive and ready to go.

3. Mix the milk, eggs, flour, xanthan gum, half of the garlic, and the salt into the yeast mixture to form a soft dough. The dough should not be sticky to the touch, but should still be moist enough so as not to be firm. Add small amounts of additional flour, if needed, just until the dough is workable by hand.

4. Separate the dough into 12 equally sized balls. Shape each ball into a flat disk by stretching it with your hands until it is about ¼ inch thick.

5. Pull the oven rack with the pizza stone on it partially out of the oven (to allow easier access to the back of the pizza stone), and place as many rounds on the stone as will fit with 1 inch of space between each. Brush the tops with butter. Push the rack back in the oven and bake the naan for 5 to 7 minutes. Meanwhile, add the remaining minced garlic to the remaining melted butter.

6. Pull the rack back out, flip the naan, and brush the tops with the garlic butter. Bake for an additional 5 minutes, or until golden brown in places.

7. Repeat with the remaining dough. Serve the naan warm.

Variation

For plain naan bread, simply omit the garlic.

NAAN IS A round flatbread that comes from central and southern Asia, including India. It is typically baked in a tandoor, or clay oven. As a yeast bread, it would normally be allowed to rise for at least 1 hour, and as such can be time-consuming to make. However, thanks to the nuances of gluten-free baking and this recipe, we find you can go straight to the oven without waiting.

biscuits

[MAKES 12 BISCUITS]

Biscuit is a word that means different things in different places. This recipe is for the American biscuit, a quick bread with a firm, browned crust and soft, moist interior. American biscuits are light and flaky, and pair well with both sweet and savory foods.

2 cups Artisan GF Flour Mix (page 15)
1 tablespoon GF baking powder
2 teaspoons sugar
1/2 teaspoon salt
6 tablespoons (3/4 stick) cold salted butter
1 cup milk

1. Preheat the oven to 450°F. Grease a cookie sheet.
2. Mix together the flour, baking powder, sugar, and salt. Cut the butter into the dry ingredients using a pastry blender or your hands, until the mixture looks like coarse crumbles. Stir in the milk to form a batter.
3. Drop rounded (heaping) tablespoons of the dough onto the prepared sheet.
4. Bake for 10 to 12 minutes, until the biscuits are golden. Serve warm.

IN NORTH AMERICA, American biscuits are the norm. They can be served with dinner (as with gravy) or with breakfast (as with butter or jam). They're especially popular in the South, where they are often made with buttermilk and paired with gravy as a common dish. Outside of North America, and particularly in Europe, biscuits are quite a different food. There, they're typically twice-baked, resulting in a hard, crunchy texture more akin to a cookie or cracker than to what most Americans think of as a biscuit. In Italy, the name for the popular treat, biscotti, is derived from the same root word, which fittingly means "twice baked." When it comes to American biscuits, however, we enjoy ours with honey butter. Simply mix equal parts softened butter and honey, and enjoy!

belgian waffles

[MAKES 5 WAFFLES]

With Pete's Belgian heritage and an Eggo waffle addiction in high school, waffles have always been important to him. They're equally important to Kelli, whose family often enjoys them when getting together on Saturday mornings. This gluten-free Belgian waffle recipe can go the distance with the best of 'em. Following a gluten-free cooking demonstration at a Denver-area Whole Foods where we featured these waffles, an attendee wrote to say, "You've made me love breakfast again." But perhaps the best testament to these waffles is that Kelli's parents now use this recipe, instead of one for standard gluten waffles, because they prefer our version. Hooray for gluten-free converts!

1¾ cups Artisan GF Flour Mix (page 15)
1 tablespoon GF baking powder
¼ teaspoon salt
2 eggs, separated
1¾ cups milk
1 teaspoon GF vanilla extract
8 tablespoons (1 stick) salted butter, melted

1. Mix together the flour, baking powder, and salt in a large bowl.
2. Add the egg yolks, milk, and vanilla and mix. Add the melted butter and mix just until combined.
3. Whip the egg whites in a separate bowl until stiff peaks form. (A handheld mixer works great for this.) Tenderly fold the egg whites into the batter.
4. Cook a waffle according to your waffle maker's instructions, but do not open the waffle iron (no peeking!) until the waffle is fully cooked.
5. Remove the waffle and repeat to make 5 waffles.

If YOU'RE SETTING aside the waffles in order to serve them all at once, keep in mind that stacking will result in soggy waffles. Instead, place them in a single layer directly on your oven's rack with the oven set to Warm to keep the waffles light and crispy. The waffles also store well in the refrigerator or freezer.

pancakes

[MAKES TWELVE 3-INCH PANCAKES]

These pancakes are the perfect demonstration of the power of a good gluten-free flour blend. Their texture is soft, moist, and chewy, and nearly indiscernible from gluten pancakes. Paired with pure maple syrup, the combination is divine.

1 cup Artisan GF Flour Mix (page 15)
1 tablespoon sugar
2 teaspoons GF baking powder
¼ teaspoon salt
1 egg
1 cup milk
1 teaspoon GF vanilla extract
2 tablespoons salted butter, melted

1. Mix together the flour, sugar, baking powder, and salt in a bowl.
2. Add the egg, milk, and vanilla and mix. Add the melted butter and mix just until the ingredients are combined.
3. Heat a griddle or skillet to medium-high. Grease with butter or nonstick cooking spray. Pour the batter into rounds on the hot griddle or skillet using a 2-ounce ladle. Cook until bubbles have formed on the surface of each pancake. Flip and cook until the other sides are golden brown. Repeat to make 12 pancakes.

crepes

Crepes are one of those wonderful foods that excel equally well as both breakfast and dessert. They're a chameleon, taking on the needs of the moment (and the meal) depending on how they're served and what you use for toppings. Either way, though, we think you'll have a hard time telling that these crepes are gluten-free. Try serving them with pure maple syrup, confectioners' sugar, or fruit and Homemade Whipped Cream (page 200) for breakfast. For dessert, try Dessert Crepes with a Trio of Sauces (page 214).

3/4 cup Artisan GF Flour Mix (page 15)
2 tablespoons sugar
2 eggs
1 cup milk
1 teaspoon GF vanilla extract
2 tablespoons salted butter, melted

1. Mix together the flour and sugar in a bowl.
2. Add the eggs, milk, and vanilla and mix. Add the melted butter and mix just until the ingredients are combined.
3. Heat a nonstick medium skillet over medium-high heat. (In this instance, you definitely want to use a skillet or frying pan, *not* a sauté pan. The straight sides of a sauté pan make it more difficult to turn the crepes.) Grease the pan with butter or nonstick cooking spray and wipe the excess out with a paper towel; you want only a very thin layer. Typically, you will only need to grease the pan for the first crepe unless your pan is sticky.
4. Pour 1/4 cup of the batter into the pan and spread to thinly cover the bottom by tilting and rotating the pan. Cook until the crepe begins to dry, about 45 seconds. Flip the crepe, using a fork to separate the crepe from the pan and to turn the crepe over. Cook the second side briefly and turn out of the pan onto a plate. The finished crepe will be light to golden brown.
5. Repeat with the remaining batter to make 10 crepes.

french toast

[MAKES 4 SERVINGS]

Something magical happens when vanilla and cinnamon come together, and this French toast is the perfect example. On a leisurely Saturday morning, we'll put some John Coltrane jazz on the stereo and whip up a batch of French toast for breakfast, preferably with some pure maple syrup, and maybe a strip of bacon or three.

> 2 eggs
> 1/2 cup milk
> 2 teaspoons sugar
> 1 teaspoon GF vanilla extract
> 1/2 teaspoon ground cinnamon
> 8 slices GF bread (page 26) or store-bought GF bread
> Salted butter

1. Whisk together the eggs, milk, sugar, vanilla, and cinnamon in a shallow bowl.

2. Dip each piece of bread into the egg mixture, leaving it in long enough to absorb some of the mixture, about 60 seconds per slice. (Note: GF bread can be dense and so needs a little extra soaking time. Also, if your plate isn't deep enough to fully submerge the slices, be sure to soak both sides of the bread.)

3. Preheat a skillet or griddle to medium-high. Liberally grease with butter.

4. Place 2 or 3 slices of the dipped bread onto the hot pan and cook until the bottoms are golden, about 5 minutes. Flip and cook the second sides until the bread is cooked through and golden, another 3 minutes or so.

5. Repeat with the remaining bread, buttering the pan between each batch.

french toast casserole

[MAKES 6 SERVINGS]

This dish gives extra mileage to food you already have in the house. We seldom make this dish in its own right. More often, we have leftover bread, or pancakes, or waffles, or French toast (or some combination thereof) that we're looking to give new life. French toast casserole fits the bill—it's super tasty, and you'd never know that you're eating "leftovers" if you weren't making the dish yourself. It's moist, and the vanilla and cinnamon trump the flavors of whatever breads you use to make it.

4 cups cut up, day-old bread/pancakes/waffles/muffins (any leftover GF bread product)

4 tablespoons (½ stick) salted butter, melted

2 eggs

1½ cups milk

1 tablespoon sugar

2 teaspoons ground cinnamon

1 teaspoon GF vanilla extract

Pure maple syrup

1. Preheat the oven to 375°F. Grease an 8- or 9-inch square baking pan or an 8- or 9-inch round cake pan.

2. Cut the bread into 1-inch pieces and put in a large bowl. Drizzle with the melted butter and toss to coat.

3. Whisk together the eggs, milk, sugar, cinnamon, and vanilla in a separate bowl.

4. Pour the egg mixture over the bread and mix roughly with a spoon to break up the bread so it can absorb most of the liquid. Scrape the mixture into the prepared pan.

5. Bake for 30 to 35 minutes, until a knife inserted in the center comes out clean. The casserole should be golden brown. Serve warm with pure maple syrup.

For a WONDERFUL homemade breakfast in the morning without a lot of work, make the casserole the night before and cover and refrigerate until morning. You will have a hot breakfast on the table with no fuss! Be sure to bake the chilled casserole for an additional 5 minutes. You can also fully bake the dish the night before, and simply reheat it in the morning.

cinnamon rolls

[MAKES 16 ROLLS]

Cinnamon rolls can feel sinfully indulgent, but the mere smell of them is a temptation we can't resist. What can we say? Sometimes our morning sweet tooth just needs to be satisfied. Fortunately, we're not alone. When our gluten-eating buddy Tom visited recently, he helped himself to not one, two, or even three, but to four cinnamon rolls, and he couldn't tell they were gluten-free! They're intensely sweet, in a good way, and bursting with cinnamon flavor.

Dough
- $3/4$ cup milk
- $1/2$ cup sugar
- 8 tablespoons (1 stick) salted butter, cut into pieces
- $1^1/2$ teaspoons salt
- $1/3$ cup warm water (about 110°F)
- $4^1/2$ teaspoons (2 packages) active dry yeast
- 3 eggs, room temperature
- $4^1/2$ to $5^1/2$ cups Artisan GF Flour Mix (page 15)
- 2 teaspoons xanthan gum

Filling
- 4 tablespoons ($1/2$ stick) salted butter, melted
- $3/4$ cup sugar
- 3 tablespoons ground cinnamon

Glaze
- $3/4$ cup confectioners' sugar
- 2 tablespoons milk

1. To make the dough: Heat the milk in a saucepan over medium-high heat until bubbles form around the edge of the pan (scald the milk), remove from the heat and stir in the sugar, butter, and salt. Cool to lukewarm, about 115°F.

2. Combine the warm water and yeast in a medium bowl and let stand until the mixture bubbles, about 5 minutes. The bubbles mean your yeast is alive and ready to go.

3. Add the lukewarm milk mixture and eggs to the yeast mixture and stir to combine. Add $4^1/2$ cups of the flour and the xanthan gum. Mix well and form the dough into a ball. Add more flour if needed to make the dough soft and smooth and only a little tacky.

4. Roll out the dough between two large sheets of plastic wrap to form a rectangle that is 24 x 16 inches. (Create large sheets of plastic by slightly overlapping the long edges of two 2-foot-long sheets of standard plastic wrap.)

5. To fill the dough: Brush the rolled-out dough with the melted butter. Combine the sugar and ground cinnamon and sprinkle on the dough.

6. Roll up the dough to form a 24-inch-long roll. Pinch the long edge to seal. Slice the roll into 16 equal cross sections, each about 1½ inches wide.

7. Grease a 13 x 9 x 2-inch baking pan. Place the rolls in the pan, cover, and set in a warm location free from drafts to rise for 30 minutes.

8. Preheat the oven to 350°F.

9. Bake the rolls for 25 to 30 minutes, until golden brown. Remove from the oven and let cool for 15 minutes.

10. To make the glaze: Mix together the confectioners' sugar and milk. Drizzle the glaze over the cinnamon rolls and serve. (Don't put the glaze on too quickly after the rolls come out of the oven or it will melt off because of the residual heat.)

summer fruit salad with yogurt sauce

[MAKES 10 SERVINGS]

This is a great dish during the height of summer, when melons and berries are at their peak. The inspiration for the salad struck when our friends Jed and Kaisa came over for dinner and brought along their fruit salad with a yogurt sauce. We enjoyed it so much, we unabashedly made our own version.

1 cantaloupe, cut into bite-size pieces

1 honeydew melon, cut into bite-size pieces

1 pineapple, peeled, cored, and cut into bite-size pieces

1 quart strawberries, halved if large

1 pint blueberries

1 cup plain yogurt

2 tablespoons honey

1 tablespoon orange juice (freshly squeezed if available)

¼ teaspoon ground nutmeg

1. Combine the cantaloupe, honeydew, pineapple, strawberries, and blueberries in a large glass bowl.
2. Mix together the yogurt, honey, orange juice, and nutmeg in a separate bowl.
3. Serve the fruit with the yogurt sauce on the side.

pepper, onion, and cheddar frittata

[MAKES 6 SERVINGS]

We first made this frittata for Wednesday Night Dinner, an informal dinner club and social get-together with our friends in Colorado's Front Range. The host house rotates and provides dinner and dessert, while the guests bring their own drinks. The frittata was such a hit one night when we hosted that Kelli later made it for a dinner at Denver's Ronald McDonald House, where she coordinates a series of quarterly dinners prepared by volunteers from the hospitality business. It was a hit there, too, with all the families staying at RMH.

1 to 2 tablespoons olive oil

½ red bell pepper, diced small

½ onion, diced small

12 eggs

¼ cup half-and-half

Salt and pepper

1 cup shredded Cheddar cheese

1. Preheat the broiler.
2. Heat the olive oil in a 12-inch oven-proof, nonstick skillet over medium-high heat. (You can use a 10-inch skillet, but you will have to cook the frittata a little longer in order to cook it through, since it will be deeper.) Add the pepper and onion and sauté until soft.
3. Whisk together the eggs, half-and-half, and salt and pepper in a medium bowl. Pour the egg mixture over the pepper and onion mixture in the skillet. Sprinkle with half the cheese and gently stir. Cook, stirring occasionally, until the eggs begin to set up but are still loose in places, 3 to 5 minutes.
4. Sprinkle the remaining cheese on top of the eggs. Place the frittata under the broiler and broil for 5 minutes longer, or until the cheese is melted and brown.
5. Remove from the oven and slide onto a serving platter. Cut into wedges and serve.

Variations

Instead of pepper, onion, and Cheddar, try these flavor combinations:

- Spinach, garlic, and feta cheese
- Bacon, onion, and Cheddar cheese
- Tomato, scallion, and Swiss cheese
- Asparagus, ham, and Parmesan cheese

A FRITTATA IS AN Italian-style omelet that frequently features meat, cheese, and vegetables. One of its trademarks is that it is partially cooked on the stove top, but then finished in the oven under a broiler.

scrambled omelet

[MAKES 4 SERVINGS]

Our friend Tom is a master omelet maker; this scrambled omelet just may be his signature version. He first made a variation of it for us while we were camping together in the Rocky Mountain backcountry. Later, he made another version at his house in Boston. The shredded potato makes this much less "eggy" than a traditional omelet, as if hash browns and an egg omelet merged. This particular version was inspired by Tom, but born of necessity—Kelli was home alone while Pete was away on a business trip. Ingredients in the house were sparse, but she did have eggs and potatoes, and the rest—as they say—is history.

> 3 tablespoons olive oil
> 1 large russet potato, shredded and squeezed of excess moisture
> 1/2 green bell pepper, diced small
> 1/2 onion, diced small
> 4 eggs
> Salt and pepper

1. Heat 2 tablespoons of the oil in a skillet over medium-high heat. Add the shredded potato and cook until semi-soft and golden, about 10 minutes.
2. Move the potato to the outside edge of the pan. In the center of the pan, add the remaining 1 tablespoon oil and the pepper and onion and cook until soft.
3. Whisk the eggs with salt and pepper in a bowl. Pour over the potato and vegetables and scramble until the eggs are cooked, about 3 minutes. Serve hot.

Variations

For a meat lover's version of this veggie omelet, add bacon or ham. Cut the ham or bacon into small pieces, cook in the skillet (discard excess bacon fat, if needed), and then add the eggs as per above. Omit the potato if you're desiring a straight-up omelet.

UNLIKE AN ITALIAN-STYLE frittata (page 39), a French-style omelet is cooked exclusively on the stove top, with the edges of the omelet folded in to the middle in order to contain the filling. In our version of the French-style omelet, though, rather than fold the edges in, we prefer to scramble the egg with the fillings.

spinach and cheese quiche

[MAKES 8 SERVINGS]

Quiche is a meal unto itself, and works great for breakfast, brunch, or dinner. We made four different quiches—including this spinach and cheese version—for our daughter Marin's baptism brunch. Not a morsel was left behind. The filling has a custard quality to it, and it's rich while still remaining light, not heavy.

1/2 recipe Pie Dough (page 191), prepared through step 4 (unbaked pie shell)

3/4 cup frozen spinach, thawed

1 tablespoon salted butter

1/2 medium onion, diced

1 garlic clove, minced

1 cup shredded mozzarella cheese

Dash of nutmeg

Salt and pepper

4 eggs

1 cup half-and-half

1/2 cup milk

1. Preheat the oven to 350°F. Roll out the piecrust and use it to line a standard 9-inch pie pan.

2. Rinse the thawed spinach in a colander and squeeze out all the excess liquid.

3. Melt the butter in a skillet over medium-high heat. Add the onion and garlic and sauté until soft, about 4 minutes. Add the spinach and sauté for 1 minute longer.

4. Sprinkle the cheese in the bottom of the piecrust. Spread the spinach mixture over the cheese. Sprinkle with the nutmeg and salt and pepper.

5. Whisk together the eggs, half-and-half, and milk in a small bowl. Pour over the spinach.

6. Bake the quiche for 50 minutes, or until the top is lightly browned.

Variations

To make alternate versions of this quiche, simply use 1 cup of any combination of cooked vegetables and/or meat, and 1 to 1 1/2 cups of any shredded cheese. For example, try broccoli with Cheddar cheese, ham with Gruyère or Swiss cheese, or bell pepper and onion with mozzarella cheese.

APPETIZERS

mango-pineapple salsa

[MAKES 2 CUPS]

This mango-pineapple salsa is fruity and refreshing. It pairs well with chicken as well as white flaky fish such as mahimahi and halibut. It also goes well with spicy foods like Jamaican Jerk Chicken (page 148), where the light freshness of the salsa balances out the spice of the dish. As an appetizer, serve with corn chips.

1 mango, pitted, peeled, and diced small
$\frac{1}{2}$ pineapple, peeled, cored, and diced small
$\frac{1}{2}$ red onion, diced small
$\frac{1}{2}$ jalapeño chile pepper, minced
$\frac{1}{4}$ bunch fresh cilantro, chopped
1 lime, juiced
Salt and pepper

Mix together all the ingredients and season with salt and pepper to taste.

WHEN IT COMES to jalapeño peppers (and chile peppers in general) most of the heat (spice) is contained within the oil of the seeds and the membrane that holds the seeds. You can dial the heat up or down according to your preference. To make a salsa milder, discard the seeds and retain only the flesh of the pepper. To maximize the kick, keep it all in there. And to moderate the spice, use just some of the seeds.

fire-roasted corn salsa

[MAKES 2 CUPS]

Whereas most of our salsas have a clean, fresh flavor, the grilled corn and tomato in this salsa add a nice smoky element. It pairs well with grilled meats, and we recommend serving it with our Mexican Spice-Rubbed Pork Tenderloin (page 172). As an appetizer, serve with corn chips.

2 tomatoes, whole
1 ears corn, husked
1/3 medium onion, chopped
1/3 bunch cilantro, chopped
1/2 jalapeño chile pepper, diced
1/2 lime, juiced
1/2 garlic clove, minced
1/4 teaspoon ground cumin
Salt and pepper

1. Heat a grill to high.
2. Grill the tomatoes and corn on the cob over high heat, turning, until lightly charred and tender, about 10 minutes.
3. Dice the tomatoes and cut the corn kernels off the cob. Combine in a bowl and add the onion, cilantro, jalapeño, lime juice, garlic, cumin, and salt and pepper. (See the box on page 44 for tips on making the salsa more or less spicy with the jalapeño.)

*I*F YOU DON'T have a grill, you can cook the tomatoes and corn under a broiler. Or, if you have a gas stove, "grill" them directly over a gas burner on the stove top.

fresh tomato-cilantro salsa

[MAKES 2 CUPS]

This is a classic fresh salsa, period. It's great with corn chips, as a topping for Turkey Tacos (page 170), Chipotle Chicken Fajitas (page 146), or anywhere else you like to use salsa.

3 vine-ripened tomatoes, diced
1/3 medium onion, finely chopped
1/3 bunch cilantro, chopped
1/2 jalapeño chile pepper, diced
1/2 garlic clove, minced
1/2 lime, juiced
1/4 teaspoon ground cumin
Salt and pepper

Combine the tomato, onion, cilantro, jalapeño, and garlic in a medium bowl. Stir in the lime juice, cumin, and salt and pepper. (See the box on page 44 for tips on making the salsa more or less spicy with the jalapeño.)

guacamole

[MAKES 1 CUP]

Throughout high school and college in Ithaca, New York, Kelli worked at a Mexican restaurant, which has sadly since closed its doors. The real loss was the restaurant's guacamole, which was Kelli's favorite item on the menu. Unfazed, she became inspired to concoct her own guacamole that could live up to the memory of her first guac love. Happily for her, and the rest of us, she succeeded. It's decadent, rich, and creamy—thanks to the good fats found in avocado.

1 avocado, pitted and peeled
½ lime, juiced
2 tablespoons diced tomato
1 tablespoon chopped cilantro
2 teaspoons diced onion
½ garlic clove, minced
½ teaspoon minced jalapeño chile pepper
Salt and pepper

Coarsely mash the avocado in a bowl. Add the lime juice, tomato, cilantro, onion, garlic, jalapeño, and salt and pepper and gently stir to combine. (See the box on page 44 for tips on making the salsa more or less spicy with the jalapeño.)

AVOCADOS HAVE A thick, dark skin and a large, smooth central pit. To pit and peel an avocado, first use a long, sharp knife to cut the avocado along its long axis until you strike the pit. Then, leaving the blade in contact with the pit, rotate the avocado so that knife slices a complete circle around the avocado lengthwise. Remove the knife and, grasping each half of the avocado, twist in order to separate. One half of the avocado will still have the pit. With the knife, carefully strike the pit with the blade, then pull back and twist to remove the pit. Finally, use a spoon to scoop the flesh of the avocado away from the skin.

cucumber dip

[MAKES 1½ CUPS]

We had our first shared bites of cucumber dip when Kelli was studying abroad in Australia. Since then she's created this version, which is light, mild (the foundational flavor is cucumber, after all), and slightly reminiscent of tzatziki, the Greek yogurt-cucumber sauce. Try serving the dip with fresh GF bread (page 26) or crudités.

1 cup sour cream
1 cucumber, peeled, quartered, and deseeded
2 scallions, coarsely chopped
1 tablespoon lemon juice
1 garlic clove, peeled
Salt and pepper

Combine all the ingredients in a food processor and blend until smooth.

red lentil dip with crudités

[**MAKES ABOUT 2 CUPS**]

We first had this dish when Pete was visiting our friends Kirk and Maury in Vermont. Pete was in town on assignment for a magazine, and he, Kirk, and two other friends skied the Teardrop Trail, a backcountry ski trail cut by the Civilian Conservation Corps in the 1930s on Mount Mansfield, the state's tallest peak. At the end of the day, everyone returned to Kirk and Maury's place in the Mad River Valley, where Maury had this delicious dip waiting. It's akin to hummus but made with red lentils, and the cumin gives the flavor a slight Middle Eastern flair. Serve with crudités.

2 teaspoons olive oil

3 tablespoons chopped cilantro

2 1/2 teaspoons ground cumin

2 teaspoons grated or minced fresh ginger

1 garlic clove, minced

1 cup red lentils, rinsed

1 1/4 to 1 1/2 cups water

1 tablespoon freshly squeezed lemon juice

Salt

1. Heat the oil in a saucepan over medium-high heat. Add the cilantro, cumin, ginger, and garlic and sauté until the garlic just begins to brown, 2 to 3 minutes.

2. Stir in the lentils and 1 1/4 cups water and bring to a boil. Reduce the heat to medium-low, cover, and cook until the lentils are soft and the water is absorbed, 20 to 25 minutes. Add an additional 1/4 cup of water if the lentils don't become soft enough to mash.

3. Mash the lentils and stir in the lemon juice and salt to taste. Let cool briefly before serving (the dip can be served warm, at room temperature, or cold).

*C*RUDITÉS IS JUST a fancy French way of saying "sliced or whole raw vegetables for dipping." Celery sticks and carrots are the most common, though you can also try bell pepper, broccoli, radishes, and cauliflower.

bruschetta

[MAKES 10 TO 12 SERVINGS]

Bruschetta is an easy, yet elegant, appetizer that's great for parties. It brings together some of the classic Italian flavors—tomato, basil, olive oil, and a touch of balsamic vinegar. Some people like to jazz it up with mozzarella cheese, but we prefer the straight-tomato version.

> 3 vine-ripened tomatoes, diced
> 6 to 8 basil leaves, chopped
> 1 tablespoon olive oil
> 2 teaspoons balsamic vinegar
> 1 garlic clove, minced
> Salt and pepper
> GF bread (page 26) or thin rounds of Polenta (page 103)

1. Combine the tomatoes, basil, olive oil, vinegar, garlic, and salt and pepper in a bowl. Cover and refrigerate for 1 hour.
2. Broil or toast the bread or polenta. (Or, if you have the grill out, place on the grill for a smoky flavor.)
3. Spoon the bruschetta topping on the slices of toast or polenta and serve.

If you don't want to make your own polenta, a quick and easy shortcut is to use store-bought, pre-cooked tubes of polenta (also known as polenta chubs), cut into "medallion" cross sections. Polenta is almost always naturally gluten-free, but check the label to be sure.

caprese salad

[MAKES 6 SERVINGS]

Like Bruschetta (page 50), Caprese salad pairs classic Italian flavors—in this case, tomato, fresh basil, and mozzarella cheese. It's best made in the late spring through summer, when tomatoes are at their peak.

3 vine-ripened tomatoes, thinly sliced
16 ounces fresh mozzarella cheese, thinly sliced
1/2 bunch fresh basil, chopped (about 1/2 cup)
Olive oil
Balsamic vinegar
Salt and pepper

Lay out alternating slices of tomato and mozzarella on a platter. Sprinkle with the chopped basil. Drizzle with olive oil and balsamic vinegar and season with salt and pepper.

Variations

In lieu of chopping the basil, you can also use whole basil leaves, alternating them with the tomato and mozzarella slices. Or, you can skewer mini-kebabs of cherry tomatoes, mozzarella cubes, and basil. As long as the tricolor trio is present—tomato, mozzarella, and basil—you've got a Caprese salad!

crab cakes

[MAKES 10 TO 12 CRAB CAKES, ABOUT 5 TO 6 SERVINGS]

Pete fondly remembers his childhood spent in and around the Atlantic Ocean, including many days and nights spent on his Uncle Joe's boat. One favorite family activity was going crabbing, usually for blue claw crabs on Long Island's South Shore. Returning home, the family would steam their haul and gather around the kitchen table, working their way through the crabs. The almost inevitable surplus of crabs resulted in a variety of tasty ways to fully utilize the meat, one of which was crab cakes. More recently, we were inspired to develop these gluten-free cakes after Pete watched Elise Wiggins, the executive chef of Panzano restaurant in Denver, make a gluten-free crab puff at a Denver beer and food festival. This is a crab cake that's all about the crab, not the breading. It tastes like seasoned crab meat, and that's the way we like it . . . meaty.

½ cup GF bread crumbs (see box, page 57)
2 teaspoons seafood seasoning (see box, below)
1 teaspoon GF baking powder
1 teaspoon mustard powder
2 eggs
2 tablespoons salted butter, melted
1 tablespoon sour cream
1 teaspoon Worcestershire sauce
1 pound lump crab meat (not imitation)
2 tablespoons olive oil

1. Preheat the oven to 375°F.
2. Mix together the bread crumbs, seafood seasoning, baking powder, and mustard powder in a bowl.
3. Mix together the eggs, melted butter, sour cream, and Worcestershire sauce in a medium bowl. Lightly mix in the crab meat, being careful not to break up the crab. Carefully mix in the bread crumb mixture.
4. Form the crab mixture into 10 to 12 patties and place on a cookie sheet. Cover and refrigerate for 1 hour, or pop the sheet in the freezer for 15 minutes.
5. Heat the olive oil in a skillet over medium-high heat. Add half of the crab cakes and cook, turning once, until browned on each side, about 10 minutes. Repeat with the remaining cakes, adding more oil if needed. Place the cakes on a cookie sheet and bake for 15 minutes, or until the outside is crispy and the center is cooked through but still moist.

WHEN PEOPLE THINK of "seafood seasoning," they often by default think of Old Bay, which is ubiquitous around Baltimore's Inner Harbor, among many other places! We prefer to make our own blend and store it in a small, airtight spice container. We started by reading the list of ingredients on a container of Old Bay, but our version isn't a direct overlap, and we played with ratios until we stumbled upon a combination of flavors that we thought blended perfectly with crab.

Follow these instructions to make your own:

1. Pulse 6 dry bay leaves in a coffee or spice grinder until the leaves are fairly well ground.

2. Add 1 teaspoon celery seeds, 1 teaspoon ground mustard, 1 teaspoon ground pepper, 1 teaspoon paprika, $\frac{1}{2}$ teaspoon ground ginger, $\frac{1}{4}$ teaspoon ground allspice, $\frac{1}{4}$ teaspoon ground cinnamon, $\frac{1}{4}$ teaspoon red pepper flakes, a pinch of ground cloves, and $\frac{1}{2}$ teaspoon salt. Pulse again, and you're good to go!

bacon-wrapped shrimp

[MAKES 4 SERVINGS]

When Pete was in high school, he and his buddies would always celebrate New Year's Eve at a party at the Sabellico household—the dad, Tom, was Pete's Little League baseball coach, and the son, Chris, was a good friend. The Sabellicos always served up an incredible spread of appetizers, which included bacon-wrapped shrimp. Arguably, bacon makes anything better, but in this case, the saltiness of the bacon and the sweetness of the shrimp really are a divine combination. There's also the play of textures at work—crispy bacon with chewy shrimp. The trick is to have the bacon and shrimp finish cooking at the same time.

10 strips GF bacon
20 medium (about 21–25 count) uncooked shrimp, peeled and deveined

Note: Shrimp naturally like to curl themselves into a half-moon sort of shape. That's okay. When wrapping the shrimp in bacon, allow enough bacon to wrap around the shrimp while they're in their curled position. Don't try to straighten out the shrimp and wrap them that way. When you skewer the shrimp, skewer first through the tail, and then through the thick, meaty portion nearest what would be considered the "head."

1. Heat a grill to medium-high.
2. Partially cook the bacon (about halfway to being done) in a skillet on the stove top, or on a plate in the microwave (with the strips of bacon between sheets of paper towel).
3. Cut the bacon strips into lengths just long enough to make one full wrap around the shrimp. The size of your shrimp will determine the length of the bacon.
4. Wrap each shrimp in a piece of bacon and thread onto wooden skewers, leaving a small gap between each shrimp. Do not press them tightly together. You can probably fit 4 to 6 bacon-wrapped shrimp on each skewer.
5. Place the skewers on the grill and cook until the bacon is becoming crispy on the grill side, about 5 minutes. Flip the skewers and grill the opposite side about 3 to 4 minutes. When the bacon is getting crispy on that side and the shrimp are pink and opaque, the bacon-wrapped shrimp are done!

shrimp cocktail
with homemade sauce

[MAKES 10 SERVINGS]

Shrimp with fresh cocktail sauce is easily one of our all-time favorite appetizers. It's a classic, and we love it. Growing up, Pete and his family would often gather 'round the kitchen sink, furiously peeling and deveining pounds of shrimp. It happened most often around the Christmas holiday, but any family get-together was a good enough excuse for them. In fact, a get-together wasn't even strictly needed—Pete's mom told him and his brother, Mike, that as long as they did the work, she'd steam the shrimp! The cocktail sauce is zippy, thanks to as much or as little horseradish as you care to use, and the flavor is bright, thanks to the fresh lemon.

2 pounds shrimp
1 cup ketchup
1 to 3 teaspoons prepared horseradish
1/2 lemon, juiced

1. If using fresh shrimp, first peel and devein them. (A combo peeler/deveining tool really expedites this process.) Shrimp have a ventral and dorsal vein—you want to remove the dorsal one (the one on the shrimp's "back"), which actually isn't a vein at all, but rather the intestinal tract. Rinse the deveined shrimp under cold water. If using store-bought, uncooked shrimp, they may already be deveined. In which case you can skip to step 2. If using precooked shrimp, skip to step 3.

2. To steam the shrimp, bring 1 to 2 inches of salted water to boil in a saucepan. Place the shrimp in a steaming basket and place in the saucepan. Cover and steam the shrimp for about 5 minutes, until pink and opaque all the way through. (Alternately, use a dedicated food steamer. Or cook the shrimp in a small amount of boiling water in a covered saucepan; technically, the shrimp on the bottom will boil, not steam, but they'll still cook.) Chill the shrimp until you're ready to serve.

3. Mix together the ketchup, horseradish, and lemon juice to make the cocktail sauce. Use more horseradish for a spicier cocktail sauce and less for a milder version.

4. Serve the chilled shrimp with the cocktail sauce.

SHRIMP ARE SOLD by the pound, and are given a "count," which refers to the number of shrimp per pound. 30 count shrimp and higher are pretty small, trending toward the popcorn shrimp size. 20–30 count shrimp are a good size for shrimp cocktail—big enough to dip, but small enough that everyone gets a few (and they're typically not too expensive). Sub-20 count shrimp are large, and the closer you get to single-digit counts, the closer you get to jumbo shrimp, which at that point are big enough to look like baby lobsters!

mozzarella sticks

[MAKES 6 SERVINGS]

Mozzarella sticks are a definite holdover from our pre-gluten-free days. In those earlier times, we were big fans of brew-pubs, both local spots and those we encountered on the road. (We suppose we're still fans of brewpubs, though the food and the beer is almost categorically off-limits these days.) If one thing was a constant from place to place, it was that pretty much every brewpub had mozzarella sticks on their appetizer menu. This is our delightful, gluten-free version of the brewpub staple. We came up with it one night while drinking some gluten-free beer. With some mozzarella in the fridge, we wondered if we could make a good mozzarella stick. Turns out the answer is yes. We're big fans of the crispy breading and the soft, melted cheese. Serve with our Marinara Sauce (page 128), the simple marinara sauce for Gnocchi (in the box on page 109), or your favorite prepared marinara sauce.

> 1 pound brick mozzarella cheese (not fresh mozzarella)
> 3/4 cup Artisan GF Flour Mix (page 15)
> 1 egg
> 2 tablespoons water
> 2 cups Italian-seasoned GF bread crumbs (see box, page 57)
> Dried basil
> Dried oregano
> Garlic powder
> Salt and pepper
> Olive oil

1. Cut the mozzarella into sticks that are about 1/2 inch square and 3 inches long.

2. Put the flour in a shallow dish. Whisk together the egg and water in a second shallow dish. Put the bread crumbs in a third shallow dish. Season each dish (flour, egg wash, and crumbs) with a dash of basil, oregano, garlic, and salt and pepper.

3. Dredge the cheese sticks in the flour, coat with the egg wash, and then coat with the bread crumbs. To keep your hands from getting too messy, use one hand for the flour and bread crumbs and the other hand for the egg.

4. Heat about 1/4 inch oil in a large skillet over medium-high heat until it is hot but not smoking (if the oil smokes, reduce the heat). In batches, add the cheese sticks and fry, turning the pieces, just until the bread crumbs are golden, about 45–60 seconds per side. Be careful not to keep the cheese in the oil for too long as it will melt and ooze out of the breading.

5. Place the finished mozzarella sticks on a plate lined with paper towels to absorb any excess oil before serving.

T O MAKE YOUR own gluten-free bread crumbs, begin with any stale gluten-free bread. In the past, we've used traditional gluten-free bread, as well as leftover waffles, pancakes, and even arepas (Venezuelan corn pancakes). Pulse the gluten-free bread in a food processor until you have small crumbs. To make Italian-seasoned bread crumbs, add salt, garlic powder, dried basil, and dried oregano to taste. Also, many specialty gluten-free companies are now offering GF bread crumbs. We recommend both the plain and Italian versions from Aleia's Gluten-Free Foods. They're the best we've tried.

chicken or beef saté with peanut dipping sauce

[MAKES 6 SERVINGS]

This saté with peanut dipping sauce is a favorite of Kelli's family for parties. In fact, Kelli made it for the first time for her college graduation party, which she self-catered. It has remained popular ever since, and we still make it for festive, celebratory occasions. The saté is seasoned, but it's the dipping sauce that really makes the dish—it's a little spicy, a little creamy, and a whole lot o' tasty.

Saté

- ¾ cup tamari wheat-free soy sauce
- ¼ cup sake
- 1 lime, juiced
- 2 tablespoons honey
- 4 garlic cloves, minced
- 1 teaspoon ground coriander
- 1 teaspoon ground turmeric
- 2 pounds chicken breast or beef sirloin, cut into thin strips

Peanut Dipping Sauce

- 1 vine-ripened tomato, quartered
- ½ cup peanut butter
- ½ cup GF chicken broth
- ½ lime, juiced
- ⅓ cup cilantro leaves
- 3 tablespoons tamari wheat-free soy sauce
- 2 tablespoons brown sugar
- 2 garlic cloves, peeled
- 1 jalapeño chile pepper

1. To make the saté: Combine the soy sauce, lime juice, honey, garlic, coriander, and turmeric in a bowl.

2. Place the chicken or beef in the soy sauce mixture and toss to coat. Cover and marinate for at least 1 hour. The meat can be marinated in the refrigerator for up to 24 hours.

3. Meanwhile, to make the peanut dipping sauce: Combine all the ingredients in a food processor and blend until smooth.

4. Heat a grill to high. Remove the chicken or beef strips from the marinade and thread onto metal skewers or bamboo skewers that have been soaked in water for several hours. Place on the grill and grill until the meat is cooked through.

5. Serve the saté with the peanut dipping sauce on the side.

Variation

For a vegetarian version, use very firm tofu in place of the chicken or beef. Before marinating, place the drained tofu between paper towels and place a pot or plate on top to weigh it down. Let the tofu sit for 1 hour to press out any excess moisture. Slice the tofu into thin strips and marinate as above.

pigs in a blanket

[MAKES 72 PIGS IN BLANKETS, ABOUT 12 SERVINGS]

There are at least two times each year that we make pigs in a blanket and devour them like a plague of locusts descending on a field of gluten-free grain. The first is for our Christmas tree trimming party. Each winter, usually in late November or early December, we buy a permit and cut down a Christmas tree in one of Colorado's national forests. Returning home that evening, we turn on the Christmas music, uncork a bottle of wine, and lay out a spread of seemingly unrelated appetizers that ranges from Shrimp Cocktail (page 55) to these pigs in a blanket. The other time of year is just two months later (give or take a few weeks), when we break out the pigs in blankets for the Super Bowl. We'll also make them at other times of the year, though not without some debate—Kelli sometimes argues that pigs in a blanket aren't "classy enough" for certain parties; Pete, ever the guy, argues that pigs in a blanket are always a crowd favorite, so why not? We say, you decide when you make 'em, and enjoy! Serve with ketchup and mustard.

3/4 cup warm water (about 115°F)

1 tablespoon honey

2¼ teaspoons (1 package) active dry yeast

4 tablespoons (½ stick) salted butter, melted

1 teaspoon salt

1 teaspoon xanthan gum

2 cups Artisan GF Flour Mix (page 15)

6 GF hot dogs (we recommend Coleman Natural or Applegate Farms)

1. Preheat the oven to 400°F.
2. Combine the warm water, honey, and yeast in a medium bowl and let stand until the mixture bubbles, about 5 minutes. The bubbles mean your yeast is alive and ready to go.
3. Stir together 2 tablespoons of the melted butter with the salt and xanthan gum, and add to the yeast mixture. Mix in the flour to form a dough that is soft but not sticky to the touch. Divide the dough in half.
4. Roll out one half of the dough between two pieces of plastic wrap to a roughly 6 x 13-inch rectangle that is about ⅛ inch thick. Cut the dough into 36 rectangles that are about 1 inch wide by 2½ inches long. Repeat with the remaining dough.
5. Cut each hot dog lengthwise into quarters. Then cut each quarter into shorter thirds to create a total of 72 small dogs.
6. Wrap each mini hot dog with a piece of dough and place on ungreased cookie sheets. Brush the pigs in blankets with the remaining 2 tablespoons melted butter.
7. Bake the pigs in blankets for 12 to 15 minutes, until the dough is cooked through.

summer rolls
with sweet and sour dipping sauce

[MAKES 12 ROLLS, ABOUT 6 SERVINGS]

We love summer rolls, not only for their own sake, but also because they have the same wonderful fillings as spring rolls, but without the frying and the grease. This is a vegetarian version, but you could also add cooked shrimp for some extra pizzazz.

Summer Rolls
6 shiitake mushrooms, de-stemmed

2 ounces rice vermicelli noodles

2 scallions

Twelve 8-inch round rice paper wrappers

1 carrot, grated

1/2 cup finely shredded cabbage

1/2 cup bean sprouts

Fresh cilantro leaves

Fresh mint leaves

Sweet and Sour Dipping Sauce
2 tablespoons agave nectar

2 tablespoons rice vinegar

2 tablespoons ketchup

2 tablespoons water

1 1/2 teaspoons tamari wheat-free soy sauce

3/4 teaspoon cornstarch

1. To make the rolls: Bring a few cups of water to a boil in a saucepan. Add the mushrooms and boil until tender, about 5 minutes. Remove the mushrooms from the water and set aside to cool. In the same water, boil the vermicelli until soft and glassy, 2 to 3 minutes. Drain and run under cold water. Cut the noodles into 3-inch segments and set aside.

2. Slice the mushrooms into thin strips. Slice the scallions in half lengthwise, and then in half lengthwise again. Cut each full-length scallion piece into 3-inch long sections.

3. To assemble a roll, soak one rice paper wrapper in warm water for a few seconds to soften. Remove from the water and set on a paper towel. Take a small amount of each of the filling items (vermicelli, mushrooms, scallions, carrot, cabbage, and bean sprouts) and arrange crosswise on the third of the rice paper closest to you. Top with a few cilantro and mint leaves. To roll up, take the side of the rice paper closest to you and roll it up and over the filling, until the edge meets the middle of the rice paper. Fold in the right and left sides. To complete the roll, finish rolling to seal the summer roll with the filling inside.

4. Repeat with the remaining wrappers to make 12 rolls. Cover and refrigerate the rolls if not serving immediately.

5. To make the sweet and sour sauce: Mix all ingredients in a saucepan and heat over high heat, stirring, until the mixture comes to a boil and thickens. Let cool. Cover and refrigerate if not serving immediately.

6. Serve the rolls with the sweet and sour sauce.

chinese chicken-lettuce wraps

[MAKES 6 SERVINGS]

When our friend Laurel returned from an educational trip to China, she went on a Chinese-cooking spree. Around the same time, she and her husband, Chris, were selling their house and made Chinese chicken-lettuce wraps as an offering to the real estate agents and potential buyers who toured their home. We tasted the leftovers, which were delicious enough that we couldn't resist making our own version. The water chestnuts add a little crunch, while the sesame, sherry, and soy really stand out in the sauce that ties the chicken and mushroom filling together.

Stir-Fry Sauce

2 tablespoons water

1 tablespoon tamari wheat-free soy sauce

1 tablespoon dry sherry

1 tablespoon dark brown sugar

2 teaspoons rice wine vinegar

2 teaspoons cornstarch

1 teaspoon sesame oil

Chicken Filling

2 teaspoons dry sherry

2 teaspoons water

1 teaspoon cornstarch

Salt and pepper

2 boneless, skinless, chicken breasts, diced small

Olive oil or peanut oil

2 garlic cloves, minced

1-inch piece fresh ginger, peeled and minced

8 shiitake mushrooms, stemmed and diced small

2 scallions, chopped

8 ounces water chestnuts, drained and diced small

1 head iceberg lettuce, leaves separated

1. To make the stir-fry sauce: Whisk together all the ingredients in a small bowl. Set aside.
2. To make the chicken filling: Combine the sherry, water, cornstarch, and salt and pepper in a medium bowl. Add the diced chicken and stir to mix. Cover and marinate for 20 minutes.
3. Heat a few tablespoons of oil in a large skillet or wok over high heat. Add the chicken and its marinade and stir-fry until the chicken is cooked through and lightly browned, about 4 minutes. Remove the chicken from the pan.

4. Add a little more oil to the pan. Add the garlic and ginger and stir-fry until aromatic but not browned, about 2 minutes. Add the mushrooms, scallions, and water chestnuts. Stir-fry the veggies until they reduce in volume and are beginning to brown (which adds a little crunch to the texture of the filling), about 10 minutes.

5. Return the chicken to the skillet and add the stir-fry sauce. Cook until the sauce is thickened, turning the mixture to evenly coat in the sauce.

6. Serve the chicken filling with the lettuce leaves. To assemble, put a few spoonfuls of the filling on the center of the lettuce leaf, roll up, and enjoy.

Variation

To make the lettuce wraps vegetarian, omit the chicken and triple the quantity of shiitake mushrooms.

STIR-FRYING INVOLVES cooking at high heat for a short amount of time. Don't be afraid to crank up the burner.

shrimp and vegetable tempura

[MAKES 2 TO 10+ SERVINGS]

(DEPENDING ON THE AMOUNT OF SHRIMP AND VEGETABLES)

We don't deep-fry often. It's not really our style. Usually, we'll sauté in olive oil and/or butter, and occasionally we'll pan- or stir-fry. But deep-fry? Almost never. Tempura is one time when we happily make an exception. The light rice-flour batter combined with the dipping sauce (where the mirin and soy shine in combination) transports us in spirit, and in flavor, to our favorite Japanese restaurants.

Shrimp and Vegetables

Uncooked shrimp, large (typically, under 20 count)

Broccoli

Asparagus

Bell pepper

Onion

Potato

Sweet potato

Dipping Sauce

¹/₄ cup + 1 tablespoon hot water

2 tablespoons mirin

1 tablespoon tamari wheat-free soy sauce

1¹/₄ teaspoons sugar

¹/₄ teaspoon fish sauce

Tempura Batter

³/₄ cup brown rice flour

¹/₄ cup cornstarch

¹/₂ teaspoon GF baking powder

¹/₂ teaspoon salt

1 egg

¹/₂ cup cold water

Canola or peanut oil for frying

1. To prep the shrimp: Peel and devein the shrimp, leaving the tails on as a "handle" or removing the tail shells in order to have a fully edible shrimp tempura.

2. To prep the vegetables: Cut the vegetables according to the following guidelines: broccoli, bite-sized pieces; asparagus, individual spears; bell pepper, long slices; onion, potato, and sweet potato, ¹/₈-inch-thick slices.

3. To make the dipping sauce, combine all the ingredients and stir until the sugar is fully dissolved. Set aside.

4. To make the tempura batter: Mix together the rice flour, cornstarch, baking powder, and salt in a bowl. Make a well in the center. Add the egg and cold water to the well, then mix together to incorporate all the dry ingredients and make a wet batter. (To make a thinner, lighter batter, add a small amount of additional water. A thin batter works well for shrimp, but will be too runny to adhere well to the vegetables.)

5. Heat 2 to 3 inches of oil in a saucepan over medium-high heat (or enough oil to fully submerge your largest tempura foods). The oil is the appropriate temperature when it passes this test: Drip a small amount of batter into the oil. If the batter sinks to the bottom of the pan and stays there, the oil is too cold. If the batter stays atop the oil and sizzles immediately (or if the oil is smoking), it's too hot. If the batter sinks, and then quickly rises back to the surface and starts to sizzle, the oil is the right temperature. Adjust your burner accordingly to maintain this oil temperature throughout the frying.

6. In batches, dip the shrimp and vegetables in the batter to coat fully and gently ease into the oil. Fry, turning the shrimp and veggies after several minutes, until light golden brown. (Regularly remix the tempura batter; sometimes it can settle and the bottom will be very thick while the top will be watery.) Transfer the shrimp and vegetables to a platter lined with paper towels to drain.

7. Serve the tempura pieces with the dipping sauce.

SOUPS

AND

SALADS

split pea and ham soup

[MAKES 4 SERVINGS]

There are certain times of year—Christmas and Easter being two of them—when a spiral cut, baked ham is our traditional family dinner. We always look forward to the ham, and maybe just as much, to the leftovers as well. In addition to the rich salty ham, those leftovers include the ham bone, and there's no better way to put it to use than in soup. Since the ham bone is cooked in the soup, the rich ham flavor permeates the split peas and the soup becomes almost smoky.

2 cups GF chicken broth

2 cups water

1 cup dried split peas, rinsed

1 ham bone (left over from spiral cut ham)

1 carrot, chopped

1 celery stalk, chopped

1 medium onion, chopped

1 bay leaf

1 cup diced GF ham

Salt and pepper

1. Combine the broth, water, peas, ham bone, carrot, celery, onion, and bay leaf in a large pot. (Add more water if needed to cover the vegetables fully.) Bring to a boil and reduce the heat. Simmer, covered, for 1 hour, or until the peas are very soft.

2. Remove the ham bone and bay leaf. Puree the soup using an immersion blender, or in batches in a standard blender, returning the pureed soup to the saucepan.

3. Add the diced ham and cook until the ham is heated through, 10 minutes.

chicken noodle soup

[MAKES 8 SERVINGS]

Chicken noodle soup has been one of our constant companions through the years. As kids, our moms would bring us a bowl to make us feel better when we were sick, or have a hot bowl waiting when we came inside from playing in the snow. More recently, shortly after moving to Colorado, we'd warm up with chicken noodle soup after a day of ice climbing, or stop by the grocery store at the end of the work day to pick up a fresh "hot loaf" of bread to pair with our Campbell's or Lipton soup. Going gluten-free ended those days, but awakened us to another chicken noodle soup pleasure. As we increasingly embraced the artisanal way of cooking, we developed a preference for a different (and healthier) kind of chicken noodle soup, one built from the ground up, starting with a whole chicken as its base. This yields a richer, more intense chicken flavor in the soup.

1 whole chicken, quartered
1 medium onion, diced
1 carrot, diced
1 celery stalk, diced
1 cup GF pasta noodles (page 122)
Salt and pepper

1. Combine the chicken, onion, carrot, celery, and enough water to cover in a large pot. Bring to a boil over high heat, reduce the heat, and simmer uncovered for 2 hours.

2. Remove the pot from the heat. Remove the chicken pieces from the broth and allow to cool. When cool enough to handle, pick the meat from the bones, discarding the skin, any pieces of fat, and the bones. Shred the meat with your fingers or two forks.

3. Spoon the fat from the top of the broth. Return the shredded meat to the broth and bring to a simmer. Add the noodles and simmer for 10 to 15 minutes. Season with salt and pepper to taste.

THIS RECIPE STARTS out with a mirepoix, a classic French combination of three aromatics: onion, carrot, and celery. Traditionally, they're in a ratio of 2:1:1 (2 parts onion, 1 part carrot, and 1 part celery). Here, though, we use them in roughly equal quantities to provide a great base for the chicken soup broth.

TO QUARTER A chicken, first remove the packet of giblets from the cavity and discard or reserve for another use. Cleave the chicken in half down the middle. Then separate the breast from the leg and thigh. A strong, sharp knife works well, but heavy-duty kitchen shears work even better to help cleave the breastbone and the ribs.

butternut squash soup

[MAKES 4 SERVINGS]

We first made this soup simply because we had a leftover butternut squash after Thanksgiving. As Kelli's dad would say, we had "a solution looking for a problem." And voilà! *Here we are. The soup is very smooth and mild-flavored, with a touch of sweetness from the apple. If you don't have a slow cooker, you can make the soup on the stove top in a large, heavy saucepan over low heat for 2 hours.*

1 medium butternut squash, peeled, seeded, and cubed
1 medium onion, chopped
1 green apple, peeled, cored, and chopped
2 cups GF chicken broth or vegetable broth
1 cup water
$\frac{1}{2}$ teaspoon curry powder
Salt and pepper

1. Combine the squash, onion, and apple in a slow cooker. Add the broth, water, and curry powder and stir to combine.
2. Cook on low for 6 to 8 hours.
3. Puree the soup using an immersion blender, or in batches in a regular blender. Season with salt and pepper.

Variation

For a richer, creamier soup, stir 1 cup half-and-half into the finished soup.

SLOW COOKERS COOK foods for long periods of time under low heat. They're great at making meats tender, melding the flavors in soups, and making your life easier—just prep the meal in the morning, let it cook while you're at work all day, and have a meal ready to eat when you get home. (Unless you work from home like Pete, and smell the delicious food cooking all day long . . . This may lead to unintended snacking to satisfy the inevitable hunger.

roasted winter vegetable soup

[MAKES 4 SERVINGS]

This recipe was one of the first we developed as newlyweds. We were recipe testing for an article about holiday cuisine we wrote for a small, upstate New York magazine—the only time, other than this cookbook, that we've genuinely worked as coauthors! At the time we lived in a tiny studio apartment in Weehawken, New Jersey, just across the Hudson River from midtown Manhattan. Our friend Chris called it the "Swiss Army apartment," because it converted to multiple uses—bedroom, kitchen, home office, and dining room for entertaining. The quarters may have felt cramped at times, but we ate many wonderful meals there with great friends. This soup was often on the menu.

1 parsnip

1 onion

1 turnip

1 acorn squash

2 carrots

2 medium russet potatoes

2 tablespoons olive oil

Salt and pepper

$1/2$ cup dry white wine (try a Pinot Gris)

$4^1/_2$ cups GF vegetable broth

$3/4$ cup half-and-half

1. Preheat oven to 400°F.
2. Peel and cut all the vegetables into large dice. Spread the veggies in a roasting pan, drizzle with the olive oil, and season with salt and pepper. Roast for 60 minutes, or until tender and browned.
3. Transfer the vegetables to a saucepan. Add the wine to the roasting pan and deglaze, scraping to remove all of the roasted bits (known as the *fond*) from the bottom of the pan. Pour the wine over the vegetables in the saucepan and add the broth.
4. Cook the vegetables and broth over medium-heat until heated through, about 10 minutes. Puree the soup using an immersion blender or in batches in a standard blender.
5. Stir in the half-and-half. Season with salt and pepper to taste.

tomato soup

[MAKES 4 SERVINGS]

Our local farmers' market has a vendor—an organic farm with amazing produce—that always has the most beautiful tomatoes we've ever seen. They're intensely flavorful, and we buy them specifically for this recipe. Other friends of ours in Colorado's Front Range either belong to a CSA (Community Supported Agriculture) organization or have a community garden plot, both of which often yield an enormous surplus of tomatoes . . . another good reason to make this recipe! We're spoiled in the sense that tomatoes—both greenhouse- and field-grown—are in season for much of the spring, summer, and early fall in Colorado. But as a fruit in general, tomatoes are very seasonal, and we recommend making this recipe in late summer, when they're at their peak.

2 tablespoons olive oil

1 onion, chopped

1 garlic clove, minced

8 tomatoes, chopped

2 cups GF chicken broth or vegetable broth

About 10 basil leaves, chopped; or 2 teaspoons dried basil

1/2 teaspoon red pepper flakes, optional

Salt and pepper

1. Heat the oil in a saucepan over medium-high heat. Add the onion and garlic and sauté until the onion is translucent. Add the tomatoes and broth. Bring to a boil, reduce the heat, and simmer uncovered, stirring occasionally, about 30 minutes.

2. Puree the soup with an immersion blender, or in batches in a standard blender, returning the pureed soup to the saucepan.

3. Bring the soup to a simmer and cook until reduced by one-third, 30 to 40 minutes longer.

4. Season with basil, red pepper flakes, and salt and pepper.

Note: The flavor of this dish hinges on the quality of the tomatoes. Don't skimp. Get fresh, ripe tomatoes. Your taste buds will thank you.

strawberry soup

[MAKES 6 SERVINGS]

From Kelli's hometown of Ithaca, New York, at the southern end of Cayuga Lake, you can drive up the western shoreline and arrive at Taughannock Falls, the highest waterfall in New York State. Just before you reach the falls, you first arrive at Taughannock Farms Inn, which has a restaurant known, in part, for its strawberry soup. It's the direct inspiration for this soup, which Kelli first made back in high school when Kay, the mother of one of Kelli's friends, helped her develop this recipe, which we've refined over time. As a chilled soup, the strawberry flavor is clean and refreshing, and this dish works not only as an appetizer, but also potentially as a breakfast or even a dessert in summer when strawberries are at their peak.

1 quart strawberries, hulled
1 cup GF vanilla yogurt
¼ cup honey
1 cup half-and-half

Combine the strawberries, yogurt, and honey in a food processor. Blend until smooth. Pour in the half-and-half while blending until incorporated. Serve chilled.

HULLING A STRAWBERRY involves removing the stem as well as a white core of tough pulp (the hull). This can be done using a knife or a strawberry huller, which looks a bit like a pair of large tweezers. Kelli, long a fan of kitchen gadgets, acquired her first strawberry huller at age 7 at a Tupperware party!

new england clam chowder

[MAKES 4 SERVINGS]

As a native of Long Island, New York, Pete spent his childhood in and around the Atlantic Ocean—surfing, fishing, crabbing, and . . . clamming. Along the South Shore, a series of bays and inlets were protected from the comparatively harsh Atlantic by a string of thin, sandy barrier beaches. In among those protected bays and coves were areas known as the Flats, broad expanses of shallow water where you could wade and dig into the sandy bottom looking for clams. The subsequent haul was divided up for all sorts of dishes, including baked clams and New England Clam Chowder, which we've modified here to make gluten-free and use fresh Colorado clams (which is to say they're canned). See the box on page 131 for more info on using fresh versus canned clams.

4 strips GF bacon

1 medium onion, diced

1 celery stalk, diced

1 garlic clove, minced

2 medium potatoes, peeled and cubed

Three 6.5-ounce cans chopped clams in clam juice, drained, juice reserved

4 tablespoons (1/2 stick) salted butter

1/4 cup Artisan GF Flour Mix (page 15)

1 cup milk

1/2 cup half-and-half

1 tablespoon red wine vinegar

Salt and pepper

1. Cook the bacon in a 12-inch or larger skillet or a saucepan over medium-high heat until crisp. Crumble and set aside.

2. Add the onion, celery, and garlic to the bacon fat and sauté until soft, about 5 minutes.

3. Add the potatoes and clam juice and simmer until the potatoes are tender, about 20 minutes.

4. While the potatoes are cooking, melt the butter in a large saucepan. Whisk in the flour until smooth. Whisk in the milk and half-and-half. Cook over medium heat, stirring constantly, until thickened.

5. Add the potato mixture to the thickened milk mixture and stir. Stir in the clams and vinegar and season with salt and pepper. Cook just until the clams are heated through (overcooking clams will make them tough and chewy). Serve topped with the crumbled bacon.

Variation

If using fresh clams, use 1¼ pounds fresh clam meat (about 5 pounds whole clams). First steam the clams in a large, covered sauté pan, and collect the fresh meat for use in the recipe (discard the sheath that covers the "foot" of the claims). Add a little extra water to the recipe in lieu of the clam juice from the canned clams.

roasted tomato and red pepper soup

[MAKES 4 SERVINGS]

Kelli "discovered" a version of this dish while studying abroad in Australia, where peppers are known as cap-sicums. The flavor of this naturally gluten-free soup is sharp and slightly acidic, and the roasting adds a depth to the otherwise clean, fresh flavors of the vegetables.

3 vine-ripened tomatoes, quartered

2 red bell peppers, seeded and quartered

1 medium onion, quartered

2 garlic cloves, unpeeled

3 tablespoons olive oil

2 tablespoons balsamic vinegar

Salt and pepper

1. Preheat the oven to 350°F.

2. Combine the tomatoes, bell peppers, onion, and garlic in a roasting pan. Drizzle with the olive oil and balsamic vinegar. Roast for 1 hour, or until all of the vegetables are soft. Let the vegetables cool for a few minutes.

3. When just cool enough to handle, peel the skin from the red peppers. If the skin does not come off easily, wrap them in plastic wrap and let sit for about 5 minutes, then try peeling them again. Squeeze the garlic from the unpeeled cloves.

4. Transfer the roasted vegetables to a food processor or blender and blend until smooth. Make sure to scrape all bits from the bottom of the pan and use them, too! Season with salt and pepper and serve. (The soup should be ideal serving temperature, but you can always reheat it if it has cooled too much or if you'd like to serve it hotter.)

honey-mustard chicken
and green apple salad

[MAKES 4 SERVINGS]

Our love of mustard dates back to the first days of our relationship, when we'd dip pretzels in a wasabi mustard as a tasty snack. More recently, Pete was on a business trip in Stowe, Vermont, and stumbled across a honey-mustard chicken and green apple salad at a local restaurant, which directly inspired this dish. The tartness of the green apple, sweetness of the honey, and spiciness of the mustard combine to form a vibrant and flavorful salad.

1/4 cup Dijon or brown mustard

1/4 cup honey

4 boneless, skinless chicken breasts

2 tablespoons olive oil

1 lemon wedge

Salt and pepper

1 tablespoon salted butter, optional

1/2 cup chopped pecans

1/2 head green leaf lettuce, chopped

1/2 to 2/3 Granny Smith apple, cored and thinly sliced

1. Heat a grill to medium-high.

2. Whisk together the mustard and honey. Combine half of the honey mustard with the chicken breasts in a shallow dish and toss to coat. Cover and marinate for 15 minutes, or until your grill is up to temperature.

3. To make the dressing, add the olive oil and a squeeze of lemon juice to the remaining honey mustard. Season with a dash of salt and pepper and mix to blend; set aside.

4. Grill the chicken breasts, turning once, until no longer pink, 8 to 10 minutes. Baste with the marinade while grilling until 5 minutes before the chicken is cooked through. Slice the chicken and set aside.

5. Melt the butter in a small skillet over medium-high heat. Add the pecans and cook until toasted and lightly golden brown, about 5 minutes. Sprinkle with salt if desired. (To toast without the butter, preheat the oven to 350°F, spread the pecans on a baking sheet and toast for 10 to 15 minutes.)

6. Toss the lettuce with the dressing. Divide the lettuce among four bowls. Top with apple slices, pecans, and chicken slices.

Variation

For a vegetarian apple salad, simply omit the chicken.

german potato salad

[MAKES 6 SERVINGS]

Each year we host an Oktoberfest party, usually in late September to coincide with the "real thing" in Munich, Germany. It's something of a meat-lovers' fest, as we fire up the grill and cook an assortment of bratwurst, sausage, and kielbasa. We also make this German Potato Salad—because, after all, what goes better with meat than potatoes? It's always a hit, and each year we decide that next time, we'll make even more German Potato Salad, but it still all gets eaten. It's a little smoky, a little tangy, and a little sweet.

5 large Yukon Gold or Red Bliss potatoes

5 slices GF bacon

1 medium onion, diced

3/4 cup water

1/4 cup apple cider vinegar

2 tablespoons sugar

1 tablespoon Artisan GF Flour Mix (page 15)

1/2 teaspoon celery seeds

1/2 teaspoon dry mustard

1/2 teaspoon salt

1/4 teaspoon pepper

1. Cover the whole, unpeeled potatoes with water in a saucepan. Bring to a boil and cook until tender, 30 to 40 minutes. Drain and let cool.

2. Peel the potatoes by scraping the skin off. It may help to hold each potato with a towel if they are too hot. Don't worry about getting every last square inch of skin. Cut the potatoes into quarters, and then cut those quarters into 1/4-inch-thick slices. Set aside.

3. Cook the bacon in a large skillet until crispy. Crumble and set aside.

4. To make the dressing, add the onion to the bacon drippings in the skillet and sauté until soft. Stir in the water, vinegar, sugar, flour, celery seed, mustard, salt, and pepper. Cook, stirring, until thickened, about 3 minutes.

5. Combine the potatoes, crumbled bacon, and dressing in a large salad bowl and toss.

shrimp-tomato-spinach pasta salad

[MAKES 6 SERVINGS]

Perhaps because the recipe calls for fresh basil, baby spinach, and vine-ripened tomatoes, this is a dish we associate with summertime. The flavors are light and refreshing, and the fresh ingredients are what the season is all about. We'll often enjoy this salad sitting on our back patio.

½ pound GF macaroni or bow-tie pasta

¼ cup olive oil

¼ cup freshly squeezed lemon juice

2 garlic cloves, minced

1 teaspoon salt

½ teaspoon pepper

6 vine-ripened tomatoes, chopped

2 cups fresh baby spinach, washed and dried

1 pound cooked large shrimp, peeled and deveined, with tails removed

¼ cup chopped fresh basil

1. Cook the pasta in salted boiling water until al dente. Immediately drain and rinse under cold water. Chill in the refrigerator.
2. Make the dressing by whisking together the olive oil, lemon juice, garlic, salt, and pepper.
3. Combine the chilled pasta, tomatoes, spinach, shrimp, and basil in a large bowl. Pour the dressing over the salad and toss to coat. Keep chilled in the refrigerator until ready to serve.

Variation

For a vegetarian salad, simply omit the shrimp.

For this pasta salad, we actually recommend going with the short-cut and using store-bought pasta since it is difficult to make these shapes at home. If you'd like to use our homemade Pasta Dough (page 122), use a whole recipe and cut the dough into short strips, about 1–2 inch long segments.

quinoa salad with vinaigrette

[MAKES 4 SERVINGS]

We first fell in love with quinoa during a high-altitude mountaineering expedition in Bolivia. In between climbing peaks in the Cordillera Real, one of the dominant mountain chains in the country, we spent time in and around La Paz, the country's administrative capital city. Our hotel there served a quinoa salad with vinaigrette very similar to this one, and upon returning to the United States, we immediately set about developing our own version.

1 cup quinoa, rinsed if necessary (see box below)

2 cups water

¼ cup red wine vinegar

¼ cup olive oil

Salt and pepper

½ red bell pepper, diced small

3 scallions, thinly sliced

1. Combine the quinoa and water in a saucepan and bring to a boil. Reduce the heat, cover, and simmer for 15 to 20 minutes, until all of the liquid is absorbed. The quinoa should be translucent and soft but not mushy. Refrigerate until cooled.

2. To make the vinaigrette, combine the vinegar and olive oil in a small bowl and season with salt and pepper.

3. Mix together the cooled quinoa, bell pepper, scallions, and vinaigrette in a serving bowl and toss. Serve chilled.

QUINOA, OFTEN BILLED as the "supergrain of the Andes" or the "gold of the Incas," is a plant native to South America that was prized in pre-Columbian cultures. It has a high protein content as well as a nutritionally well-balanced blend of amino acids. It's gaining popularity today for those reasons, and also because it is gluten-free.

In its most natural form, quinoa grains have a coating called *saponin* that is mildly toxic and a deterrent to birds and other would-be eaters. If your quinoa still has saponin, the water will develop soapy bubbles or a film, and the quinoa will taste bitter. Most prepackaged quinoa will have already been rinsed. Some people recommend rinsing it again anyway. We use the Ancient Harvest brand, and have never found the need. On the other hand, if you buy your quinoa from bulk bins you'll likely need to rinse it—either in a generous pot of water for several hours, or if you don't have the time, under running water in the sink. Either way, when it's time to drain the quinoa, the small grains will fall through most colanders and other strainers. We recommend using a strainer or sieve with a very fine mesh to get the job done.

mesclun salad with candied walnuts, dried cranberries, and goat cheese

[MAKES 2 SERVINGS]

When Kelli worked in New York City, she'd often head out for lunch to one of Manhattan's many gourmet food markets, which she called "the everything deli." They did indeed serve everything, from pasta to sandwiches to sushi (and lots more). And they also made salads, where the sky was the limit for customization with top-pings. More often than not, though, Kelli went with her tried and true . . . this recipe. Arguably, no combination is more classic than a green salad with candied nuts, dried fruit, and a bit of cheese. The interplay of tex-tures—the crunch of the walnuts, the sweet chew of the cranberries, and the creaminess of the cheese—really makes the dish. It's one of Kelli's favorites, and we hope you enjoy it as much as she does.

Mesclun Salad

2 tablespoons sugar

1/4 cup walnuts

8 ounces mesclun salad greens

1/4 cup dried cranberries

2 ounces goat cheese, crumbled

Balsamic Vinaigrette

3 tablespoons balsamic vinegar

1 tablespoon olive oil

1/2 teaspoon dried basil

1/4 teaspoon garlic powder

Salt and pepper

1. To make the salad: Melt the sugar in a small non-stick skillet over low heat. Add the walnuts and toss to coat. Immediately remove the nuts from the heat, spread out on a cookie sheet, and let cool. Break apart any nuts that have stuck to-gether so that there are no large clumps.

2. Toss together the salad greens, cranberries, goat cheese, and candied walnuts in a salad bowl.

3. To make the vinaigrette: Combine all the ingredi-ents in a small bowl and whisk to combine. If you like, transfer the vinaigrette to a salad dressing jar or other container for easier pouring and storage.

4. Drizzle the dressing over the salad and toss.

*T*RADITIONAL BALSAMIC VINE-GAR hails from two regions of Italy—Modena and Reggio Emilia—and isn't vinegar in the usual sense, in that it hasn't been distilled. Instead, traditional balsamic is made from wine *must* that is boiled down and then aged for years in wooden barrels. Most commercially available balsamic vinegars, on the other hand, start with a red wine vinegar base that is amended with "real" balsamic vinegar to emulate the traditional version. Often labeled as Balsamic Vinegar of Modena (confusing, isn't it, since it sounds like the traditional stuff?), it's widely available and commonly used in salad dressings and other cooking applications. Other than the method of production, and arguably, the taste, the other major difference you'll notice is price—"true" Balsamic vinegars will give you a major case of sticker shock, while the commercial Modena balsamics are reasonably priced.

bok choy salad

The original version of this recipe comes from our friend Kate. We've modified it somewhat to suit our own tastes, and to make it gluten-free, but we still owe Kate a big thanks for turning us on to the joys of bok choy— the dark, leafy greens are rich in iron, calcium, and vitamins A and C, while the bright white "stalks" of the leaves provide a sharp visual contrast. The bok choy is delightfully crunchy, and the vinaigrette has a great balance of sweet and salty. When an apartment fire tragically claimed many of Kate's belongings, including her family cookbook, she sent out a request for recipes. We were glad to be able to share with her a recipe that she originally shared with us, and in so doing, hopefully giving her back one small piece of what was lost.

Sweet Soy Vinaigrette

- ½ cup olive oil
- ⅓ cup sugar
- ¼ cup rice vinegar
- 2 tablespoons tamari wheat-free soy sauce

Salad

- 1 tablespoon olive oil
- ¼ teaspoon garlic powder
- Salt and pepper
- ¼ cup sesame seeds
- 4 ounces sliced almonds
- 1 medium head bok choy, cut into bite-size pieces
- 1 bunch scallions, cut into bite-size pieces

1. To make the vinaigrette: Bring all the ingredients to a boil in a saucepan and boil for 30 seconds, until the sugar is fully dissolved. Set aside to cool.

2. To make the salad: Heat the olive oil in a skillet and season with the garlic powder and salt and pepper. Add the sesame seeds and almonds and sauté until light brown and toasted. Remove from the heat and set aside to cool.

3. Mix together the bok choy, scallions, sesame-almonds, and vinaigrette in a large bowl. Serve immediately. (The salad also stores well in the refrigerator—combine the bok choy, scallions, and sesame-almonds, but store the dressing separately to prevent the salad from becoming soggy.)

caesar salad

[MAKES 2 SERVINGS]

Caesar salad comes in many shapes and sizes, from jarred dressings and bagged lettuce, to elaborate salads that are made fresh before your eyes tableside at restaurants. This version is much more in line with the latter, and comes from Kelli's brother Scott, who—like Kelli—has worked in the restaurant and hospitality biz for a long time. Caesar salad would traditionally have a raw egg yolk in the dressing, but when Scott's wife, Sandy, was pregnant with their first child, they modified the recipe to omit the egg. They didn't miss it, and neither do we. We think this Caesar salad is first rate as is.

1/4 cup olive oil
1 tablespoon Dijon mustard
2 teaspoons prepared horseradish
1/2 lemon, juiced
3 anchovies or 1 inch anchovy paste
1 garlic clove, passed through a press or finely minced
1/4 teaspoon red wine vinegar
1/4 teaspoon Worcestershire sauce
4 cups romaine lettuce
2 tablespoons grated Parmesan cheese
20 GF croutons (see box below)
Freshly ground pepper

1. Whisk together the olive oil, mustard, horseradish, lemon juice, anchovies, garlic, vinegar, and Worcestershire sauce in a salad bowl. The dressing should be creamy.
2. Tear the lettuce into bite-size pieces and add to the bowl. Toss the salad with the dressing until all the pieces of lettuce are evenly coated.
3. Add the cheese, croutons, and pepper and toss a second time. Serve.

To MAKE YOUR own gluten-free croutons, start with gluten-free bread (either our recipe on page 26, or store-bought). Cut the bread into slices, and then the slices into cubes. Lightly drizzly the cubes with olive oil and sprinkle with salt, pepper, and garlic powder (and, if you like, dried basil, dried oregano, and/or finely grated Parmesan). Toast in a 400°F toaster oven or regular oven for 10 minutes. Alternatively, many gluten-free bakeries—and an increasing number of companies you'll find in the grocery store—are offering GF croutons as well, including Aleia's Gluten-Free Foods.

SIDES

jasmine rice

[MAKES 4 SERVINGS]

If there's one rice we make more than any other, it's jasmine rice. We love the taste and texture, and it pairs well with a wide variety of dishes.

1 cup jasmine rice
1¹/₂ cups water
1 tablespoon olive oil
1 teaspoon salt

1. Combine the rice, water, olive oil, and salt in a saucepan and stir briefly. Bring to a boil over high heat, uncovered. Immediately reduce the heat to low, cover, and simmer without opening the lid to check on the rice—let the steam and heat contained within do their work! Check on the rice after 15 to 20 minutes. When all of the water is absorbed, the rice should be tender. Confirm by tasting for texture and moistness. Depending on altitude and the day's humidity, the rice may require additional water and cooking time.

2. Let the rice sit in the covered pot, off the heat, for another 5 to 10 minutes. Fluff the rice with a fork and serve.

caribbean rice

[MAKES 4 SERVINGS]

There are times when, as much as we love the mountains, we're ready for a break from the cold and the snow. Typically, we set our sights on points farther south, and we're especially fond of the Caribbean. We first traveled there together for our honeymoon—to the island of St. Lucia—and have returned several times since. Such trips are not just about relaxation, warm weather, sunshine, and turquoise waters, though. They're also about food—travel for us is a culinary experience as much as it is a cultural one. In the Caribbean in particular, it's a way to more fully experience island life, and just as much so, a way to bring that experience back home with us, as in this Caribbean Rice. Try pairing it with our Jamaican Jerk Chicken (page 148).

1 tablespoon olive oil

½ medium onion, diced

1 garlic clove, minced

1 cup long-grain rice

1 cup GF chicken broth or vegetable broth

1 cup coconut milk

1 teaspoon dried thyme

½ teaspoon ground turmeric

½ teaspoon salt

¼ teaspoon pepper

½ cup canned kidney beans, rinsed and drained

1 ripe mango, peeled, pitted, and cut into ½-inch cubes

1. Heat the olive oil in a large saucepan over high heat. Add the onion and garlic and sauté until translucent.

2. Add the rice, broth, and coconut milk. Stir in the thyme, turmeric, salt, and pepper. Bring to a boil and reduce the heat to low. Cover and simmer for 15 minutes, or until the rice is tender and the liquid is absorbed.

3. Add the beans and mango and cook for an additional 5 minutes, or until heated through.

mexican rice

Recipes for Mexican rice can vary from cook to cook, but most agree on one thing: toast the rice in olive oil before adding a few spices and canned tomatoes (with the liquid from the can). Beyond that, the devil's in the details, as they say. We like to serve our version with Mexican Spice-Rubbed Pork Tenderloin (page 172).

1 cup long-grain rice

¼ cup olive oil

½ medium onion, diced

½ bell pepper, diced

1 garlic clove, minced

¾ cup canned no-salt-added diced tomatoes (about half of a 14.5-ounce can)

1¾ cups GF chicken broth or vegetable broth

1 teaspoon salt

1. Rinse the rice in a colander under cold water until the water runs clear (and free of excess rice starch).

2. Heat the olive oil in a large saucepan over medium heat. Add the rinsed rice and sauté until slightly toasted. Add the onion, pepper, and garlic and sauté until slightly soft. Add the tomatoes, broth, and salt and stir to combine.

3. Bring to a boil, cover, and reduce the heat. Simmer for about 20 minutes without lifting the lid, until the rice is tender and the liquid is absorbed. Fluff with a fork and serve.

brown rice

[**MAKES 4 SERVINGS**]

This recipe is as basic as they come, but it's well suited for pairing with a variety of main dishes. Try it with our Orange Chicken (page 157) or Chicken Piccata (page 161).

1 cup brown rice
2½ cups water
1 teaspoon salt

1. Rinse the rice thoroughly under cold water until the water runs clear.
2. Dry sauté the rice in a skillet over medium heat until the grains are opaque. Meanwhile, combine the water and salt in a saucepan and bring to a boil over high heat.
3. Add the sautéed rice to the boiling water, reduce the heat to low, and cover. Simmer for 45 to 50 minutes, until the rice is tender and the liquid is absorbed.
4. Remove the pan from heat and let sit covered for 10 minutes longer (no peeking). Fluff the rice and serve.

Variation

For a richer flavor, cook the brown rice in GF chicken broth instead of water.

BROWN RICE IS rice that has only had the hull removed (compared to the further milling and polishing that white rice requires). Consequently, brown rice has better nutritional content than its white rice counterpart. It's heartier, and has a slightly nutty flavor.

wild rice

[MAKES 8 SERVINGS]

We met in college—at Cornell University—and despite vastly different majors (Kelli in hospitality, Pete in natural resources) we were coincidentally enrolled in the same Native American studies class. The final for the course was a practicum of each student's choosing. Kelli's, not surprisingly (given her lifelong love of cooking), was an authentic Native American meal, which included wild rice. Although Pete has eaten it since childhood (his mom used to make it often), it was Kelli's first time trying it. She loved it, and we have been eating it together ever since.

1 cup wild rice
4 cups GF chicken broth or vegetable broth
1 teaspoon salt

1. Combine the rice, broth, and salt in a saucepan and bring to a boil over high heat. Reduce the heat to low and cover. Simmer for 50 to 60 minutes, until the rice is tender and the liquid absorbed.
2. Remove the pan from the heat and let sit for 10 minutes with the lid on.

ECHNICALLY, WILD RICE is an aquatic plant and is not related to common rice. Although it can be served "straight up," it's more often mixed with "regular" rice. And did you know that wild rice is Minnesota's state grain?

sushi rice

[MAKES 4 CUPS]

Okay, we admit it. We're nuts about sushi. From Sapporo Sushi on Long Island to Hapa Sushi and the Sushi Den in Colorado, and lots of restaurants in between, we can't get enough. Every now and then, though, we get the craving to make our own (page 140). One of our earliest dates, in fact, was making sushi together at Pete's old apartment outside Albany, New York, many years ago. Making fresh sushi, though, starts with this rice.

2 cups sushi rice (Japanese short grain rice)
2 cups water
¼ cup rice vinegar
2 tablespoons sugar
1 teaspoon salt

1. Rinse the rice under cold water until the water runs clear.

2. Combine the rice and water in a saucepan and bring to a boil over high heat. Reduce the heat to low and cover. Simmer for 15 minutes, or until the rice is tender and the liquid is absorbed. Remove from the heat and let set for 15 minutes longer, keeping the cover on at all times.

3. Meanwhile, heat the vinegar, sugar, and salt over medium heat in a separate small saucepan, stirring until the sugar and salt have dissolved. Allow to cool.

4. Put the cooked rice in a large, nonmetallic bowl (glass or wooden will do) and pour the vinegar mixture over the rice. Fold and turn the rice until the vinegar mixture is incorporated, but do not mash the rice by stirring.

5. Let the rice cool. It is best to use sushi rice right away.

grilled asparagus

[MAKES 4 SERVINGS]

Asparagus is one of those vegetables where one or the other of us could easily finish an entire pound solo. There's no self-restraint, especially when it comes to this simple yet delicious recipe.

1 pound asparagus
1 tablespoon olive oil
Garlic powder
Salt and pepper

1. Heat a grill to medium-high.
2. Wash the asparagus and cut away the woody bottoms (see box below). Drizzle the asparagus with the olive oil and season with garlic powder, salt, and pepper. Toss with your hands to evenly coat all the spears.
3. Grill the asparagus, turning occasionally, until tender and slightly charred. If possible, spread the asparagus in a single layer on the rack, rather than in a pile. When piled, the asparagus that are not in contact with the grill tend to get steamed by the other asparagus rather than grilled by the fire. If space on the grill is limited and you have to pile 'em up, rotate the pile every so often so that everyone gets a turn by the heat.

THE BOTTOM, WIDE ends of asparagus spears can be tough and woody, and are always discarded before cooking. But where to cut the spears, and what to keep and what to discard? Our sister-in-law Sandy (and Harold McGee, in a "Curious Cook" piece for the *New York Times*) mentions bending the spears with your hands and letting them naturally snap. We find this seldom happens in the ideal spot on the asparagus. McGee also mentions cutting the spears 6 to 7 inches down from the tip, which, he notes, often leaves too much asparagus behind. We prefer to cut off and discard the bottom third of each spear. Any remaining woody texture is usually broken down by the high heat of the grill, and you have nice, long, delicious asparagus spears to boot.

$\int$OMETIMES, IT'S THE simpler preparation that yields the best results. This recipe is a great example—the combination of olive oil, garlic powder, salt, and pepper is one of our all-time favorites. In addition to using this prep to grill asparagus, try the same thing with sliced zucchini, or heads of baby bok choy, sliced in half, seasoned on the sliced side, and grilled sliced-side-down.

$\mathcal{G}$ROWING UP IN a household of partly Sicilian heritage, Pete learned early on some important rules of life. For example, olive oil was to the kitchen what holy water was to church. Translation: it's good for you, you should use it regularly, you should use it liberally, and it makes everything it touches better! Throughout this cookbook, we recommend using extra light olive oil, rather than extra virgin olive oil. While the extra virgin is a good choice for salad dressings (and to a degree, for low-temperature cooking), it's not a great choice when it comes to grilling. Extra-light olive oil has a higher smoke point than extra virgin, meaning it stands up better to the intense heat of a grill. If you buy only one olive oil, go with the extra light. If you buy more than one type, feel free to get extra virgin for your salad dressings and extra light for grilling, sautéing, and other cooking.

grilled fajita vegetables

[MAKES 4 SERVINGS]

Some vegetables are simply meant to go together, and peppers and onions would definitely qualify. They're like yin and yang; they complete one another. They both start out crunchy and become softer as you cook 'em, they take similar amounts of time to cook (thanks in part to their similar water content), and they both caramelize well at similar rates, becoming sweeter in the process. And while this recipe for grilled fajita vegetables (code for "tasty peppers and onions") would pair well with any Mexican or Latin American dish (not to mention many Italian dishes), we particularly recommend it with our Chipotle Chicken Fajitas (page 146).

1 red bell pepper
1 green bell pepper
1 yellow onion
Olive oil
Salt and pepper

1. Heat a grill to medium-high.
2. Core the peppers and slice lengthwise into 1/2-inch-thick slices. Slice the onion into 1/2-inch-thick rings.
3. Drizzle the vegetables with olive oil and season lightly with salt and pepper.
4. Grill the vegetables over medium to high heat, turning, until they are tender and have grill marks, but are not so cooked as to be soft, translucent (for the onion), or overly caramelized.

IF GRILLING ISN'T an option, you can sauté the peppers and onions in olive oil in a skillet or sauté pan over medium-high heat.

prosciutto-wrapped asparagus and mozzarella

[MAKES 4 SERVINGS]

We were first inspired to make this dish after Pete had a similar side at a Mediterranean restaurant years ago. It takes three things we love—asparagus, mozzarella, and prosciutto—and brings them together wonderfully.

16 asparagus spears
4 ounces fresh mozzarella, quartered
8 slices prosciutto
3 tablespoons olive oil
2 tablespoons balsamic vinegar
Salt and pepper

1. Steam the asparagus in a steaming basket on the stove top for 3 to 4 minutes until mostly cooked and bright green.

2. Set 2 asparagus spears on your work surface (kitchen counter, table, cutting board, you get the idea). Put a piece of mozzarella on the asparagus and then 2 more spears on top. Wrap the aspara-gus-mozzarella combination with 2 slices of pro-sciutto. Skewer a toothpick through the prosciutto at each end of the wrap to hold the prosciutto in place and everything together as a package. Repeat with the remaining ingredients to make 4 asparagus packages.

3. Heat 1 tablespoon of the olive oil in a skillet over medium-high heat. Add the asparagus packages and sauté, turning once, until the prosciutto is slightly brown and crispy.

4. To make the vinaigrette, mix together the remain-ing 2 tablespoons olive oil, the vinegar, and salt and pepper.

5. Arrange the asparagus packages on a plate and drizzle with the balsamic vinaigrette.

yuca

[MAKES 4 SERVINGS]

Before moving to Colorado, we lived in Weehawken, New Jersey. That particular corner of northeastern New Jersey is home to the second-largest Cuban American population in the United States, behind only Miami. There were bodegas on the street corners near our apartment, extensive Latin sections in the supermarkets, and an assortment of superb Cuban restaurants to choose from. All had yuca—either in the store aisles, or on the menu. Yuca is the Cuban word for cassava, the same plant whose roots are used to make tapioca. It's starchy, like a potato, and can be used in many of the same ways. We recommend serving this boiled yuca with Garlic-Lime Skirt Steak with Cuban Mojo (page 177).

1 pound fresh or frozen yuca

If using fresh yuca, peel first and cut in half lengthwise. Cover the yuca with water in a saucepan. Bring to a boil and cook for 45 to 60 minutes, until very soft and clear (the yuca begins opaque and becomes clearer as it is boiled).

Note: Never eat raw yuca. Naturally occurring compounds and enzymes in the root conspire to produce cyanide, a potent toxin. Only proper cooking, boiling, and/or frying renders yuca safe to eat. Always discard the boiled water.

ANOTHER GREAT WAY to prepare yuca is to make yuca *frita*, which are basically Cuban French fries. Boil the yuca as above, but pull it out of the water a little early. Cut the yuca into steak-fry-sized pieces, and deep fry in oil until golden brown. Serve the yuca *frita* lightly salted, with a cilantro dipping sauce on the side. To make the dipping sauce, pulse ½ bunch cilantro and 2 garlic cloves juice in a blender. Then, drizzle in ⅓ cup olive oil while blending. Season with a dash of salt and pepper and squeeze of fresh lime juice. Transfer to a small bowl to serve.

tostones

[MAKES 4 SERVINGS]

As much as we love yuca (page 96), we also love plantains, another staple of Cuban cuisine. When we moved to Colorado from New Jersey, we felt like we left much of Cuban American culture behind . . . until we discovered Cuba Cuba restaurant in Denver, where the tostones took us right back to our newlywed days in northeast Jersey, when we were immersed in the influence of Cuban cuisine.

2 green (under-ripe) plantains
½ cup olive oil
Salt

1. Peel the plantains and slice into 1-inch-thick silver-dollar discs.
2. Heat the olive oil in a medium to large skillet. Add the plantain slices and fry, turning halfway through, until tender and slightly golden, about 6 minutes. Remove from the oil and place on a paper towel.
3. Flatten each piece by pressing down with the bottom of a pan, making each plantain about ¼ inch thick.
4. Refry each flattened plantain, turning once, until golden and crispy, 5 to 7 minutes.
5. Remove from the oil, drain on a paper towel, and season with salt. (Traditionally, the flattened plantains are dipped in warm salt water *before* they are fried the second time, but we prefer to season with salt after the plantains are cooked the final time.)

WHILE TOSTONES ARE made with under-ripe plantains, *maduros* are made with overripe plantains. They're equally tasty, but in a very different way. Start with brown, overripe plantains. Peel them and cut into slices on a bias. Pan-fry the slices once (as opposed to twice for the *tostones*), sprinkle with salt, and serve. That's it!

PLANTAINS ARE SIMILAR to bananas, but unlike bananas, which are eaten raw, plantains are almost always cooked first (either starting with a green, under-ripe, and starchy plantain or with a brown, overripe and sweet plantain). They're a standard dish throughout tropical regions of the world, hence their popularity in Cuba. Like yuca, they can be prepared in several ways, but our favorite remains the *tostone*.

applesauce
[MAKES 6 SERVINGS]

Homemade applesauce is so tasty and easy to make, we have a hard time figuring out why anyone would buy it in a jar. It's especially good to make in fall (such as for Oktoberfest or Thanksgiving), when it's harvest time and apples are at their peak.

6 apples
2 to 4 tablespoons water
¼ cup sugar

1. Peel, core, and cube the apples.
2. Combine the apples, water, and sugar in a saucepan. Cook over medium-low heat until the apples are very soft, about 30 minutes.
3. Mash the apples with a potato masher or ricer and serve warm.

Note: Use McIntosh apples for a smooth apple-sauce, or Granny Smith apples for a chunkier sauce. Those two varieties may be some of the most widely available nationally. But don't be afraid to experiment with other types of apples. If you've spent a little time in a supermarket with a well-stocked produce section, or at your local farmers' market, you've surely noticed that the apple family tree has branched out lately, and that there's more apple choices than there used to be. In our eyes, this is both a good and a bad thing. Some of those "new" apple varieties are in fact old, and are part of a resurgence in the popularity of historical and heirloom varieties (this is a good thing). But other varieties are indeed genuinely new—some are quite good. Others, though, have been bred for traits that have little to do with the quality of their taste, and much more to do with how well the apples stand up to the rigors of transportation, and how quickly they spoil. (Both factors are influenced by agribusiness and profit margins, rather than what is the most nutritious and delicious.) Our recommendation: chat with the produce manager of your store, or have a candid conversation with the growers at your local farmers' market. You just might discover an apple variety (or several) that makes wonderful applesauce.

sauerkraut

[MAKES 6 SERVINGS]

Each year we host an Oktoberfest, complete with assorted cooked meats such as Bratwurst, Italian Sausage, and Kielbasa (page 175), Applesauce (page 98), and German Potato Salad (77), but it wouldn't be complete without sauerkraut. We find it's a love it or hate it kind of food (Kelli loves it, Pete not so much). But for the sauerkraut lovers out there, this version will thoroughly please the palate (and maybe even earn a few converts).

One 32-ounce jar sauerkraut (see box below)
1 tablespoon olive oil
1 Granny Smith apple, peeled, cored, and diced
1 medium onion, diced
1 teaspoon caraway seeds
Salt and pepper

1. Drain and rinse the sauerkraut well.
2. Heat the olive oil in a large skillet over medium-high heat. Add the apple and onion and sauté until tender. Season with caraway seeds and salt and pepper. Stir in the sauerkraut and cook for about 5 minutes, until heated through.

FOR EXTRA CREDIT, try making your own sauerkraut. Be forewarned, however. Unlike other from-scratch recipes in this book, which can be made on-demand, sauerkraut requires planning ahead (typically a few weeks) to allow for fermentation. Start by grating 2 large heads of cabbage, then toss with 3 tablespoons or so of Kosher salt. Pack the cabbage tightly into a crock, glass container, or food-grade plastic bucket (approximately 1-gallon capacity). Press down on the cabbage firmly with a plate that's well-fitted to your container. The pressing (combined with the salt) encourages water to come out of the cabbage. If enough water doesn't come out during pressing to completely submerge the cabbage and plate, add enough brine (very salty water) to get the job done. Place a weight on the plate to maintain pressure, cover the container with a cloth towel, and set it in a location where it won't be in the way. Check on your sauerkraut-to-be every few days, skimming any "scum" off the surface of the brine. Depending on the temperature where you're storing the container, fermentation may take anywhere from a few weeks to a month and a half. Periodically taste test your kraut, and enjoy it when the flavor profile is to your liking. (Drain the sauerkraut as you use it, allowing the remainder to continue fermenting in the juices.)

costa rican slaw

[MAKES ABOUT 10 SERVINGS]

This recipe comes from our friends Kirk and Maury. We met them in Colorado, but they now live in Vermont, though not before first spending a year in Costa Rica, working as teachers high in the cloud forests and moun-tains of Central America. There, refrigeration was sometimes spotty, and access to certain ingredients was difficult. This slaw became their "go to" salad—the ingredients were inexpensive, and the dressed slaw (made with a vinegar-based dressing, as opposed to a slaw with mayonnaise) kept well. The recipe includes cabbage, as well as raw beets, which add a nice crunch.

½ head green cabbage, thinly sliced and chopped

½ head red cabbage, thinly sliced and chopped

1 medium carrot, peeled and grated

1 raw beet, peeled and grated

3 tablespoons chopped fresh cilantro

¼ cup olive oil

2 tablespoons apple cider vinegar

1 to 2 teaspoons honey

Salt and pepper

1. Combine the green and red cabbage, the carrot, beet, and cilantro in a large bowl.

2. Whisk together the olive oil, vinegar, honey, and salt and pepper in a small bowl. Drizzle the dress-ing over the salad, toss, and serve.

For a quick shortcut, substitute the ½ head each of green and red cabbage with one large (1-pound) bag of pre-chopped cabbage/slaw mix.

corn on the cob

[MAKES 4 SERVINGS]

Corn on the cob is one of those foods that for us is wholly evocative of the summer season. In fact, when the corn is fresh and in season, we may eat it most nights of the week, simply because we can't get enough of it and want to try to eat our fill while it lasts. Kelli's family even has their own corn lingo: there's Fourth of July corn (early season corn that's sweet), and there's Grandfather corn (late season corn that's a little past its prime). Eat enough corn on the cob, it seems, and you'll develop a strong corn preference, as Pete's family did. They overwhelmingly preferred corn from Long Island's East End, the North Fork in particular, where roadside farm stands sold fresh Butter and Sugar Corn (a hybrid variety with white and yellow kernels, resulting in a blend of sweetness and hearty corn flavor). Now, living in Colorado, we've traded in our earlier biases for a new love: Colorado's Olathe Sweet, a corn variety that, we're convinced, is indeed the best corn on the cob you can eat (the town of Olathe even hosts a festival every year to celebrate its corn). Depending on our mood, we'll typically cook it using one of four methods.

4 ears corn
Salted butter
Salt

To steam: If you have a steaming basket large enough for ears of corn, go ahead and use it. Otherwise, boil to 1 inch of water over high heat in a saucepan deep enough for the ears. Shuck the ears and remove all the silk. Place the ears in the saucepan (or steaming basket), and cover with a tight-fitting lid. Steam over medium-high heat for 10 to 15 minutes, until the corn is tender.

To boil: Fill a large pot with enough water to fully submerge the ears. Bring the water to a boil. Meanwhile, shuck the ears and remove all the silk. Place the corn in the water and reduce the heat to a simmer. Cover and cook for 7 to 8 minutes, until the corn is tender.

To grill in the husks: Heat a grill to medium-high. Place the ears (in their husks) directly on the grill rack. Grill, turning every 5 minutes, for 10 to 15 minutes, until the corn is tender. Don't worry if the outside of the husks blacken or the ends of the silk singe. Remove the corn from the grill and carefully remove the husks and silks. The corn will be very hot!

To grill in foil: Heat a grill to medium-high. Shuck the ears and remove all the silk. Wrap each ear in tin foil and place on the grill rack. Grill, turning every 5 minutes, for 10 to 15 minutes, until the corn is tender.

For all methods, serve the corn with a side of butter and salt to taste.

corn bread stuffing

[MAKES 6 TO 8 SERVINGS]

Ask most Americans (including us), and we think they'd tell you that Thanksgiving isn't complete without a side of stuffing. Thanks to this recipe, gluten-free foodies can have our stuffing, and eat it, too. Our moist, savory stuffing showcases the sage and sausage (and corn bread, too).

1 pound GF pork sausage, caseless, or with casings removed
8 tablespoons (1 stick) salted butter
1 medium onion, diced
2 tablespoons chopped fresh sage
1¹⁄₂ teaspoons salt
1 teaspoon pepper
GF Corn Bread (page 28), one whole recipe, cut into ¹⁄₂-inch pieces
2 cups GF chicken broth

1. Preheat the oven to 350°F. Grease a 2-quart baking dish.
2. Cook the sausage in a large skillet over medium-high heat until browned. Transfer to a plate and set aside.
3. Melt the butter in the same skillet. Add the onion and sauté until translucent. Return the sausage to the skillet along with the sage, salt, and pepper and stir to mix.
4. Combine the sausage mixture and corn bread in the prepared baking dish and toss to mix. Pour the broth over the stuffing.
5. Cover the dish with foil and bake for 30 to 40 minutes, until the stuffing is heated through completely and the top is crispy.

cranberry relish

[MAKES 8 TO 10 SERVINGS]

Cranberry relishes and sauces come in many shapes and sizes, from ones made with fresh cranberries, to the log/tube of jellied cranberry sauce so ubiquitous around Thanksgiving. This cranberry relish balances the sweet and the tart, and has just the right amount of "bite." We were first introduced to a similar version by a family friend at a Thanksgiving dinner years ago, and we haven't looked back since.

12 ounces fresh cranberries
1 large navel orange, well washed and quartered
1 cup sugar

Combine the cranberries, orange quarters (including the peel/rind), and sugar in the food processor. Blend until the relish is uniformly chopped into very small pieces, but not smooth. (Remember: you want cranberry relish, not cranberry paste!)

polenta

[**MAKES 6 TO 8 SERVINGS**]

Polenta is a versatile corn-based dish. At its most basic, it's a cornmeal mush or porridge that you can serve as a simple side dish as you would mashed potatoes. But that doesn't nearly do it justice. When spread into a thin layer in a pan and chilled in the refrigerator, it can be cut into different shapes, then sautéed or grilled. In gluten-free cooking, it can be a great substitute for croutons on salad, or as the base for Bruschetta (page 50), as just two examples.

1 quart (4 cups) milk
1 tablespoon salted butter
1 cup yellow or white cornmeal
Cream, grated cheese, and/or additional butter, optional
Salt and pepper
Chopped fresh herbs or other seasonings, optional

1. Boil the milk and butter in a saucepan. Add the cornmeal slowly, stirring constantly to prevent lumps from forming. When all the cornmeal has been added, simmer, stirring occasionally, until very thick, 25 to 30 minutes.

2. If you like, stir in cream, cheese, or additional butter along with salt and pepper to taste. The base flavor of polenta is very mild, and can also be enhanced as much as you'd like with herbs, spices, and other seasonings.

3. Spread the polenta in a buttered pan to a uniform thickness using a spatula dipped in water (to prevent the polenta from sticking). Cover and refrigerate until chilled and firm, about 45 to 60 minutes.

4. Unmold the polenta by tipping it out of the pan and cut into desired shapes.

5. Sauté the polenta pieces on both sides in a small amount of butter in a skillet until golden brown, or grill the shapes or toast in a toaster oven.

Note: For subtle variations in the flavor of the polenta, you can substitute either GF chicken broth or water for the milk. Also, keep in mind that the size of your pan will determine the depth of the polenta. Use smaller pans for thicker pieces, and large pans for thinner ones (as when you want to make thin polenta rounds for Bruschetta, page 50).

mashed potatoes

[MAKES 6 SERVINGS]

This is a classic, straight-up mashed potato recipe. We've made it creamy without using cream, instead opting for evaporated milk, which provides richness without all the fat of cream. It pairs well with meat dishes, and with gravy!

6 Yukon Gold or other all-purpose potatoes, peeled and cubed
3 tablespoons salted butter
¾ cup evaporated milk
Salt and pepper

1. Combine the potatoes and enough water to cover in a saucepan. Bring to a boil and cook until the potatoes are very tender, about 30 minutes. Drain well.

2. Return the potatoes to the saucepan and add the butter. Mash the potatoes using a potato masher or ricer. Stir in the evaporated milk and season with salt and pepper to taste.

Variations

- **Garlic Mashed Potatoes:** Add 3 cloves of roasted garlic with the evaporated milk. To roast garlic, leave the cloves in their peels and place in a pocket of aluminum foil. Drizzle with olive oil, close the aluminum foil, and roast in a 400°F oven or toaster oven for 15 to 20 minutes, until the cloves are soft when pressed. Squeeze the flesh out of the garlic skins.

- **Potato Pancakes:** Leftover mashed potatoes can be formed into patties and cooked in butter or olive oil in a heated skillet until lightly browned on each side, making a quick and easy potato pancake.

ALL POTATOES ARE not created equal, and there are many to chose from. In Bolivia alone, more than 200 varieties are cultivated! Generally, potatoes fall into two categories: starchy and waxy. Starchy potatoes, as their name suggests, are high in starch, and generally dry. They're great for baking, mashing, and frying. Examples include the Idaho/russet. By comparison, waxy potatoes are moist, with a high sugar content but low starch content. They're good for soups and potato salads, but not the best choice for mashed potatoes, which tend to turn out thick and lumpy, instead of smooth and creamy. Examples include the Red Bliss potato. Then you have the in-between potatoes that have characteristics of both starchy and waxy potatoes. They're good all-around performers, and a great example is the Yukon Gold, which is what we often use for this mashed potato recipe.

seasoned, roasted potatoes

[MAKES 4 SERVINGS]

Pete started making these seasoned, roasted potatoes in a toaster oven as part of his lunches years ago. Since then, he's made them for family and friends, who started calling them "Pete Potatoes." They can be as mild or as spicy as you like—it all depends on how liberal you are with the seasonings (feel free to add or omit spices as per your preference).

4 Yukon Gold potatoes (see box, page 104), cubed (bite-sized, about 1-inch square)
Olive oil
Paprika
Chili powder
Dried basil
Garlic powder
Salt and pepper

1. Preheat the oven or a toaster oven to 375°F.
2. Combine the potatoes and olive oil in a roasting pan and toss to coat. Season to taste with the spices. Generally, a light to modest sprinkling of each spice will be plenty. Toss the potatoes again to redistribute the spices.
3. Roast for 20 minutes, then toss and turn the potatoes. Roast for an additional 20 minutes. They should be fork tender and lightly browned, or if you prefer, leave them in longer and allow them to get golden brown and crunchier.

Note: When roasting the potatoes, use a pan large enough so that the potatoes are in a single layer. If the potatoes are piled on one another, they won't crisp up, and instead will turn out a little on the soggy side.

homemade french fries

[MAKES 4 SERVINGS]

Growing up, Pete's family didn't frequent fast food restaurants much. But that didn't stop him and his brother from developing a healthy love of French fries. Every once in a while, Pete's mom would make them from scratch. Her method involved both frying and baking, resulting in a French fry that had all the qualities of a good fried potato without as much of the grease. And her method uses a brown paper bag . . . a technique you're unlikely to find used for most French fries. The bag absorbs some of the oil from the frying, while still leaving enough for the salt to stick.

4 russet potatoes (see box, page 104)
Canola or peanut oil for frying
Salt

1. Preheat the oven to 375°F.
2. Cut the potatoes into desired shape (see box below). Submerge the potatoes in cold water as you slice to keep them from oxidizing (turning brown).
3. Heat 2 to 3 inches of oil to 375°F in a saucepan that is deep enough to submerge the potatoes.
4. Drain the potatoes thoroughly. Fry the potatoes in batches (you don't want to overcrowd them in the oil) until golden brown. (Frying time will depend upon the size of the fry you cut.) Remove the fries and drain on a paper bag or paper towels.
5. Spread the fries into a single layer on a baking sheet lined with a brown paper bag and season with salt. Bake for 10 to 15 minutes.

USING A CUTTING board and knife you can cut the potatoes into long, thin strips to make shoestring fries, or wide thick strips to make steak fries, or a standard French fry. Alternatively, you can use a mandoline and its slicing attachments to make a variety of shapes, including crinkle cut.

belgian waffles (page 31)

lemon poppy seed bread (page 27)

blueberry muffins with streusel topping (page 22)

cinnamon rolls (page 36)

scrambled omelet (page 40)

mesclun greens with candied walnuts, dried cranberries, and goat cheese (page 80)

meatballs with spaghetti and marinara sauce (page 128)

margherita pizza (page 119)

chicken pad thai (page 155)

chili (page 116)
with corn bread (page 28)

summer rolls with sweet and sour
dipping sauce (page 60)

chipotle chicken fajitas (page 146)
with fresh corn tortillas (page 145),
grilled fajita vegetables (page 94),
and fresh tomato-cilantro salsa
(page 46)

pesto pasta (page 124)

garlic-lime skirt steak
with cuban mojo (page 177)
and tostones (page 97)

pan-seared scallops (page 136)
with grilled asparagus (page 92)

general chang's chicken (page 163)

gnocchi with marinara sauce
(page 108)

curry-glazed pork tenderloin (page 171) with jasmine rice (page 86)

whole roasted turkey with gravy (page 168), corn bread stuffing (page 102), mashed potatoes (page 104), and cranberry relish (page 102)

jamaican jerk chicken (page 148) with mango-pineapple salsa (page 44) and caribbean rice (page 87)

honey-soy chicken with spicy sauce
(page 166) with jasmine rice (page 86)
and grilled zucchini (page 93)

kolachkis (page 221)

chocolate chip cookies (page 182)

blueberry pie (page 193)

angel food cake with strawberries and
homemade whipped cream (page 200)

dessert crepes (page 214)

carrot cake (page 211)

zucchini cake with cream cheese frosting
and fresh fruit (page 206)

ENTRÉES

gnocchi

[**MAKES 6 SERVINGS**]

Gnocchi is a beautiful thing—it's essentially a pasta made with potatoes. Think of it this way: if a mashed potato dumpling and a fresh pasta noodle had a love child, gnocchi would be it. We were inspired to make a gluten-free gnocchi after seeing the beautiful traditional version made by our friend Rebecca, who writes the delightful (though not gluten-free) food and travel blog, From Argentina with Love. In Argentina, she notes, the 29th of every month is celebrated by eating gnocchi! (As one version of the story goes, money was traditionally tight by the end of each month, and so Argentineans made inexpensive gnocchi to carry them through to the next paycheck.)

> 2 pounds (3 to 5) starchy potatoes (see box, page 104)
> 2 eggs, beaten
> 1 to 1½ cups Artisan GF Flour Mix (page 15)
> Salt
> Marinara Sauce (see box below) or your favorite sauce

1. Heat the oven to 350°F.

2. Pierce the potatoes multiple times on each side with a fork and place directly on a rack in the oven. Bake for about 1 hour, until soft. (Alternatively, you can microwave them on high for 10 to 15 minutes.) Let cool.

3. When cool enough to handle, cut open each potato and scoop out the flesh. Put the flesh through a ricer or Foley mill or mash with a potato masher, being careful to create a smooth, but not pasty, consistency.

4. Mound the potatoes on a work surface and create a well in the middle. Add the beaten eggs, 1 cup of the flour, and salt. Work the mixture with your hands to form a dough. Add additional flour as needed to form a smooth dough that is not sticky, but not too stiff.

5. Divide the dough in quarters and squeeze/roll the dough into a snakelike roll about ½ inch in diameter. The dough will be tender. Cut the snake into ¾-inch segments and roll each segment over the tines of a fork to create grooves (these are purely cosmetic and not strictly necessary, though they will make your gnocchi look nicer and hold more sauce!). Set the completed gnocchi aside, tossing with flour to prevent them from getting sticky. Repeat with the remaining dough.

6. Bring a large pot of salted water to a boil. Add the gnocchi in batches. When you initially drop them in the water, they will sink. Once they float, let them continue to boil for 2 to 3 minutes. Remove them from the water with a slotted spoon and place in a colander to allow any excess water to drain.

7. Toss the gnocchi with the sauce and serve.

To MAKE A quick and easy marinara, use an immersion blender to puree one 14.5-ounce can of no-salt-added diced tomatoes. Add about 1 tablespoon dried basil, 2 teaspoons garlic powder, and 2 teaspoons salt. Heat in a saucepan. Serve over the gnocchi. Or, for a more well-rounded marinara sauce, try the version with our Meatballs with Spaghetti (page 128).

THIS RECIPE USES a Foley mill, which is also known as a food mill. It's shaped like a saucepan, but the bottom has many small holes. A crank handle attaches to a blade that you turn to press food through the holes. The mill can be used to rice potatoes, make applesauce, or make jam—to name just a few possibilities. We remember when Carol, a close family friend who wasn't exactly best friends with the kitchen, was using Pete's mom's Foley mill. "I don't know how you do this," she said. "You must have arms of steel." She simply couldn't get the potatoes through the mill. Upon inspection, we discovered that she hadn't boiled the potatoes first, and was trying to press them through the mill raw!

stuffed squash

What do you do when the refrigerator's empty, save for an acorn squash and a pound of sausage? If you're Kelli, you make dinner. Like our Scrambled Omelet (page 40), this recipe was born out of circumstance. We've since jazzed it up a bit, but the history of the dish is humble.

1 pound GF sausage, casings removed

1/2 cup GF bread crumbs (see box, page 57)

1 egg

1 Granny Smith apple, peeled, cored, and diced

1/2 medium onion, diced

1/2 teaspoon dried thyme

1/2 teaspoon garlic powder

1/2 teaspoon dried basil

Salt and pepper

2 medium acorn squash

1. Preheat the oven to 375°F.

2. Combine the sausage, bread crumbs, egg, apple, onion, thyme, garlic powder, basil, and salt and pepper in a bowl and toss to mix.

3. Cut each acorn squash in half along the equator and remove all the seeds and stringy fibers. If a squash half does not set level, cut a small amount off the rounded bottom to create a flat surface.

4. Divide the filling among the four halves, mounding it in the squash. Place the squash in a baking dish, add 1 cup of water to the dish, and cover with aluminum foil.

5. Bake for 60 minutes. Remove the foil and bake for 10 minutes longer, or until the squash is tender and the sausage is thoroughly cooked.

Variation

If desired, top with shredded cheese after removing the foil, and then finish baking uncovered as per the recipe.

stuffed peppers

[MAKES 6 SERVINGS]

Kelli's mom made stuffed peppers for Kelli and her siblings growing up. Back then, they ate the filling but left the pepper behind. These days, we happily devour the whole thing.

3 bell peppers (green, yellow, orange, or red)

Olive oil

1/2 medium onion, diced

1 garlic clove, minced

1 pound ground turkey

One 14.5-ounce can no-salt-added diced tomatoes

1 cup Jasmine Rice (page 86)

1 teaspoon Worcestershire sauce

1 teaspoon dried oregano

1/2 teaspoon dried basil

Salt and pepper

1 cup shredded Cheddar or mozzarella cheese

1. Preheat the oven to 350°F.
2. Cut the peppers in half lengthwise and remove the stems, seeds, and membranes.
3. Drizzle a little bit of olive oil in the bottom of a baking pan. Place the peppers cut-side down in the baking pan and rub olive oil on the back sides. Bake for 25 minutes, or until the flesh is tender and the skin starts to brown.
4. Meanwhile, heat a small amount of olive oil in a skillet. Add the onion and garlic and sauté until the onion is translucent. Add the ground turkey and cook until browned. Drain off any excess fat. Stir in the tomatoes (including the liquid from the can), rice, Worcestershire sauce, oregano, basil, and salt and pepper.
5. Remove the peppers from the oven and turn them over so the cut sides are facing up (like a bowl). Fill each pepper half with the filling. Sprinkle the cheese on top.
6. Bake for an additional 20 to 25 minutes, until the cheese is melted and brown.

Variation

To make vegetarian stuffed peppers, substitute 2 cups (one 15-ounce can) rinsed chickpeas (also known as garbanzo beans) for the ground turkey.

margherita empanadas

[MAKES 4 SERVINGS]

In a lot of ways, empanadas are like mini-calzones made with pie dough instead of pizza dough. They're popular throughout Spain and Latin America, and look slightly different from place to place. Our empanadas most resemble the Argentinean version, thanks to the influence of our friend and fellow food blogger, Rebecca, who married an Argentinean. The Margherita version is filled with tomato, basil, and mozzarella cheese. We thought those fillings sounded awfully Italian for an Argentinean empanada . . . then we learned that Argentina has a prominent Italian immigrant population!

1 cup diced tomatoes (either fresh tomatoes or no-salt-added, canned tomatoes)
$\frac{1}{2}$ cup shredded mozzarella cheese
8 to 10 fresh basil leaves, chopped
1 garlic clove, minced
Pie Dough (page 191), prepared through step 3
1 egg
2 tablespoons water

1. Preheat the oven to 350°F.
2. Mix together the tomatoes, mozzarella, basil, and garlic in a bowl.
3. Roll out one of the pieces of dough between two sheets of plastic wrap to a thickness of about $\frac{1}{8}$ inch. Invert a 6-inch diameter bowl with a narrow lip and use it like a giant cookie cutter to cut out 4 rounds of dough. Repeat with the remaining dough.
4. Scoop about 3 tablespoons of the filling onto one half of a dough round, taking care to leave a border of naked dough for sealing. Use a wet fingertip to wet the naked dough edge. Fold over the remaining half of the dough onto and overlapping the filling, creating a half-moon. Seal the edge using the *repulgue* technique, which results in a beautifully scalloped edge: Starting at one end of the crescent, use your fingers to fold over a small section of the edge and press down to seal. Repeat, moving over slightly each time until you've reached the other end of the crescent. Place the empanada on an ungreased cookie sheet.
5. Repeat with the remaining dough and filling to make 8 empanadas.
6. Make an egg wash by whisking together the egg and water with a fork. Brush the top of each empanada with the egg wash.
7. Bake the empanadas for 10 to 15 minutes, until light golden brown.

Variation

For Cinnamon Peach Empanadas, a sweet and tasty dessert, use a filling of 1 thinly sliced peach, 1 tablespoon sugar, and 1 teaspoon ground cinnamon.

hoppin' john

[MAKES ABOUT 10 SERVINGS]

Hoppin' John is a Southern version of rice and beans. The recipe comes straight from our friend Maury, a native of Mississippi. She now lives in New England, but says, "this is a traditional Southern dish that I grew up eating and continue to eat because it always reminds me of home." Black-eyed peas, the beans in the dish, are a Southern symbol of good luck, and so the dish is a popular offering on New Year's Day (nothing wrong with starting the year off on the right foot!). As a vegetarian, Maury doesn't include bacon. We've included it in the recipe, but you decide.

1 cup (8 ounces) dried black-eyed peas

10 cups water

3 slices GF bacon, optional

1 small onion, chopped

1 green bell pepper, chopped

1 cup uncooked white or brown rice

1½ teaspoons salt

Scallions, chopped

Tomatoes, chopped

1. Rinse and sort the peas (pick through them to remove any stones or other debris). Soak for 8 hours in a bowl of cold water. Drain.

2. Bring the peas and 7 cups water to boil over high heat in a Dutch oven (or heavy pot with a lid). Reduce the heat to medium and simmer, uncovered, for 1½ hours, or until the peas are tender.

3. Cook the bacon in a large skillet until crisp. Remove the bacon, reserving the drippings in the skillet. Crumble the bacon and set aside.

4. Add the onion and bell pepper to the bacon drippings (or in 1 to 2 tablespoons olive oil if you're omitting the bacon). Sauté over medium heat until tender.

5. Add the onion and pepper to the split peas, along with the remaining 3 cups water, the rice, and salt. Cover and cook over medium-low heat for 20 minutes (longer if using brown rice), or until the rice is tender. Remove from the heat, and let stand, covered, for 10 minutes.

6. Garnish with the reserved bacon, scallions, and tomatoes and serve.

pork tamales

[MAKES 3 DOZEN-PLUS TAMALES, ABOUT 12 SERVINGS]

From spring through summer and into fall, on many Saturday mornings you'll find us wandering the stalls of the Boulder Farmers' Market, a locavore's delight nestled between the downtown pedestrian mall and Boulder Creek. If we've slept in and wandered over to the market around lunchtime (always dangerous), there's a section of food vendors ready and willing to serve up lunch. One vendor sells gluten-free tamales—veggie, chicken, or pork. By and far, the pork is our favorite, and we've created our own version here. Serve with Fresh Tomato-Cilantro Salsa (page 46), Guacamole (page 47), and sour cream.

The recipe has four major stages: cooking the pork, seasoning the pork, making the masa paste, and assembling and steaming the tamales.

Cook the Pork

One 2- to 3-pound pork roast
1 onion, quartered
3 garlic cloves, peeled
1 teaspoon ground cumin
1 teaspoon chili powder
Salt and pepper

1. Cut the roast into 4 pieces. Place the roast quarters, onion, garlic, cumin, chili powder, and salt and pepper in a large pot. Cover with water, then fill the pot with a few extra cups of water beyond what is needed to cover the ingredients completely. Bring the mixture to a boil and reduce the heat to medium. Boil, uncovered, for 2½ hours, or until the pork can easily be shredded.
2. Remove the pork from the broth and let cool. When cool enough to handle, shred with your fingers or two forks.
3. Puree the cooking broth with an immersion blender and set aside.

Season the Pork

½ teaspoon ground cumin
½ teaspoon chili powder
¼ teaspoon garlic powder
Salt and pepper

Season the shredded pork with the cumin, chili powder, garlic powder, and salt and pepper. Toss to coat. Feel free to increase the quantities if you would like a spicier pork! Pour a small amount of the reserved cooking broth over the meat to keep it moist but not dripping wet.

Make the Masa Paste

4 cups instant corn masa flour (we recommend the Maseca brand)
2 teaspoons salt
1 cup corn oil
4 cups reserved pork stock

1. Season the masa flour with the salt, and mix to combine thoroughly.
2. Use your hands to mix in the corn oil until evenly distributed. Add the 4 cups of the pork cooking broth 1 cup at a time to form a smooth paste. You may need a little bit more or less liquid. You want the paste to be soft enough to spread with your hands, but not very sticky.

Assemble and Cook the Tamales
Corn husks

1. Soak the corn husks in warm water for at least 2 hours. (We recommend starting the husks soaking at the same time you put the pork roast on to boil.)
2. Remove one corn husk and pat dry. Spread 3 to 4 tablespoons masa paste on the husk, leaving bare about one-third of the narrow end and a 1-inch strip along the long edge. Spread the paste into a thin layer, about 1/4 inch thick.
3. Place 1 to 2 tablespoons of seasoned pork along the middle of the masa paste.
4. Roll up the tamale, rolling toward the long edge that is free of masa paste, which will overlap the corn husk. Fold the narrow end (also free of masa paste) up to enclose the filling.
5. Place the rolled tamales in a steaming basket standing upright (we use a pasta steaming insert in our pot, with the narrow, folded end of the tamale on the bottom). Make sure your steamer is deep enough to accept a tight fitting lid without the interference of the tamales. Heat the water in the bottom of the pot, but not too much that the tamales boil instead of steam. Place the steaming basket in the pot and steam the tamales for 1 to 1 1/2 hours, until the masa paste is firm. Check every 30 minutes to make sure there is still water to steam the tamales in the pot.
6. Remove the tamales from the steamer and let cool. Serve hot, refrigerate until serving, or freeze for later use.
7. To reheat the tamales, steam in the same method they were cooked, or microwave.

FOR AS MANY tamales as this recipe makes (and believe us, they are worth the effort, and any extra tamales can be saved for later and enjoyed in the future), you may also be left with some surplus seasoned, pulled pork roast. It's basically *carnitas,* and makes a great alternative meat filling for tacos (page 170).

THE CORN HUSKS used in this recipe are dried, single layers of husk, and as such as typically available year-round. (You can find them in the ethnic aisle of many supermarkets.)

chili

[MAKES 8 SERVINGS]

Chili must easily be one our favorite dishes for cold nights. When you need to warm up fast with some good old comfort food, this is the way to go. This particular version comes from our friends Greg and Emily. As so many of our beloved friends do, they happily cook gluten-free dinners to accommodate Pete's needs, even though they normally don't eat a gluten-free diet. Gluten or not, this chili is one of the best, and we recommend pairing it with our Corn Bread (page 28). If you don't have a slow cooker, you can make the chili on the stove top in a large, heavy saucepan; simmer it covered for at least two hours.

Two 14.5-ounce cans diced tomatoes with green chilies
One 28-ounce can no-salt-added, diced tomatoes
1 medium onion, diced
1 green bell pepper, diced
2 garlic cloves, minced
1 tablespoon chili powder
1 tablespoon ground cumin
2 teaspoons dried oregano
One 1-pound beef round roast
One 15-ounce can kidney beans, drained and rinsed

1. Combine the tomatoes with chilies, diced tomatoes, onion, bell pepper, garlic, chili powder, cumin, and oregano in a slow cooker. Put the roast in the middle of the pot. Cover and cook on low for 8 to 10 hours. Remove the roast from the pot. Allow the roast to cool until you can handle the meat.

2. Discard the fat and shred the beef with two forks. Return the shredded meat to the slow cooker. Add the kidney beans, cover, and cook on low for an additional 30 minutes.

deep dish pizza dough

[MAKES 1 PAR-BAKED CRUST]

In contrast to the Thin Crust Pizza Dough (page 118) this deep dish crust is chewy, in a good way, reminiscent of the Sicilian pizzas Pete ate as a kid on Long Island. We use this deep dish crust to make a Chicago-Style Pizza (Page 121).

3/4 cup warm water (about 115°F)
1 tablespoon honey
2 1/4 teaspoons active dry yeast
1 tablespoon olive oil
1 teaspoon xanthan gum
1 teaspoon dried basil
1/2 teaspoon dried oregano
1/2 teaspoon garlic powder
1 teaspoons salt
1 1/3 cups Artisan GF Flour Mix (page 15)
additional olive oil

1. Preheat the oven to 400°F, with a pizza stone inside.
2. Combine the warm water, honey, and yeast in a large bowl and let stand until the mixture bubbles, about 5 minutes. The bubbles mean your yeast is alive and ready to go.
3. Stir in the olive oil, xanthan gum, basil, oregano, garlic powder, and salt. Mix in the flour to form a dough that is very soft and sticky, almost wet.
4. Drizzle about 1 tablespoon of olive oil into the mixing bowl, and roll the dough ball to evenly coat it. Cover, set in a warm location, and let rise for 20 minutes.
5. Drizzle a small amount of olive oil into an 8-inch round cake pan. Use your fingers to spread the oil and evenly coat the bottom and sides of the pan. Transfer the dough to the cake pan, and use a spatula or your hands to press the dough into the pan.
6. Par-bake the dough for 13 minutes, docking with a fork if necessary to eliminate any large air bubbles. When finished par-baking, use a spatula to remove the pizza from the pan, and complete the pizza by adding toppings and baking directly on the pre-heated pizza stone in the oven.

SICILIAN-STYLE AND Chicago-style pizzas are a bit like Long Island and New Jersey . . . so close and so similar, and yet so different and so culturally distinct. Both have a hearty, inch-thick crust, and both usually put the sauce *on top* of the cheese. But Sicilian-style pizzas are rectangular, and often go lighter on the toppings (and actually, true Sicilian pizzas—which originated in Palermo, Sicily—don't even use cheese!). Meanwhile, Chicago-style pizzas—which were first created in 1943—are round, with a raised lip of crust that helps to retain a hefty portion of sauce, cheese and other toppings.

thin crust pizza dough

[MAKES 1 PAR-BAKED CRUST]

Some recipes have earned a regular spot in our weekly rotation of dinners and become tradition. Pizza is one of them. Typically, we'll make it for dinner on a Sunday night (that tradition dates back in Kelli's family for as long as she's been eating pizza). In our division of kitchen labor, Kelli makes the dough, and then hands off to Pete, who forms the crust, tops the pizza, and pops it in the oven. When it's all said and done, though, we're both at the table to enjoy the fruits of our labors. This thin crust is lightly chewy, and also reminiscent of a cracker. Use it to make Margherita Pizza (page 119) and New York–Style Thin Crust Pizza (page 120).

3/4 cup warm water (about 115°F)

1 tablespoon honey

2 1/4 teaspoons (1 package) active dry yeast

1 tablespoon olive oil

1 teaspoon xanthan gum

1 teaspoon dried basil

1/2 teaspoon dried oregano

1/2 teaspoon garlic powder

1 teaspoon salt

1 1/3 cups Artisan GF Flour Mix (page 15)

1. Preheat the oven to 400°F with a pizza stone inside.

2. Combine the warm water, honey, and yeast in a large bowl and let stand until the mixture bubbles, about 5 minutes. The bubbles mean your yeast is alive and ready to go.

3. Stir in the olive oil, xanthan gum, basil, oregano, garlic powder, and salt. Mix in the flour to form a dough that is soft but not sticky to the touch.

4. Drizzle about 1 tablespoon of olive oil into the mixing bowl, and roll the dough ball to evenly coat it. Cover, set in a warm location, and let rise for 20 minutes.

5. Drizzle a small amount of olive oil onto a 13-inch pizza pan. Use your fingers to spread the oil and evenly coat the pan. Transfer the dough to the pan, and use a spatula or your hands to spread the dough over the pan.

6. Par-bake the dough for 10 minutes, docking with a fork if necessary to eliminate any large air bubbles. When finished par-baking, use a spatula to remove the pizza from the pan, and complete the pizza by adding toppings and baking directly on the preheated pizza stone in the oven.

margherita pizza

[MAKES 1 MEDIUM PIZZA]

Unlike a pizza with a rich, traditional sauce, this Margherita Pizza has clean, simple flavors—fresh tomato, garlic, and fresh basil. Although the base ingredients are very similar, it tastes worlds apart.

Thin Crust Pizza Dough (page 118)
8 ounces fresh mozzarella cheese, thinly sliced
1 to 2 tomatoes, thinly sliced
5 to 6 fresh basil leaves, cut into chiffonade (see box below)
1 tablespoon olive oil
1 garlic clove, minced
Dried basil
Dried oregano

1. Begin with the par-baked thin crust pizza dough on wooden pizza paddle. (If you don't have a pizza paddle, you could use another large, flat surface—such as a cookie sheet—that would make it easy to transfer the pizza with toppings from your work surface to the oven.) Your oven should already be preheated to 400°F from par-baking the crust.

2. Arrange the mozzarella slices on the par-baked crust. Arrange the tomato slices on top of the cheese. Sprinkle with the fresh basil.

3. Mix the olive oil and garlic in a small bowl, cup, or ramekin. Drizzle over the pizza using a spoon. Top with a sprinkling of dried basil and oregano.

4. Bake on the pizza stone for 10 to 15 minutes, until the cheese is melted and slightly browned. Remove from the oven and let set for 5 minutes. Slice and serve.

CHIFFONADE IS A technique in which green, leafy vegetables are cut into long, thin strips. To chiffonade basil, stack all the basil leaves one on top of the other. Then roll the stack of basil leaves into a tight roll. Finally, thinly slice the roll. When the cross sections unroll, you'll have beautiful, long, thin strips of basil!

TWO ESSENTIAL TOOLS for making thin crust pizza are the pizza stone and the pizza paddle. A stone transfers heat to the crust differently than a metal pan, resulting in a crust more like those at good pizzerias. Always preheat your oven with the stone inside on a middle oven rack, allowing at least 30 minutes for the stone to reach temperature. A wooden pizza paddle is equally important—it allows you to easily and effectively get the pizza in and out of the oven.

new york–style thin crust pizza with traditional sauce

[MAKES 1 MEDIUM PIZZA]

As a native New Yorker, it was almost inevitable that Pete would inherit (or be indoctrinated with, depending on your point of view!) a love for New York–style thin crust pizza. This version includes Pete's signature pizza sauce, and puts the sauce on top of the cheese, a practice we picked up from a Long Island pizzeria in Pete's hometown of Farmingdale.

Thin Crust Pizza Dough (page 118)

Sauce

> **One 14.5-ounce can no-salt-added diced tomatoes**
> **1 teaspoon dried basil**
> **1 teaspoon dried oregano**
> **1 teaspoon garlic powder**
> **Salt and pepper**
> **1 tablespoon cornstarch**
> **1 tablespoon cold water**

Toppings

> **8 ounces mozzarella cheese, thinly sliced**
> **Turkey pepperoni**

1. Begin with the par-baked thin crust pizza dough on a wooden pizza paddle. (If you don't have a pizza paddle, you could use another large, flat surface—such as a cookie sheet—that would make it easy to transfer the pizza with toppings from your work surface to the oven.) Your oven should already be preheated to 400°F from par-baking the crust.

2. To make the sauce: Puree the tomatoes in a medium saucepan with an immersion blender. (Blend more for a smoother sauce, or less for a chunky sauce.) Add the basil, oregano, garlic, and salt and pepper. Mix together the cornstarch and cold water and add to the saucepan. Heat the sauce over medium heat just until it comes to a boil. Reduce the heat and simmer, stirring occasionally, for 5 minutes, until thickened slightly.

3. Arrange the mozzarella slices on the par-baked crust. Ladle the sauce onto the cheese and spread evenly. Top the pizza with pepperoni (or your choice of toppings).

4. Bake on the pizza stone for 13 minutes, or until the pepperoni is crispy and the cheese is melted under the sauce. Remove from the oven and let set for 5 minutes. Slice and serve.

Variation

For a vegetarian version, simply omit the pepperoni.

chicago-style deep dish pizza

[MAKES 1 PIZZA]

Going gluten-free, you sometimes get a craving for foods you used to eat but no longer do. For us, one of the persistent cravings was for deep dish pizza. Yet, when we looked around at pizzerias that offered gluten-free pizzas, even the ones that specialized in deep dish regular pizzas offered only thin crust gluten-free pizza. It soon became clear that it would be up to us to make our own deep dish pie, and in the end, it was a craving satisfied.

Deep Dish Pizza Dough (page 117)
One 14.5-ounce can no-salt-added diced tomatoes
1 teaspoon dried basil
1 teaspoon dried oregano
1 teaspoon garlic powder
Salt and pepper
8 ounces mozzarella cheese, shredded
Olive oil, for brushing

1. Begin with the par-baked pizza crust on a wooden pizza paddle. (If you don't have a pizza paddle, you could use another large, flat surface—such as a cookie sheet—that would make it easy to transfer the pizza with toppings from your work surface to the oven.) Your oven should already be preheated to 400°F from par-baking the crust.

2. Puree the tomatoes in a medium saucepan with an immersion blender. (Blend more for a smoother sauce, or less for a chunky sauce.) Add the basil, oregano, garlic powder, and salt and pepper. Heat the sauce over medium heat just until it comes to a boil. Reduce the heat and simmer, stirring occasionally, for 5 minutes, until thickened slightly.

3. Spread two thirds of the sauce on the par-baked crust and sprinkle the shredded cheese over the sauce. (Reserve the remaining third of the sauce for another use.) Brush the exposed crust (the perimeter with no cheese or sauce) lightly with olive oil.

4. Bake for 15 minutes, or until the cheese is melted and starting to brown in places. Remove from the oven and let set for 5 minutes. Slice and serve.

pasta dough

Shortly after we were married, we inherited an Italian-made, manual pasta maker from Pete's mom. It was the kind that clamped on to your kitchen table, and used a hand crank to feed pasta dough through a series of rollers and cutters. We adored it, making long sheets of beautiful pasta dough, and then transforming that pasta dough into linguine, fettuccine, and other types of noodles. Now, we happily continue the tradition of making fresh pasta from scratch with this gluten-free recipe.

3 cups Artisan GF Flour Mix (page 15)
2 teaspoons xanthan gum
1 teaspoon salt
4 eggs, beaten

1. Mix the flour and xanthan gum together. Form the flour mix into a mound on your work surface and make a well in the center.

2. Add the salt and eggs to the well. Using the index and middle finger of one hand, swirl the eggs, slowing pulling in dry flour from the perimeter. Work the dough, pulling in more flour as needed until you have a smooth, moist dough that is not tacky. Clean your work surface and give it a fresh sprinkling of flour before moving on to the next step.

3. Roll the dough out very thin ($1/16$ inch thick or less) on a floured surface with a rolling pin. Use a long, sharp knife or pizza cutter to cut the pasta into the desired shape (see Variations below). Lightly flour the blade of the knife or pizza cutter to prevent the dough from sticking. Note: If you have difficulty working with a single large sheet of pasta dough, you can always divide the dough ball and roll out several smaller sheets that are more manageable. (Also see the box below for notes on using pasta makers.)

Variations

- **Linguine:** Cut the pasta into long, straight noodles not much wider than standard spaghetti.
- **Fettuccine:** Cut the pasta two to three times as wide as linguine.
- **Lasagna:** Divide the dough into 3 or 4 equal pieces (depending on how many layers of noodles you want in your lasagna). Roll each piece of dough out into a broad, flat sheet that is $1/16$ inch thick. Cut the pasta to fit the size and shape of your pan. Depending on the pan size and the number of layers of lasagna you'd like, you may need to double the recipe.
- **Ravioli:** Cut into 2- or 3-inch squares. You can use a square or round cookie cutter if you're worried about getting uniform and exactly shaped ravioli halves. However, this will also result in wasted dough. We recommend using a long knife or pizza cutter (our preference). Some specialty stores sell a ravioli rolling pin for making ravioli en masse—ignore this contraption built for people who cook with gluten.

*A*LTHOUGH MAKING FRESH pasta can require a little practice in the beginning, once you become proficient it doesn't take much longer than using store-bought, premade pasta. The difference is that you spend 15 minutes making fresh pasta and 2 to 5 minutes boiling it, versus spending 30 seconds to open a package of dried pasta and then 15 to 20 minutes boiling it.

Having said that, there may be times when you'll prefer to use store-bought pasta. Keep in mind that gluten-free pasta can be made from a variety of flours: rice, corn, quinoa, and others. We recommend using rice pasta, and in particular recommend the Tinkyáda brand organic brown rice pasta. We think it's the best on the market. Also, a word of advice: it's easy to overcook gluten-free pasta, and when that happens, it quickly turns to mush. Cook the pasta until it's al dente. Then strain it and immediately rinse under cold water to halt the cooking process. Then add it back to your recipe to finish the dish.

*W*HEN MAKING FRESH gluten-free pasta from scratch, our secret weapon is an offset spatula, the kind you'd use to ice a cake. It's perfect for sliding under the pasta dough to separate it from the work surface when the dough sticks (this is especially helpful when rolling out broad sheets of pasta dough). It's also helpful for easily picking up and manipulating lasagna sheets, ravioli, etc.

*I*N ADDITION TO making pasta from scratch strictly by hand, you can also try using a pasta maker (either a hand-cranked manual maker or an electric maker). Pasta makers come in two varieties: roller pasta makers (which form the pasta by passing it through a series of rollers and cutters) and extruder pasta makers (which press the pasta dough through a die with shaped holes or cutouts). Extruded pasta is denser than rolled pasta—as a result it takes longer to boil and doesn't pick up the sauce as well. However, both styles of pasta can work. If using a pasta maker to make your fresh GF pasta from scratch, knead a little extra flour into the dough to make the dough just a touch drier, so that it doesn't stick to the pasta maker. We've done this with great success using our inherited Italian pasta maker from Pete's mom.

pesto pasta

[MAKES 4 SERVINGS]

We've both been fans of pesto for a long time, but we became pesto fanatics thanks to one of the vendors at our local farmers' market. They made a variety of pestos that we became absolutely addicted to. Motivated to make our own, we bought a live basil plant from an organic farm at the market that produced an entire summer's worth of leaves for our pesto cravings (sadly, Pete's green thumb failed to yield a basil plant grown from seed, hence our need for someone else's green thumb to get it started for us).

1¼ cups fresh basil leaves

¼ cup olive oil

¼ cup walnuts

2 tablespoons grated Parmesan cheese

2 garlic cloves, peeled

Salt and pepper

Pasta Dough (page 122), cut into shape of choice, or store-bought GF pasta

1. Puree the basil, olive oil, walnuts, Parmesan, garlic, and salt and pepper in a food processor until smooth.
2. Cook the pasta in a large pot of salted boiling water until al dente. Drain.
3. Toss the hot pasta with the pesto in a large bowl and serve.

Note: you can heat the pesto in a pot on the stove, but be careful—too much heat is evil for pesto (the cheese in the pesto sauce sticks to the pan).

mediterranean lasagna

[MAKES 9 SERVINGS]

Lasagna is a great go-to dish for hosting dinner groups, but when we're joined by vegetarian friends, our Meat Lovers' Lasagna (page 126) obviously won't do. This inspired us to create a vegetarian Mediterranean Lasagna. The tomatoes, peppers, pine nuts, and nutmeg speak to Pete's Sicilian heritage (and the Mediterranean influences on Sicily's cuisine over the centuries). Spinach and mushrooms round out this hearty yet light dish.

Béchamel
- 3 tablespoon salted butter
- 4 tablespoons + 1 teaspoon Artisan GF Flour Blend (page 15)
- 3 cups milk
- Salt, pepper, and ground nutmeg to taste
- 1½ cups whole milk ricotta cheese

Spinach Filling
- 1 tablespoon olive oil
- 2 garlic cloves, minced
- 6 ounces fresh baby spinach
- Salt and pepper to taste

Tomato-Pepper-Mushroom Filling
- 1 tablespoon butter
- ½ medium onion, finely diced
- 1½ cups sliced button mushrooms (about 4 ounces, or 5 medium mushrooms)
- ½ cup sun-dried tomatoes, thinly sliced
- ½ cup roasted red peppers, thinly sliced

- ¼ cup pine nuts, dry roasted
- 8 ounces mozzarella cheese, shredded
- Pasta Dough (page 122), formed into 4 thin sheets of lasagna

1. To make the béchamel: Melt the butter in a medium saucepan over medium-high heat. Add the flour and stir to combine. Cook until frothy and bubbly, about 2–5 minutes. (The sauce should be pale, not golden.) Add the milk, whisking to combine and prevent lumps. Season to taste with salt, pepper, and ground nutmeg. Bring to a boil, reduce heat, and simmer for 10 minutes. Remove from the heat, stir in the ricotta cheese, and set aside.

2. To make the spinach filling: Heat the olive oil over medium-high heat in a medium non-stick skillet. Sauté the garlic until fragrant. Add the spinach, season with salt and pepper, and turn the spinach until all leaves are wilted. Remove from the heat and set the spinach aside.

3. To make the tomato-pepper-mushroom filling: Melt the butter over medium-high heat in the same skillet used for the spinach. Add the onions and sauté until translucent. Add the mushrooms and sauté until soft. Add the tomatoes and peppers and sauté for 2 minutes. Remove from the heat and set the filling aside.

4. To dry roast the pine nuts: Heat a clean, dry non-stick skillet over high heat. Add the nuts, and gently toss or stir until lightly golden, about 1–2 minutes.

5. Preheat the oven to 375°F.

6. To assemble the lasagna: Spread a thin layer of the béchamel in the bottom of a greased 9 x 9-inch baking pan. Add a sheet of lasagna. Spread half of the tomato-pepper-mushroom filling over the noodle. Cover with one quarter of the remaining béchamel and one quarter of the mozzarella. Add a second sheet of lasagna, spread with all of the spinach filling and one third of the pine nuts, then cover with one quarter of the béchamel and one quarter of the mozzarella. Repeat the steps for a second tomato-pepper-mushroom layer. Lastly, top with the fourth lasagna sheet and the remaining béchamel and mozzarella, and sprinkle with the remaining pine nuts.

7. Bake for 40 minutes in the preheated oven, until the cheese is golden on top. Cover with tin foil, and bake for an additional 15–20 minutes.

meat lovers' lasagna

[MAKES 9 SERVINGS]

There's Italian food, and then there's Italian comfort food. This dish definitely falls into the latter category. It's a hearty meal that's great for feeding a table full of guests (or any hungry mouths). The balance of sauce, cheese, meat, and a few veggies makes this the perfect pasta dish for meat lovers, though you could easily scale back on the meat and pump up the vegetables if you prefer. Best of all, this lasagna is neither too dry, nor too runny—not always the easiest line to walk with this type of dish! When Kelli field-tested this dish with two of her coworkers, one of whom is a self-proclaimed foodie, neither could tell it was gluten-free, and both loved it.

1 tablespoon olive oil

1/2 red bell pepper, diced

1 medium onion, chopped

2 garlic cloves, minced

1/2 pound ground turkey

1/2 pound Italian seasoned GF sausage, casings removed

2 teaspoons dried basil

2 teaspoons dried oregano

Salt and pepper

Two 14.5-ounce cans no-salt-added diced tomatoes

Pasta Dough (page 122), formed into 3 sheets of lasagna

1 pound mozzarella cheese, shredded

7 ounces ricotta cheese (about half of a 15-ounce container)

1. Heat the olive oil in a large skillet over medium-high heat. Add the pepper, onion, and garlic and sauté until softened. Add the ground turkey and sausage meat and cook until browned. Stir in the basil, oregano, and salt and pepper.

2. Puree the tomatoes in a large bowl with an immersion blender. Add to the skillet. Reduce the heat and simmer for 10 minutes.

3. Preheat the oven to 375°F.

4. For the assembly of the lasagna, remember the 4-3-4-3 rule. There are 4 layers of sauce, 3 layers of ricotta, 4 layers of mozzarella, and 3 layers of noodles. Begin by ladling a layer of sauce into the bottom of a 9 x 9-inch baking pan. Spoon one-third of the ricotta over the sauce. Then sprinkle one-fourth of the mozzarella on top of that. Place one sheet of pasta over the cheese.

5. Repeat two times, building layers of lasagna.

6. To finish the assembly, ladle the remainder of the sauce over the top, and top with mozzarella.

7. Bake the lasagna for 30 to 40 minutes, until the mozzarella on top has started to brown and the lasagna is cooked through. Remove from the oven and let set for 5 to 10 minutes. Slice into 9 equal portions and serve.

To MAKE A great vegetarian version of this lasagna, omit the meat and instead use 1 zucchini and 1/2 an eggplant, all thinly sliced. Sauté the vegetables in a skillet until al dente and continue as per the recipe.

ravioli

[MAKES ABOUT TWENTY-FIVE 2-INCH RAVIOLI OR FIFTEEN 3-INCH RAVIOLI, ABOUT 3-4 SERVINGS]

Gluten-free ravioli may easily be the least-made GF dish out there. People perceive it as being too difficult to make (or are at least too intimidated to try), or they fret that they can't find premade GF ravioli in the stores (a select few companies and bakeries are making GF ravioli these days, but not many). But for anyone who's tried to make GF ravioli from scratch, their responses all tend to fall along the lines of, "it was time consuming, but totally worth it." We'll let you in on a little secret—it's a little time consuming, yes, but it is indeed worth it. And by breaking the process down into simple, manageable steps, making fresh GF ravioli from scratch isn't any more involved than making lasagna (page 126) or Linguine with Clam Sauce (page 131). Go ahead and give it a try . . . you won't regret it. Try pairing with a marinara-style sauce for cheese- and meat-based raviolis, or with a brown butter sauce for vegetable-filled raviolis.

³/₄ cup ricotta cheese
Dried parsley
Salt and pepper
Pasta Dough (page 122), cut into 2- or 3-inch ravioli squares

1. Season the ricotta to taste with parsley and salt and pepper.
2. Spoon a small dollop (about 2 teaspoons) of the ricotta filling onto the center of one 2-inch pasta square. (Use more filling for 3-inch squares.) Using your finger dipped into a ramekin of water, wet all four edges of the square. Place a second ravioli square directly over the first, enclosing the filling. Firmly press down around all four edges with your fingers to seal.
3. Using the tines of a fork, press the tines flat onto each edge and corner of the ravioli, taking care only to press the dough edges together, and not to press down on the filling. The resulting pattern is both cosmetic and structural, ensuring a tight seal of the ravioli.
4. Bring a saucepan of salted water to a boil. Add the ravioli (in batches, if necessary). After a minute or two, the ravioli will float. From this point, cook for 5 to 7 minutes longer, depending on the size of your ravioli, until cooked through.
5. Drain and serve.

Variations

There are easily more than three dozen varieties of fillings for ravioli. In addition to the classic ricotta above, try these fillings:

- **Garlic Chicken:** Season cooked, minced chicken with salt, pepper, and garlic.
- **Basil Pesto:** Just what it sounds like. Try our Pesto recipe on page 124.
- **Butternut Squash with Nutmeg:** Puree cooked butternut squash and season with a little salt, pepper, and nutmeg.

THERE ARE A variety of tools available to facilitate making ravioli—ravioli cutters, ravioli rolling pins, ravioli makers. In the end, we still think the fork is the best way to go. (So did Pete's grandmother, who tried every tool under the sun before returning to the tried-and-true fork method.)

meatballs with spaghetti
and marinara sauce

[MAKES 3 TO 4 SERVINGS]

We can't think of a more classic Italian dish than meatballs with spaghetti in a marinara sauce. (Okay, a few other Italian dishes do come to mind, but this is still a classic. And who can forget that scene from Lady and the Tramp, *when the movie's namesake pooches lock canine lips after slurping up opposite ends of the same pasta noodle from a bowl of spaghetti with meatballs?) You'll notice that this recipe is called Meatballs with Spaghetti, and not Spaghetti with Meatballs, as is usually written. That should be an indication of how important the meatballs are to us! (But don't let that stop you from making it vegetarian, by omitting the meatballs. We won't be offended.)*

Italian Meatballs

- 1 pound ground turkey
- 2 eggs
- 1$\frac{1}{3}$ cups GF bread crumbs (see box, page 57)
- $\frac{1}{2}$ medium onion, chopped
- 2 teaspoons dried basil
- 1$\frac{1}{2}$ teaspoons dried oregano
- 1 teaspoon garlic powder
- 1$\frac{1}{2}$ teaspoons salt
- 1 teaspoon pepper
- Olive oil

Marinara Sauce

- 1 tablespoon olive oil
- $\frac{1}{2}$ medium onion, chopped (use the onion left over from the meatballs)
- 2 garlic cloves, minced
- 1 teaspoon dried basil
- 1 teaspoon dried oregano
- One 14.5-ounce can no-salt-added diced tomatoes
- Salt and pepper

Pasta Dough (page 122), cut into shape of choice, or store-bought GF pasta

1. Preheat the oven (or toaster oven) to 350°F.
2. To make the meatballs: Combine the turkey, eggs, bread crumbs, onion, basil, oregano, garlic powder, salt, and pepper in a large mixing bowl. Mix thoroughly with your hands. Form into 16 meatballs that are slightly larger than the size of golf balls.
3. Heat an approximate heavy-handed tablespoon of olive oil in a large skillet over medium-high heat. Add the meatballs, and cook (in batches, if needed), turning occasionally, until browned on all sides.
4. Transfer the meatballs to an ungreased rimmed baking sheet and bake for 15 minutes, or until cooked through.
5. To make the sauce: Heat the olive oil in a medium saucepan over medium heat. Add the onion and garlic and sauté until soft. Add the basil and oregano, and sauté another minute or so. Add the tomatoes and salt and pepper. Simmer over medium heat to let the flavors meld, at least 5 minutes.
6. Blend the sauce using a handheld immersion blender. Simmer for 5 to 10 minutes longer, adding additional salt and pepper to taste.
7. Cook the pasta in a large pot of salted water until al dente. Drain and return to the pot.
8. Add the marinara sauce to the pasta and mix well. Add the meatballs. Mix and serve.

basic asian-inspired noodle bowl

[MAKES 2 SERVINGS]

We call this dish "Asian-inspired" because it blends Thai, Chinese, and Japanese influences. It's great by itself as a simple noodle bowl (Pete often makes it for lunch), or it can serve as a great foundation to build upon with extra vegetables and flavor combinations.

Noodles
- 5 cups water
- 6 ounces (about a 2-inch diameter bunch) thin, straight-cut rice noodles

Chicken
- 1 large boneless, skinless chicken breast, thinly sliced
- Garlic powder
- Salt and pepper
- 3 tablespoons olive oil

Sauce
- 1/2 cup water
- 2 tablespoons + 1 teaspoon tamari wheat-free soy sauce
- 2 tablespoons honey
- 2 teaspoons ground fresh chili paste
- 1 teaspoon red curry paste

- 15 to 20 sugar snap or snow peas
- 1 tablespoon cornstarch
- 1/4 cup cold water

1. To cook the noodles: Bring the water to a boil in a medium saucepan. Add the rice noodles and reduce the heat to medium-high. Cook until al dente. Drain in a colander and rinse under cold water. Set aside.

2. To cook the chicken: Lightly season the chicken with garlic powder and salt and pepper. Heat the olive oil in a skillet or wok over medium-high heat. Add the chicken and sauté until it is just cooked through and lightly browned. Set the chicken aside in a bowl.

3. Make the sauce: Combine the water, soy sauce, honey, chili paste, and red curry paste in the skillet and mix with a spoon, fork, or whisk. Bring to a light boil over medium-high heat.

4. Return the chicken to the skillet, along with the sugar snap peas. Stir together the cornstarch and water, then stir into the chicken mixture. Cook, stirring, until the sauce begins to thicken. Add the noodles, remove from heat, and toss to thoroughly mix all the ingredients. Serve in bowls (chopsticks optional).

Variation

Make this a light vegetarian meal by omitting the chicken.

linguine with clam sauce

[MAKES 4 SERVINGS]

Linguine with clam sauce is one of Pete's signature dishes, and he'll often make it for special occasions or when we have a craving for a seafood and pasta dish. In the early days of our relationship, we spent a long holiday weekend on Block Island, a picturesque and pastoral island in the Atlantic Ocean off the East End of Long Island and south of Rhode Island. It's the kind of place where a bicycle is the primary mode of transportation, and fresh seafood is always on the menu. At the end of the weekend, the ferry returned us to Point Judith, Rhode Island, where our car was waiting. But before heading home to New Jersey, we stopped at a dockside fish market to pick up some fresh clams, which we used to make this dish later that night for dinner.

One 6.5-ounce can chopped clams
One 6.5-ounce can minced clams
1 tablespoon olive oil
1 tablespoon salted butter
2 garlic cloves
1 lemon, juiced
¼ cup milk
¼ cup white wine (we like using a Riesling or Gewürztraminer, but most un-oaked
     whites will work well)
2 tablespoons water
Salt and pepper
Pasta Dough (page 122), cut into linguine, or store-bought GF pasta

1. Drain and reserve the clam juice from the chopped and minced clams. Set the clams and the clam juice aside.
2. Heat the olive oil and butter in a large skillet over medium-high heat. Add the garlic and sauté until golden. Add the reserved clam juice, lemon juice, milk, wine, water, and salt and pepper. Bring to a boil, reduce the heat, and simmer until the sauce is reduced by about one-fourth.
3. Add the clams and cook just long enough to heat through. (An overcooked clam gets tough and chewy.)
4. Meanwhile, cook the pasta in a large pot of salted boiling water until al dente. Drain.
5. Add the pasta to the clam sauce and toss.

Since WE LIVE in Colorado, we tend to make this dish exclusively with canned clams. But if you have access to fresh clams, by all means, use them! When we lived near the ocean, we'd use fresh clams, but would still use the chopped and minced clams as a base for the sauce. Separately steam the fresh clams (about one dozen), and serve them atop linguine.

grilled halibut with lemon, garlic, and olive oil

[MAKES 4 SERVINGS]

We firmly believe that if you have truly fresh, high-quality fish (and especially flaky white fish, such as halibut), then the best thing you can do is to prepare the fish simply. This allows the natural flavors of the fish to shine through. The goal is just to accentuate what's already there. In fact, when Pete's family would go fishing on his Uncle Joe's boat, they'd often eat the fresh catch of the day right on the boat, or the beach, or the dock. They'd make a "baking pan" out of tinfoil, and cook the whole fish (gutted and cleaned first, of course) in little more than straight seawater over a propane stove or open fire. The meat, eaten right off the bone, was divine. This recipe takes that same ethos into the kitchen or backyard. The first time we made the recipe, though, we weren't home, but rather visiting our friends Sarah and Jeff in Seattle. We made a requisite visit to the Pike Place Fish Market, where the vendors literally toss the fish orders to customers. Jeff handled the catch like a pro, and later that night, this halibut recipe was born over their grill in Seattle's University District.

Four 6-ounce halibut fillets with skin, washed and patted dry
Olive oil
2 garlic cloves, minced
Salt and pepper
1 lemon, halved

1. Rub the fillets with olive oil and season with the garlic and salt and pepper. Squeeze one lemon half over the fillets. Let the fish sit for 30 minutes, if you have the time.

2. Slice the remaining lemon half and place the slices on the fish fillets.

3. Heat a grill to medium-high.

4. Grill the fillets, skin side down, without turning, until the fish flakes easily with a fork and the meat is cooked through (fully opaque).

Note: When grilling fish, such as halibut, always grill the fillets skin-side down, and do not flip the fish. Ever. Let the fillets cook on the one side only until the fish is fully cooked. Skin-on fillets can be cooked directly on the grill grate. If your fillets don't have skin, they can be cooked on tinfoil. Trying to flip fish on a grill rarely, if ever, results in a positive outcome. Trust us.

shrimp marinara over pasta

[MAKES 4 SERVINGS]

Pete's family in Belgium is mainly centered in and around two cities: Brugge and Antwerp. Among the Antwerp clan, there are several restaurateurs, and during one of Pete's visits "across the pond" he had the chance to eat at one of their restaurants, an Italian bistro just outside of Antwerp. Dinner was a dish called Gambas le Bistro, which were giant prawns in a tomato broth. This recipe, served over pasta, pays homage to that meal, which Pete still remembers fondly (and with some small amount of salivating), albeit with marinara sauce instead of tomato broth, and shrimp in lieu of Belgian giant prawns. You could also make the dish with cubed chicken or vegetables instead of shrimp. Serve over your favorite store-bought GF pasta or pasta made from Pasta Dough (page 122).

1 tablespoon olive oil
½ medium onion, chopped
2 garlic cloves, minced
12 ounces shrimp, peeled and deveined
One 14.5-ounce can no-salt-added diced tomatoes
1 teaspoon dried basil
1 teaspoon dried oregano
Salt and pepper

1. Heat the olive oil in a medium saucepan over medium-high heat. Add the onion and garlic and sauté until softened. Add the shrimp and cook until the shrimp turn pink, about 5 minutes. Remove the shrimp, leaving behind most of the onion and garlic.

2. Add the tomatoes, basil, and oregano to the sauce. Cook over medium-low heat until the flavors meld, about 5 minutes.

3. Blend the sauce using a handheld immersion blender. Let simmer for 5 minutes longer, adding salt and pepper to taste.

4. Return the shrimp to the sauce and serve.

Variation

For a vegetarian version, substitute vegetables such as sliced zucchini or broccoli florets for the shrimp.

slow-cooked tilapia in spicy tomato broth

[MAKES 4 SERVINGS]

Ironically enough, we first made this dish not when we lived near the ocean, but rather upon moving to Colorado. For everything that we loved about the Rocky Mountains and the Centennial State when we first moved here, we were utterly landlocked, and missed our beloved Atlantic Ocean and the fresh seafood bounty it provided. We made a trip to our local Whole Foods supermarket, which imports fresh, never-frozen fish, and promptly set about making this dish. We've loved it ever since. The subtle spiciness and tomato-based broth complement the mellow flavors of white fish very well. Serve over Jasmine Rice (page 86) or Brown Rice (page 89).

1 tablespoon olive oil

1 medium onion, diced

One 14.5-ounce can no-salt-added diced tomatoes

$1/2$ cup GF chicken broth

1 lemon, juiced

2 garlic cloves, minced

1 small red chile, seeded and minced

$1/4$ teaspoon ground ginger

$1/4$ teaspoon curry powder

$1/4$ teaspoon ground turmeric

Salt and pepper

2 pounds tilapia

1. Heat the olive oil in a sauté pan over medium heat. Add the onion and sauté until translucent.

2. Transfer the onion to a slow cooker and add the tomatoes, broth, lemon juice, garlic, chile, ginger, curry powder, turmeric, and salt and pepper. Stir and cover. Cook on high for $1/2$ hours.

3. Add the fish to the sauce and turn the slow cooker to low. Cover and cook for 45 to 60 minutes, until the fish is flakey and cooked through.

WHEN WE FIRST made this dish years ago, we used orange roughy, but since we've switched to other types of fish. Over the years, the orange roughy fishery has suffered some serious setbacks: people are discouraged from eating roughy because of high mercury concentrations; overfishing has decimated the population; and the "standard" method of fishing for roughy—bottom trawling—is notoriously harmful to marine ecosystems. We now use tilapia, and you can also try substituting flounder, halibut, or other white fish.

If you're interested in checking on the status of different fisheries, we highly recommend the Monterey Bay Aquarium's Seafood Watch program (www.montereybayaquarium.org/cr/seafoodwatch.aspx) where you can download a handy pocket guide for supermarket shopping, and much more. You can also check out the Marine Stewardship Council (www.msc.org) which certifies sustainable seafood.

pan-seared scallops

[MAKES 2 TO 3 SERVINGS]

In the Sicilian tradition, Christmas Eve is celebrated with a wide-ranging seafood feast. For us that traditionally involves polpo (octopus), calamari (squid), squingili or scungilli (conch), and a variety of fish. But it also involves cappesante, or scallops. In recent years, Pete's brother, Mike, has handled cooking the scallops, which he pan sears in butter. In short, they're divine. The lemon butter sauce brightens the flavor of the dish, without overpowering the delicate, sweet flavor of the scallops. And as if that weren't enough, scallops are the state shell of our native New York. What's not to love?

2 tablespoons salted butter, plus more if needed
1 tablespoon olive oil
2 garlic cloves, minced
1 pound fresh sea scallops, rinsed and patted dry
1 lemon, juiced
Salt and pepper

1. Heat the butter and olive oil in a sauté pan over medium-high heat. Add the garlic and sauté until golden. (Do not overcook or the garlic will become bitter.)

2. In batches, add the scallops to the pan and cook until browned on one side. Flip and cook until browned on the other side, about 10–12 minutes total (but dependent on the thickness of the scallops). For larger scallops you may need to cover the pan and cook over medium heat to cook the scallops through without overcooking the edges. When the scallops are cooked they should be golden brown on each side and opaque all the way through (the centers should not be translucent). If needed, add more butter to the pan to cook all of the scallops. Transfer the scallops to a plate.

3. Add the lemon juice to the pan and season with salt and pepper. Make sure to scrape up all the good bits from the bottom of the pan. (This is called the *fond,* and it adds great flavor to the sauce!) Pour the pan sauce over the scallops and serve.

porcini-encrusted scallops

[**MAKES 2 SERVINGS**]

During a recent New York City reunion with college friends, we all went out to dinner on Manhattan's Upper East Side, to a seafood restaurant named Atlantic Grill. Pete's dinner was porcini-encrusted shrimp and scallops, which our server informed us could be prepared gluten-free. The porcini mushrooms proved a fantastic twist on sautéed scallops, and we simply had to come up with our own version. The porcini bits almost take on the character of a woodsy bread crumb, offering both flavor and texture contrast to the scallops.

1 to 1½ ounces dried porcini mushrooms
Salt and pepper
1 tablespoon salted butter
1 tablespoon olive oil
1 pound sea scallops (about 8 very large scallops)

1. Preheat the oven or toaster oven to 350°F. Soak the dried porcini mushrooms in hot water for 5 minutes.

2. Drain the mushrooms and transfer to a food processor. Pulse the mushrooms until they break down into large crumbs.

3. Add a dash of salt and pepper to the mushrooms. Transfer them to a baking pan or cookie sheet and spread into a thin layer. Toast in the oven or toaster oven for about 10 minutes, or until dried out. You want to evaporate off excess moisture so that you get dry porcini crumbs, but don't want to toast or burn the mushrooms.

4. Return the mushrooms to the dry food processor and pulse to form dry crumbs. Transfer to a plate or flat-bottomed bowl.

5. Heat the butter and olive oil in a sauté pan over medium heat. Firmly press one side of each scallop, and then the other, into the porcini crumbs. Gently put half the porcini-encrusted scallops in the sauté pan and cover. Cook for 5 minutes. Flip the scallops and cook on the other side, again covered, for an additional 5 minutes, or until opaque all the way through (the centers should not be translucent).

6. Repeat with the remaining scallops.

IT IS ALSO possible to process dried porcini mushrooms directly in a food processor, spice grinder, or coffee grinder, without first soaking them in hot water. This tends to yield porcini powder (more often used as a spice than to encrust a recipe), and we prefer the coarser porcini crumbs created in this recipe. However, as a shortcut, you can substitute store-bought porcini powder, which is available in jars.

If you're having difficulty with the porcini crumbs not sticking to your scallops, you can always use standard breading procedure—first press each side of the scallop into GF flour, then an egg wash, and lastly the porcini crumbs.

fresh steamed lobster

[MAKES 4 SERVINGS]

Answering the question "If you had to choose one favorite food, what would it be?" is not always easy. But for Pete, the answer has always been obvious: fresh steamed lobster. He was a notoriously picky eater as a toddler, and so his mom was understandably surprised when he devoured lobster, which he called "lobster chicken." That was the beginning of a lifelong love affair with lobster . . . from Long Island, from the coast of Maine. That love affair continues to this day, and this recipe is love in its purest form.

Salt
Four 1¼-pound lobsters

Bring about 1½ to 2 inches of salted water to boil in a large pot. Add the live lobsters to the pot and cover with a tight-fitting lid. Steam the lobsters for 15 to 20 minutes. (Hard-shell and larger lobsters may take more time, soft-shell and smaller lobsters less.) Alternatively, periodically check the lobsters, and steam for 10 to 15 minutes once the lobster shells turn bright orange-red (again, cooking for longer or shorter within the time range, depending on your lobsters).

*Y*OU'LL NO DOUBT have noticed that this recipe includes nothing but the lobster and salt water. That's intentional. A fresh, steamed lobster has tender, delicate meat, and we firmly believe that a naked lobster is the best lobster. Sure, there are other ways to serve lobster—with drawn butter, in bisque, with only the tail as part of a surf-and-turf platter. But to us, these are all crimes and an unnecessary distraction, like ordering a nice filet mignon and slathering it with ketchup. Why would you do that to such a nice piece of meat and mask the flavor? Leave the lobster naked and let the flavor of the meat shine. You're of course free to do otherwise, but trust us on this one.

*A*s YOU CAN tell from our strong opinion about how to serve a lobster, it can be a polarizing food. People form strongly held viewpoints, and tend not to budge from their positions. Case in point: what's the best part of a lobster? The tail? Claws? Legs? Body? Our take: the whole thing. Another example: what's the best size to order? From where we stand, a $1\frac{1}{4}$ to $1\frac{1}{2}$ pound lobster is ideal. It's better to order two $1\frac{1}{2}$-pound lobsters than a single 3-pounder. The meat is more tender and sweeter.

*H*ERE ARE A few things to keep in mind when buying fresh lobster: *Chick* is not a chauvinistic way to refer to a female lobster. It's a word for a 1-pound lobster of either sex. *Culls* are lobsters that have lost one of their claws (either the crusher or seizer). Lobsters periodically molt. Ones that have recently molted will have soft shells. Ones that have not recently molted will have hard shells. The hardness of the shell is not an indication of the lobster's age. The soft shells typically have a bit less meat and a bit more water, since they haven't fully grown into their shells. For that same reason, they're often priced cheaper than hard shells, and many people agree that soft shells yield the more tender and tasty lobster meat.

sushi rolls

[MAKES ABOUT 32 ROLLS]

(WITH ONE RECIPE OF SUSHI RICE, PAGE 91, AND 4 SHEETS NORI)

We've both been addicted to sushi for years, long before we were married, or dating, or even knew each other. But we started making our own sushi together for the first time when we were dating. Pete was living outside Albany, New York, and Kelli was in northeast New Jersey. Making sushi together, we thought, was a great way to spend quality time doing something we both loved: cooking and then eating the fruits of our labors. Skilled sushi chefs take years to master the craft, but you can still have fun, as we did, and enjoy sushi rolls of your own making.

Fillings
Tuna (sushi grade)
Salmon (sushi grade)
Cooked crab (real crab meat only; imitation crab meat often contains gluten)
Cooked shrimp
Cucumber
Avocado
Asparagus

Nori (seaweed sheets)
Sushi Rice (page 91)
Sesame seeds (optional)
Tamari wheat-free soy sauce
Pickled ginger
Wasabi

1. Prep your fillings by slicing into long, thin pieces. The shrimp and crab should already be cooked. Other ingredients should be left raw.

2. Prepare a bamboo sushi rolling mat by wrapping it in plastic wrap.

3. Lay out one sheet of nori on the bamboo mat. Note: Nori has two sides—one has a shiny finish, the other has a matte finish. Place the nori shiny side down.

4. Cover about three-fourths of the sheet with a thin layer of sushi rice, leaving about 1 inch of nori free of rice along the end farthest from you. Place your chosen fillings in a line across the rice, about 1 inch in from the end closest to you. Then, carefully roll the sushi, starting at the end nearest you, and rolling away from your body. As you roll, compress the bamboo mat with your hands to ensure a tightly compacted sushi roll that won't fall apart. Before you reach the naked edge of the nori, use your fingertip to apply a little bit of water to the bare area to help seal the roll. Finish rolling and press to seal the roll.

5. To slice the rolls, first wet your knife blade in rice vinegar and water. Slice the roll in half, then each half in half, and then each in half again, resulting in eight equal size pieces.

6. Serve the rolls with sides of soy sauce, pickled ginger, and wasabi.

Variation

For an inside-out roll (rice on the outside of the roll), cover the entire sheet of nori with rice. Sprinkle the rice with sesame seeds. Then, flip the nori over, so that the rice is face down on the bamboo mat, and the naked nori is face up. Add your fillings, and then roll up.

SUSHI RICE IS a short grain rice that's very starchy. That's why it's so sticky, which makes it great for making sushi. But it's also a pain when the rice sticks to your fingers like glue. Keep a small bowl of rice vinegar on hand, and dip your fingers in the vinegar and spread on your palms to prevent the rice from sticking.

sesame-seared ahi tuna

[MAKES 2 SERVINGS]

The city of Hoboken, New Jersey, sits just across the Hudson River from midtown Manhattan. It is only one square mile in area, but has one of the highest concentrations of ethnically diverse, outstanding restaurants of any town we've visited. We lived just a few miles north, in Weehawken, but made the short trip to Hoboken frequently to sample its many eats. One spot we frequented was City Bistro, a restaurant on the north end of Washington Street, the main drag. It served an exceptional sesame-seared ahi tuna, which directly inspired this dish.

Two 6-ounce sushi-grade tuna steaks
¼ cup black and white sesame seeds
1 tablespoon olive oil

1. Coat the tuna steaks on all sides with the sesame seeds.

2. Heat the olive oil in a sauté pan over high heat. Add the tuna steaks and cook for about 30 seconds on each side, including the ends. This will produce a steak that is rare, but that has seared edges.

3. Serve whole, or cut the steaks into thin slices and fan out the slices on each plate for an artistic presentation. Slicing the steak reveals the beautiful deep color of the rare tuna, with the seared edges and sesame seeds.

maple-glazed salmon

[MAKES 4 SERVINGS]

This salmon glaze—primarily maple syrup, but also with a touch of soy sauce—has a wonderful blend of sweet and salty.

¼ cup pure maple syrup
2 tablespoons tamari wheat-free soy sauce
1 garlic clove, minced
1 teaspoon minced fresh ginger
Salt and pepper
Four 6-ounce salmon fillets with skin

1. Whisk together the maple syrup, soy sauce, garlic, ginger, and salt and pepper in a small bowl.
2. Place the salmon in a shallow dish and pour the maple glaze over the salmon. Cover and marinate for 30 minutes.
3. Heat a grill to medium-high.

4. Grill the salmon skin side down, without turning, until it flakes easily with a fork, 7 to 10 minutes for 1-inch-thick fillets. Baste the salmon with any remaining glaze until 5 minutes before the salmon is done. Note: See our tip about grilling fish in the note on page 132.

Variation

You can also make this recipe in a baking dish in the oven. Bake the salmon at 400°F for about 20 minutes, or until it flakes easily.

salmon and dill

[MAKES 4 SERVINGS]

We met in college, and in fact were housemates, along with four other close platonic friends. It wasn't until roughly two years after graduation that we began dating. This dish, though, dates back to our days of friendship, when we made the recipe at our apartment not far from the Cornell University campus. The kitchen wasn't anything to write home about, but the recipe is well worth revisiting after all these years. We usually use a typical sweet onion, but if Vidalias are in season, we'll opt for them—the added sweetness makes the recipe just a touch extra special.

1 lemon, juiced
⅓ to ½ cup chopped fresh dill
¼ cup diced sweet onion
Four 6-ounce salmon fillets
Olive oil
Salt and pepper

1. Preheat the oven to 400°F.
2. Mix together the lemon juice, dill, and onion in a small bowl.
3. Rub the salmon fillets with olive oil and season with salt and pepper. Place the salmon in a shallow baking dish and pour the dill mixture over it.
4. Bake for about 20 minutes, or until the salmon flakes easily with a fork.

fresh corn tortillas

[MAKES 16 TORTILLAS]

After being deeply dissatisfied with store-bought, premade corn tortillas, which tended to be dry and somewhat flavorless, Kelli started making her own and we've never looked back. They're quick and easy to make, and there's no comparison to the tortillas you find on grocery store shelves. Pair these fresh tortillas with our recipes for Turkey Tacos (page 170), Chipotle Chicken Fajitas (page 146), or Cinnamon Sugar Tortillas (page 213).

2 cups instant corn masa flour
1 teaspoon salt
1¼ cups water, plus more if needed

1. Combine the masa flour and salt in a medium bowl, then add the water.

2. Mix using your hands for about 2 minutes, or until the mixture forms a soft dough. Add more water if needed, 1 tablespoon at a time. The dough should be soft, but not sticky. Nor should the dough be dry or crumbly.

3. Divide and shape the dough into 16 equal balls.

4. Heat a sauté pan, griddle, or *comal* (Mexican cast-iron plate) over medium-high heat.

5. Cover each half of a tortilla press with plastic wrap, and press each dough ball until it is 5 to 6 inches in diameter. Turn the flattened tortilla a quarter turn and press it again. Repeat this process until you've pressed the tortilla a total of four times, resulting in an evenly shaped tortilla.

6. Cook each tortilla, one at a time, in the heated sauté pan, griddle, or *comal* for about 1 minute each side, until cooked, but not crisp. (An over-cooked tortilla will break, instead of bend, when you try to fold it in your hand to add fillings.)

7. Store the cooked tortillas in a clean kitchen towel on a plate to keep warm until serving.

A TORTILLA PRESS is an inexpensive and invaluable tool for making fresh tortillas. Typically made of metal (for example, aluminum), they're comprised of two hinged metal halves with a lever for "pressing" each dough ball into a perfectly formed tortilla. We'll admit, though, that a tortilla press is a specialty item for many kitchens. If you don't have a press, you can still roll out or press fresh tortillas between pieces of plastic wrap using a rolling pin, heavy book, or flat-bottomed pan. Or, if you simply want to save time, you can use store-bought soft or hard 100% corn tortillas. But we still think you should give the homemade versions a try. Sure, they take a little extra time to make, but they're fresh, tasty, and store well in the refrigerator or freezer to use with leftovers.

chipotle chicken fajitas

[MAKES 4 SERVINGS]

A few years ago, we spent a weekend visiting friends at their log cabin in the Rocky Mountain high country. For dinner one night, our hosts made a chipotle-marinated steak. When we returned to Boulder, Kelli was inspired to make a chipotle-based marinade, which resulted in this fajitas recipe. It has since become a staple of our dinner menu.

1 cup cranberry juice

1/4 cup lime or lemon juice

2 tablespoons red wine vinegar

2 to 4 canned chipotle chiles in adobo sauce (use more or less, depending on how spicy you like your fajitas)

4 garlic cloves, peeled

2 teaspoons dried oregano

1 teaspoon ground cumin

Salt and pepper

4 boneless, skinless chicken breasts

Warm Fresh Corn Tortillas (page 145)

Grilled Fajita Vegetables (page 94)

Optional Toppings

Shredded Monterey Jack cheese

Sour cream

Sliced avocado

Shredded lettuce

Jasmine Rice (page 86)

1. To make the marinade, combine the cranberry juice, lime juice, vinegar, chiles, garlic, oregano, cumin, and salt and pepper in a food processor and blend until smooth.

2. Transfer the marinade to a shallow dish and add the chicken, turning to coat. Cover and marinate for 30 to 60 minutes.

3. Preheat a grill to medium-high heat.

4. Grill the chicken, turning once, until no longer pink, 8 to 10 minutes. Baste with the marinade while grilling until 5 minutes before the chicken is cooked through. Let the chicken rest for 10 minutes.

5. While the chicken rests, put the remaining marinade in a small saucepan and bring to a boil over high heat. Cook for 5 minutes (to both reduce the sauce and kill any bacteria from the raw chicken).

6. Slice the chicken into 1/2-inch thick slices. Serve the reduced marinade on the side (to be drizzled over the chicken, rice, and other fillings.)

7. Serve the chicken with the tortillas, vegetables, and your choice of toppings.

*D*ON'T YOU HATE it when you're craving a recipe, but you don't have all the right ingredients in-house, and you don't feel like running out to the store? Us too! It's happened more than a few times with this recipe, and especially with the juice for the marinade. But not to worry. Try this tip: if you don't have cranberry juice on hand, you can successfully substitute many other juice flavors to make the marinade. Instead of cranberry, try using apple or white grape juice. Similarly, if you don't have lemons or limes, try substituting orange juice. The important thing is that you have an acid/citrus component. Also, when finished making the marinade, transfer the remaining chipotles (smoked jalapeño peppers) in adobo sauce into a reusable container and freeze for future use.

jamaican jerk chicken

[MAKES 4 SERVINGS]

After getting married in Ithaca, New York, in November (it snowed the morning of our wedding), we jetted off to the warmth and sunshine of the Caribbean, to the island of St. Lucia in particular, for our honeymoon. One of our fond memories of that trip was experiencing the vibrant flavors of the island's cuisine. When it came to a local version of Jamaican jerk chicken, we couldn't help but notice that it was made with a wet rub. This was in sharp contrast to the Jamaican jerk dry spice mixes we commonly saw in American supermarkets. The wet rub resulted in some of the best jerk chicken we've had (before or since). This recipe, we think, comes pretty darned close. Yes, the ingredients list is long, but it's also mostly comprised of herbs, spices, and other seasonings, many of which you may already have in your pantry (especially if you've stocked up according to our Complete Essentials on page 16). Serve with Caribbean Rice (page 87) and Mango-Pineapple Salsa (page 44).

6 scallions

2 shallots, peeled

2 garlic cloves, peeled

1 tablespoon peeled and chopped fresh ginger

1 habanero chile pepper, seeded

1 tablespoon dark brown sugar

1 tablespoon allspice

1 tablespoon dried thyme

1 teaspoon ground cinnamon

1 teaspoon ground nutmeg

1/4 teaspoon cayenne pepper

1 teaspoon salt

1 teaspoon ground black pepper

1 lime, juiced

1/4 cup orange juice

1/4 cup rice vinegar

1/4 cup tamari wheat-free soy sauce

1/4 cup olive oil

4 boneless, skinless chicken breasts

1. Combine the scallions, shallots, garlic, ginger, and habanero in the food processor. Blend until smooth. Add the brown sugar, allspice, thyme, cinnamon, nutmeg, cayenne, salt, and black pepper and pulse to combine. Add the lime juice, orange juice, vinegar, soy sauce, and olive oil and blend well.

2. Transfer the marinade to a shallow dish. Add the chicken, turning to coat. Cover and marinate in the refrigerator for 1 hour.

3. Heat a grill to high.

4. Grill the chicken, turning once, until no longer pink, 8 to 10 minutes. Baste with the marinade while grilling until 5 minutes before the chicken is cooked through

THE HABANERO CHILE pepper—also known as a scotch bonnet pepper in the Caribbean—is one of the hottest peppers on earth. Treat it with respect! The hotness of peppers is gauged in Scoville units, which measure the amount of capsaicin (the compound that gives peppers their heat). To put it in perspective, a jalapeño pepper measures between 2,500 and 8,000 on the Scoville scale. By comparison, a typical habanero weighs in around 400,000! When handling the habanero pepper, consider wearing latex or similar gloves to prevent irritating the skin on your hands, and be very careful not to touch your eyes or other sensitive parts of your body. If you do handle the habanero with bare hands, wash your hands thoroughly and repeatedly, ensuring that you've removed all the oils from your skin.

whole roasted chicken
with root vegetables
[MAKES 3 TO 4 SERVINGS]

When we say that a dish "feels" like a certain season, this recipe is the perfect example. We associate it with one specific time of year: winter. Fresh vegetables are out of season in winter, and so we migrate toward the root vegetables. In addition, who wants their oven cranked up for a few hours in the summertime, heating up the house? We'll make roasted chicken for our Wednesday Night Dinner, an informal dinner club group made up of friends in and around Colorado's Front Range who take turns hosting Wednesday dinners. One thing is for sure, though: no matter what season you make this dish, and no matter for what occasion, it's intensely soul-satisfying. Instead of seasoning the outside of the bird, we put the seasonings between the skin and breast meat, which infuses the chicken with flavor.

1 whole roasting chicken (about 4–5 pounds)
$\frac{1}{2}$ lemon, sliced into cross sections
4 tablespoons ($\frac{1}{2}$ stick) salted butter
2 garlic cloves, sliced
1 onion, diced large
4 carrots, cut into 2-inch segments
4 medium to large Yukon Gold potatoes, cubed
$\frac{1}{2}$ cup white wine or GF chicken broth

1. Remove the top rack from your oven. Preheat the oven to 350°F.
2. Remove the packet of giblets from the cavity of the chicken and discard or reserve for another use. Rinse the outside and cavity of the chicken and pat dry with paper towels.
3. Leaving the skin intact and in place, separate the skin of the chicken from the breast meat by carefully inserting and sliding your fingers under the skin. Place lemon slices on the breast meat under the skin, and then inside the body cavity. Place pats of butter between each lemon slice and the breast meat. Distribute the sliced garlic between the skin and the meat.

4. Arrange the onion, carrots, and potatoes around the perimeter of a roasting pan and pour the wine over them. Place the chicken in the center of the vegetables, breast side up.
5. Roast the chicken for 50 to 70 minutes, until an instant-read thermometer registers 160°F when inserted deeply into a thigh and the vegetables are tender. Note: See the box on page 178 for information about carry-over cooking.
6. Carve the chicken and serve with the vegetables.

chicken parmesan

[MAKES 2 SERVINGS]

Chicken Parm is a dish that, more than any other, permeates Italian cuisine in the United States. Every Italian restaurant seems to have a version on its menu, from the national franchise chains, to the high-end local Italian restaurant run by your favorite, hot-blooded Sicilian. This version is as good as any we've had, and Pete's Sicilian American grandfather, Joe Sr., isn't shy about licking the plate clean when he's done. Serve with a side of GF pasta (page 122), if desired.

2 boneless, skinless chicken breasts

1/3 cup Artisan GF Flour Mix (page 15)

1 egg

2 tablespoons water

1/2 to 2/3 cup GF bread crumbs (see box, page 57)

Dried basil

Dried oregano

Garlic powder

Salt and pepper

1/4 cup olive oil

Marinara Sauce (see box, page 109, or about 2 cups store-bought)

6 ounces mozzarella cheese, shredded

1. Preheat the oven to 375°F. Grease a 9 x 9-inch baking pan.

2. Place the chicken breasts, one at a time, between two sheets of plastic wrap and pound thin with the flat side of a meat mallet. (If you don't have a meat mallet, a rolling pin, your favorite dictionary, the bottom of a heavy sauté pan, or even the heel of the hand can work, too.) Set the chicken aside.

3. Put the flour in a shallow dish. Whisk together the egg and water in a second shallow dish. Put the bread crumbs in a third shallow dish. Season each of the three dishes (flour, egg wash, and crumbs) with a little basil, oregano, garlic powder, and salt and pepper.

4. Heat the oil in a large skillet over medium-high heat.

5. Next, follow Standard Breading Procedure: Dredge each chicken breast in flour, then the egg wash, and then the bread crumbs. To keep your hands from getting too messy, use one hand for the flour and crumbs, and the other hand for the egg.

6. Add the breaded chicken to the hot oil and cook until browned on each side. The chicken doesn't need to be fully cooked through at this point, just browned. The rest of the cooking will take place in the oven.

7. Place the browned chicken in the prepared pan. Pour the marinara sauce over the chicken and sprinkle the shredded mozzarella cheese on top.

8. Bake for 15 to 20 minutes, until the cheese is melted and lightly browned and the chicken is cooked through.

Variation

For a vegetarian Eggplant Parmesan, substitute 1/4-inch-thick slices of eggplant for the chicken.

indian red curry

[MAKES 4 TO 6 SERVINGS]

Ever since college, when we frequented an Indian restaurant in Collegetown, near the campus of Cornell University, we've had a serious love of Indian food. We frequently find ourselves needing to indulge the craving. And never was that craving stronger than the first months of Kelli's pregnancy with our daughter, Marin. At the time, we happened to live just one mile from the Tandoori Grill, the Indian restaurant routinely voted Best of Boulder by the Boulder Weekly. *In this instance, we became creatures of habit, mostly because we adored one particular dish: chicken tikka masala. We rarely, if ever, strayed from the tikka masala straight and narrow . . . until we developed this recipe. We haven't been back to Tandoori Grill since. Seriously. Serve over Jasmine Rice (page 86), with a side of Garlic Naan (page 29). Garnish with additional fresh cilantro, if desired.*

4 large boneless, skinless chicken breasts, cubed

2 teaspoons salt

¼ cup olive oil

1 medium onion, finely chopped

1 large garlic clove, minced

1 tablespoon minced fresh ginger

1 teaspoon ground cumin

1 teaspoon ground turmeric

1 teaspoon ground coriander

½ teaspoon ground cayenne pepper

½ cup water

One 14.5-ounce can no-salt-added diced tomatoes

½ cup plain GF yogurt

3 tablespoons chopped fresh cilantro

1 teaspoon garam masala

1. Sprinkle the chicken with 1 teaspoon salt. Heat the olive oil in a skillet over high heat. Add the chicken and cook, stirring occasionally, until browned. Remove the chicken from the skillet and set aside.

2. Add the onion, garlic, and ginger to the remaining oil in the skillet and sauté until the onion is translucent, about 8 minutes. Stir in the cumin, turmeric, coriander, cayenne, and 1 tablespoon of water. Cook for 1 minute. Stir in the remaining water, the tomatoes, yogurt, cilantro, garam masala, and remaining 1 teaspoon salt. Puree the sauce with a handheld immersion blender.

3. Return the chicken to the sauce and bring to a boil. Reduce the heat, cover, and let simmer for 20 minutes.

Variation

Rich Tomato Curry: To make a red curry with a strong tomato component and more subtle Indian spice flavors, omit the garam masala and substitute ground ginger for the fresh ginger.

coconut red curry stir-fry

[**MAKES 4 SERVINGS**]

At Cornell University's School of Hotel Administration, every student is required to take a restaurant manage-
ment course that includes a rite of passage known as TCAB—Themes, Cuisines, and Beyond. In TCAB, groups
of three students take over a restaurant for an evening, totally reconceptualize the theme and decor, plan the
menu, and then execute the concept for 100 or more guests, all while managing the restaurant staff, which for
the evening is comprised of their fellow classmates. When it was Kelli's turn to tackle TCAB, she and her two
teammates chose Thai for their theme, naming their restaurant The Thai Kitchen. Coconuts filled with colored
water and floating votive candles graced the tables as centerpieces. Kelli managed the kitchen as executive chef,
and coconut red curry was the featured entrée. Her TCAB challenge may have only lasted for that one night,
but the recipe has endured. Serve over rice noodles or Jasmine Rice (page 86).

Olive oil
1 red bell pepper, chopped
1 onion, chopped
2 boneless, skinless chicken breasts, cubed
One 14-ounce can coconut milk
1 tablespoon red curry paste
1/2 lime, juiced
1/2 cup water
1 tablespoon tamari wheat-free soy sauce
1 tablespoon brown sugar

1. Heat a generous tablespoon of olive oil in a large
   sauté pan over medium-high heat. Add the pepper and onion and sauté until tender but not
   mushy, about 5 minutes. Remove from the pan
   and set aside.

2. Add a little more olive oil to the pan. Add the
   chicken and sauté until just cooked through, 5
   minutes or so. Remove from the pan.

3. Pour the coconut milk into the sauté pan and stir
   in the red curry paste. Cook for about 5 minutes.
   Add the lime juice, water, soy sauce, and brown
   sugar and simmer until sauce is reduced by approximately one quarter, about 8 minutes.

4. Return the pepper and onion and the chicken to
   the pan and simmer for about 3 minutes to meld
   the flavors.

Variation

For a vegetarian stir-fry, omit the chicken or substitute tofu (extra firm, pressed dry, and cubed).

peanut sauce stir-fry

[MAKES 4 SERVINGS]

When we were shopping in the supermarket one day, a packet of gluten-free peanut sauce in the Asian aisle caught our eye. We couldn't resist giving it a try. It was good, but the taste was a little . . . manufactured. The sauce was overly salty, and frankly, listed some pretty funky ingredients. But it left us motivated to make our own healthy and tasty version. After a handful of false starts, we succeeded. Serve the stir-fry over Jasmine Rice (page 86) or Brown Rice (page 89).

> 1 heavy tablespoon olive oil
> 1 garlic clove, minced
> 1 teaspoon minced fresh ginger
> 2 boneless, skinless chicken breasts, cubed
> 20 sugar snap peas
> 1 carrot, julienned
> ½ cup water
> ¼ cup peanut butter
> 2 tablespoons tamari wheat-free soy sauce
> 2 tablespoons rice vinegar
> 1 tablespoon brown sugar

1. Heat the olive oil in a sauté pan over medium-high heat. Add the garlic and ginger and sauté until fragrant. Add the chicken and cook, stirring for 5 minutes. Add the snap peas and carrot and sauté until the chicken is cooked through and the veggies are tender.

2. Meanwhile, mix together the water, peanut butter, soy sauce, vinegar, and brown sugar in a small bowl.

3. Add the sauce to the chicken and vegetables and cook until just heated through.

Variation

For a vegetarian stir-fry, omit the chicken or substitute tofu (extra firm, pressed dry, and cubed).

THIS RECIPE CALLS for *julienning*, which is simply cutting an ingredient (usually a vegetable, such as carrots or celery) into long, thin strips. The strips are sometimes referred to as *matchsticks.* To julienne a carrot, cut it in half lengthwise, and then place the cut side down on your cutting board so the carrot doesn't roll while you make the remaining cuts. The ideal length for julienned vegetables is about 2 inches, and that is what we recommend for this stir-fry.

chicken pad thai

[**MAKES 4 SERVINGS**]

Chicken Pad Thai must be the classic Thai dish in America. For our part, we've eaten it in easily 25 restaurants or more, from Phuket on the upper east side of Manhattan (since closed), to Republic in Union Square, to The Corner Office in Denver, and many, many more. How could we not make our own Pad Thai so that we could enjoy the dish at home, too? The sauce, egg, crushed peanuts, bean sprouts, cilantro, and fresh-squeezed lime work together like a finely tuned machine of tastes and textures.

2 tablespoons tamari wheat-free soy sauce

2 tablespoons water

2 tablespoons brown sugar

2 tablespoons peanut butter

2 tablespoons rice vinegar

2 teaspoons ground fresh chili paste (adjust to taste for level of spiciness)

8 ounces wide rice noodles

Olive oil

2 garlic cloves, minced

2 teaspoons minced fresh ginger

2 boneless, skinless chicken breasts, cut into strips

1 egg

1/2 cup bean sprouts

1/4 bunch fresh cilantro leaves

1/4 cup peanuts, crushed

1 lime, quartered

1. Whisk together the soy sauce, water, brown sugar, peanut butter, rice vinegar, and chili paste in a small bowl and set aside. The peanut butter will not mix in completely.

2. Place the raw rice noodles in a bowl and pour very hot water over them. Let soak for 15 minutes, until al dente. Drain well.

3. Heat about 1 heavy tablespoon olive oil in a large skillet or wok over medium-high heat. Add the garlic and ginger and sauté until fragrant, about 30 seconds. Add the chicken and cook, stirring, until cooked through. Remove the chicken from the pan and set aside.

4. Add a little more oil to the pan and cook the egg, stirring, for about 45 seconds. Add the noodles and stir-fry for 30 seconds to separate the noodles. Add the sauce and chicken, and cook for about 1 minute longer, until heated through.

5. Remove from the heat and stir in the bean sprouts, cilantro, and peanuts. Toss. Squeeze one-quarter of lime over each serving.

GROUND FRESH CHILI paste (also known as sambal oelek) is a condiment popular in Thai cooking typically made from chiles, vinegar, salt, and in some versions, garlic. It is bright red in color and has a good amount of heat.

How to know when your chicken is "done"? When cooking boneless, skinless chicken pieces, simply cook the chicken until the pieces are no longer pink throughout. This is most easily tested by using a knife to cut into one of the pieces and checking for pink. If your pieces aren't uniform in size, choose one of the larger, thicker pieces for your litmus test.

When cooking a whole bird, the internal temperature (as measured deep in the thigh with a meat thermometer) should read between 160° and 180°F. Cook to a higher temperature for absolute safety (but rubbery chicken), or to the lower end of the range for tasty, juicy chicken (but a very slight risk of food poisoning). Regardless, the juices should run clear.

orange chicken

[MAKES 4 SERVINGS]

During college, Kelli spent roughly nine months studying abroad in Australia. While she was over in the "other" hemisphere, she took a two-week trip to China. After being introduced to truly authentic Chinese cuisine (as when she had a breakfast of scrambled eggs with black specks that looked like cracked pepper, but which turned out to be the eyes of dozens of tiny, clear fish), Kelli unexpectedly found herself craving Americanized Chinese dishes, like this orange chicken. Americanized or not, we still think it tastes great. Serve over Jasmine Rice (page 86) or Brown Rice (page 89).

2/3 cup orange juice
1/4 cup tamari wheat-free soy sauce
2 tablespoons dry sherry
1 tablespoon + 1 teaspoon brown sugar
2 teaspoons cornstarch
1–2 tablespoons olive oil
3 garlic cloves, minced
1 tablespoon minced fresh ginger
Zest of 1/2 orange, julienned
4 boneless, skinless chicken breasts, cubed

1. Mix together the orange juice, soy sauce, sherry, brown sugar, and cornstarch in a saucepan. Stir to dissolve the cornstarch. Heat over medium heat until the mixture comes to a boil and thickens, stirring occasionally. Remove from the heat.

2. Heat the olive oil in a skillet over medium-high heat. Add the garlic, ginger, and zest and sauté until fragrant. Add the chicken and sauté until browned and cooked through.

3. Add the orange sauce to the chicken and heat through.

WHEN REMOVING THE zest from an orange, make sure you cut off only the orange part. The white pith is very bitter; leave it behind. A very sharp vegetable peeler is a handy tool for removing just the colored parts. As an alternative to using julienned orange zest, you can use a fine grater and grate the zest and add that to the sauce instead. It makes for an equally tasty modification!

sweet and sour chicken

[MAKES 4 SERVINGS]

Deep-fried sweet and sour chicken makes us think of every cheap New York City Chinese takeout joint we've ever eaten from. Colorado sadly seems to lack even one such restaurant (maybe that's not such a bad thing . . .), leaving us to our own devices—and this recipe—when it comes to sweet and sour chicken. Serve over Jasmine Rice (page 86).

1/4 cup agave nectar

1/4 cup rice vinegar

1/4 cup ketchup

1/4 cup water

1 tablespoon tamari wheat-free soy sauce

1 1/2 teaspoons cornstarch

1/2 cup Artisan GF Flour Mix (page 15)

1 teaspoon GF baking powder

1 tablespoon olive oil

1 cup cold water

4 boneless, skinless chicken breasts, cubed

Peanut or canola oil for frying

1. Mix together the agave nectar, vinegar, ketchup, water, soy sauce, and cornstarch in a saucepan. Heat over high heat, stirring, until the mixture boils and thickens, about 2 minutes. Set aside.

2. Stir together the flour and baking powder. Add the olive oil and enough cold water to make a smooth, wet batter the consistency of thin pancake batter (the 1-cup measurement in the ingredients list is only a baseline—use your judgment).

3. Heat enough peanut oil (about 4 inches) in a saucepan so the chicken can be completely submerged. The oil should be about 375°F; test by dripping a small amount of batter in the oil. It should sizzle. If it sinks, the oil is too cool. If the oil is smoking, it is too hot.

4. In batches, dip the chicken pieces in the batter to coat and then fry them, dipping new chicken pieces as there is room in the pan to fry them. Fry each piece until cooked through, then remove from the oil and place in a bowl that is lined with paper towel to absorb any excess oil.

5. Add the chicken to the sweet and sour sauce and stir to coat.

chicken cordon bleu

[MAKES 4 SERVINGS]

This dish was a regular for Kelli growing up. Her mom's version was a far cry from traditional chicken cordon bleu—for one thing, she used beef instead of ham. But it did start Kelli, and us, down the road that eventually led to this rich French classic.

4 boneless, skinless chicken breasts
4 tablespoons Artisan GF Flour Mix (page 15)
Salt and pepper
4 pieces deli-sliced GF ham
4 pieces Swiss cheese
2 tablespoons salted butter
1 tablespoon olive oil
$2/3$ cup white wine
$2/3$ cup milk
$1/4$ teaspoon ground nutmeg

1. Preheat the oven to 350°F. Grease an 8 x 8-inch or 9 x 9-inch baking dish.

2. Pound each chicken breast between two pieces of plastic wrap using the flat side of a meat mallet until they are about $1/4$ inch thick.

3. Put 2 tablespoons of the flour in a shallow dish and season with salt and pepper. Dredge one side of each chicken breast in the seasoned flour.

4. Place the floured side of the chicken facedown on your work surface and lay one piece of ham and one piece of cheese on top of each piece. Roll up the chicken breasts to enclose the ham and cheese and secure with toothpicks.

5. Heat 1 tablespoon of butter and the olive oil in a sauté pan over medium-high heat. Add the chicken and cook, turning, until browned on all sides, using tongs to handle the chicken if needed.

6. Place the browned chicken seam-side down in the prepared baking dish and remove the toothpicks.

7. Melt the remaining 1 tablespoon butter in the sauté pan that you used for the chicken. Add the remaining 2 tablespoons flour and whisk until smooth and golden brown. Whisk in the white wine and milk. Season with nutmeg and salt and pepper.

8. Pour the sauce over the chicken. Bake for 15 minutes, or until the chicken is cooked through and the cheese is melted.

chicken marsala

[MAKES 6 SERVINGS]

When our daughter Marin was born, all the grandparents flew to Colorado to visit—Bob and Linda, Kelli's parents, and Georgann, Pete's mom. We made this chicken marsala for dinner, and it proved to be a real crowd-pleaser. Serve over GF pasta (page 122).

6 boneless, skinless chicken breasts
¼ cup Artisan GF Flour Mix (page 15)
Salt and pepper
2 tablespoons salted butter
2 tablespoons olive oil
1 medium onion, diced
12 ounces button mushrooms
3 tablespoons cornstarch
1½ cups GF chicken broth
1½ cups marsala wine

1. Pound each chicken breast between two pieces of plastic wrap, using the flat side of a meat mallet, until they are about ¼ inch thick.
2. Put the flour in a shallow bowl and season with salt and pepper.
3. Melt 1 tablespoon of the butter and 1 tablespoon of oil in a large sauté pan over medium heat. Dredge 3 chicken breasts in the seasoned flour, making sure to dust off any excess. You just want a thin cover of flour. Place the chicken breasts in the sauté pan and cook until golden brown on each side and just cooked through, about 5 minutes per side. Transfer to a plate.
4. Repeat with the remaining butter, oil, and chicken breasts.
5. Add the onion to the oil remaining in the pan and sauté until soft. Add the mushrooms and sauté until soft. If necessary, drizzle a small amount of additional olive oil in the pan.
6. Mix the cornstarch with 3 tablespoons of the broth. Add the remaining broth and the marsala to the pan. Add the cornstarch mixture. Simmer, stirring occasionally, until thickened, 10 minutes.
7. Return the chicken breasts to the sauce, turn to coat, and serve.

Variation

The ratios in the recipe above assume you're using cooking marsala wine, which tends to be a little weaker in flavor than "the real thing." If you're using strong marsala wine, instead use only 1 cup wine, and increase the chicken broth to 2 cups.

chicken piccata

[MAKES 4 SERVINGS]

When we got engaged—at sunset on a largely deserted beach on the South Shore of Long Island—we celebrated with dinner at Il Classico, an Old World Italian restaurant. It was the kind of place that often forwent printed menus. Instead, the owner visited each table and explained, "Tonight, I got a chicken, I got a beef, and I got a fish." The chicken that night was chicken piccata, made to order. Our version features a super-flavorful pan sauce, defined by the lemon and capers.

4 boneless, skinless chicken breasts

¼ cup Artisan GF Flour Mix (page 15)

Salt and pepper

4 tablespoons (½ stick) salted butter

1 tablespoon olive oil

2 garlic cloves, minced

1 teaspoon lemon zest

1 lemon, juiced (you can use the same lemon that you zested)

2 tablespoons nonpareil capers, rinsed

1 cup GF chicken broth

1 teaspoon cornstarch

2 teaspoons cold water

1. Pound each chicken breast between two pieces of plastic wrap, using the flat side of a meat mallet, until they are about ¼ inch thick.

2. Put the flour in a shallow bowl and season with salt and pepper.

3. Melt 1 tablespoon of the butter and the olive oil in a large sauté pan over medium-high heat. Dredge the chicken breasts in the seasoned flour, making sure to dust off any excess. You just want a thin cover of flour. Place the chicken breasts in the sauté pan, reduce the heat to medium, and cook until the chicken is golden brown on each side and just cooked through, about 5 minutes each side. Use a very large skillet or cook the chicken in two batches. Transfer the chicken to a plate.

4. Melt the remaining 3 tablespoons butter in the pan. Add the garlic and sauté until fragrant. Add the lemon zest, lemon juice, capers, and broth. Mix together the cornstarch and cold water. Stir into the sauce and simmer for 5 minutes.

5. Return the chicken to the pan, turn to coat in the sauce, and serve.

lime-cilantro chicken

[MAKES 6 SERVINGS]

Here's an admission: Kelli loves everything cilantro. She uses it in marinades. She uses it fresh in dishes. She uses it as a garnish. Pete thinks Kelli even would have used a bunch of cilantro as her wedding bouquet, except that cilantro was out of season in November. Two of Kelli's sisters, Karen and Kim, love it, too. Perhaps it's a genetic predisposition. Regardless, we both love cilantro on this chicken. We think of it as a summer grilling recipe, but we're not shy about grilling year-round, and have been known to make this lime-cilantro chicken with two feet of snow on the ground, as long as we can get our hands on some fresh cilantro. Serve with Jasmine Rice (page 86) or Brown Rice (page 89).

1/4 cup + 2 tablespoons olive oil
1/2 medium onion, diced small
2 tablespoons garlic, minced
1 cup orange juice
1 lime, juiced
1/4 cup roughly chopped fresh cilantro
1 1/2 teaspoons salt
2 teaspoons pepper
6 boneless, skinless chicken breasts

1. Heat 1/4 cup of the olive oil in a skillet over medium-high heat. Add the onion and garlic and sauté until soft. Add the orange and lime juices, and cook for 5 minutes. Transfer to a blender and blend on high until smooth. Drizzle in the remaining 2 tablespoons oil and add the cilantro, salt, and pepper. Blend until smooth.

2. Place the chicken in a shallow dish and cover with the marinade. Cover and marinate for at least 1 hour, or in the refrigerator for up to 24 hours.

3. Heat a grill to medium-high.

4. Remove the chicken from the marinade and grill, turning once, until cooked through, 8 to 10 minutes.

general chang's chicken

[MAKES 4 SERVINGS]

The name for this dish is a hybrid of Chang's Spicy Chicken and General Tso's Chicken. Chang's Spicy Chicken is a popular dish available gluten-free at P.F. Chang's China Bistro. But Chang's Spicy Chicken in truth is just one version of a dish more widely known as General Tso's Chicken, the broader inspiration for our dish. General Tso's combines a little sweet and a fair bit of heat in a heavily Americanized version of Hunan-style Chinese cuisine that grew out of New York City in the 1970s. True to the "heat plus sweet" rule for General Tso's Chicken, our General Chang's Chicken uses a blend of juices and brown sugar to supply the sweet, and a blend of soy sauce, rice vinegar, and most importantly, ground fresh chili paste, to supply the heat. Serve over Jasmine Rice (page 86).

Olive oil
4 boneless, skinless chicken breasts, cubed
Cornstarch
3 to 4 garlic cloves, minced
$^3/_4$ cup orange juice
$^3/_4$ cup cranberry juice
$^1/_4$ cup rice vinegar
3 tablespoons tamari wheat-free soy sauce
3 tablespoons brown sugar
2 tablespoons ground fresh chili paste
$^1/_4$ cup water
Chopped scallions for garnish

1. Heat 4 to 5 tablespoons olive oil in a skillet or wok. Meanwhile, dredge the cubed chicken breasts fully in cornstarch.

2. Add the chicken to the oil and cook, turning, until cooked through, lightly browned, and crispy on all sides. Transfer to a bowl lined with paper towels.

3. Add the garlic to the remaining olive oil in the skillet (add a little more olive oil, if needed) and cook until fragrant. Add the orange juice, cranberry juice, vinegar, soy sauce, brown sugar, and chili paste and stir to mix well. Mix 2 teaspoons cornstarch with the water and stir into the sauce. Bring to a boil.

4. Return the chicken to the skillet and cook until the sauce thickens and the chicken is heated through. Garnish with chopped scallions and serve.

thai coconut-cilantro chicken

[MAKES 4 SERVINGS]

Over time we've made this dish for a wide variety of people, ranging from old friends from college to Kelli's sister Karla. Everyone has walked out of our house with the recipe—they refused to leave without it! To us, this dish is evocative of Thai cooking's marriage of the five components of taste: sweet, sour, salty, bitter, and umami (not to mention the trigeminal component, which includes hotness or spiciness). They come together magically in the recipe. Serve over Jasmine Rice (page 86).

One 14-ounce can coconut milk
¼ cup tamari wheat-free soy sauce
½ bunch fresh cilantro
4 garlic cloves, peeled
2 jalapeño chile peppers, seeded
2 tablespoons chopped fresh ginger
Grated zest and juice of 2 limes
1 tablespoon brown sugar
4 boneless, skinless chicken breasts

1. Combine the coconut milk, soy sauce, cilantro, garlic, jalapeños, ginger, lime zest and juice, and brown sugar in a food processor and blend until smooth.

2. Transfer to a shallow dish, add the chicken, and turn to coat. Cover and marinate in the refrigerator for at least 2 hours or up to 24 hours.

3. Heat a grill to medium-high heat.

4. Grill the chicken breasts, turning once, until no longer pink, 8 to 10 minutes. Baste with the marinade while grilling until 5 minutes before the chicken is cooked through.

5. Bring the remaining marinade to a boil in a small saucepan over high heat and cook for 4 minutes. Serve the chicken with the sauce.

cider bacon chicken

[MAKES 4 SERVINGS]

Kelli used to subscribe to a variety of cooking magazines (always good sources of inspiration for new recipes!). Years ago, she read an article about different types of pan sauces. It inspired her to develop this version, which includes one of her favorite beverages: apple cider. Not to mention one of Pete's favorite meats: bacon. Kelli is convinced Pete would eat bacon ice cream if offered (he's not so sure). On one memorable occasion, we prepared to make this recipe, only to discover that what we thought was a package of bacon in our fridge turned out to be a package of salmon instead. "Cider Salmon Chicken" didn't sound nearly as appetizing as Cider Bacon Chicken, so we omitted the bacon and made simply cider chicken. But ever since, we've stayed true to Kelli's original cider bacon chicken recipe. Serve with Seasoned, Roasted Potatoes (page 105).

4 boneless, skinless chicken breasts
2 tablespoons olive oil
4 strips GF bacon
1 medium onion, chopped
1 cup GF chicken broth
1 cup apple cider
2 teaspoons brown sugar

1. Flatten each chicken breast between two pieces of plastic wrap using the flat side of a meat mallet.

2. Heat 1 tablespoon of the olive oil in a sauté pan over medium-high heat. Add 2 chicken breasts and cook until browned on each side and cooked through. Repeat with the remaining 1 tablespoon olive oil and chicken breasts. Set the cooked chicken aside.

3. Cook the bacon until crispy in the sauté pan. Remove, crumble, and set aside.

4. Add the onion to the bacon drippings and sauté until soft. Add the broth, cider, and brown sugar and simmer for about 5 minutes to allow the sauce to reduce and thicken slightly.

5. Return the chicken to the sauce and add the crumbled bacon.

honey-soy chicken with spicy sauce

[MAKES 2 SERVINGS]

In our attempts to adopt the locavore ethic of eating—to eat local, seasonal foods whenever it's reasonably possible to do so—we discovered the Madhava company, which makes honey just up the road from us in Lyons, Colorado. We discovered that the honey is fabulous. We're not sure if that was purely a psychological reaction, because we wanted to love our local honey, or if it really was better (we're leaning toward the latter). We do know that we use it lots—both as honey for honey's sake, and as a sweetener in different sauces and marinades. This honey-soy chicken became one more good reason to break out the bottle of honey. Serve over Jasmine Rice (page 86) or Brown Rice (page 89).

Chicken

⅓ cup honey

3 tablespoons tamari wheat-free soy sauce

2 tablespoons olive oil

2 garlic cloves, minced

2 boneless, skinless chicken breasts

Spicy Sauce

Tamari wheat-free soy sauce

GF hot Chinese mustard

Ground fresh chili paste

1. Combine the honey, soy sauce, olive oil, and garlic in a medium bowl. Add the chicken breasts and turn to coat. Cover and marinate for 30 minutes.

2. Preheat a grill to medium-high. Grill the chicken, turning once, until no longer pink, 8 to 10 minutes. Baste with the marinade while grilling until 5 minutes before the chicken is cooked through.

3. Combine 2 to 3 tablespoons soy sauce with one dollop each of hot Chinese mustard and chili paste in a small bowl. Stir until well mixed.

4. Serve the chicken drizzled with the spicy sauce.

turkey burgers

[MAKES 2 SERVINGS]

This is one of our easy, go-to weeknight dinners. When we've had a long, tough day at work, and we're looking for a super-quick and simple meal to make, turkey burgers are the way to go. Serve sans bun on a plate with fork and knife, or follow in the tradition of Larkburger (our favorite natural, organic, eco-friendly, high-quality burger joint) and wrap your burger in green leaf lettuce (Bibb or Boston lettuce can also work well).

½ **pound lean ground turkey**
½ **teaspoon garlic powder**
Scant ¼ **teaspoon salt**
¼ **teaspoon ground pepper**

1. Mix the turkey, garlic powder, salt, and pepper in a bowl with your hands. Form the meat into 2 equal patties.
2. Heat a grill to medium-high.
3. Grill the burgers, turning once, until cooked through, 10 to 12 minutes. Alternatively, the burgers can be cooked in a skillet over medium-high heat. If using a skillet, cover the burgers with a lid or an inverted metal bowl. Doing so will retain some of the moisture, resulting in a juicier burger.

Variations

Instead of the standard seasonings above, try substituting these combinations:

- **Spicy Burgers:** ¾ teaspoon hot sauce (we recommend Frank's RedHot Original—it's gluten-free and the base flavor for Buffalo chicken wings) plus ¼ teaspoon ground pepper
- **Easy Jamaican Jerk Burgers:** ½ teaspoon ground cumin plus ½ teaspoon chili powder (or, you can use a store-bought Jamaican jerk dry spice mix)

whole roasted turkey with gravy

Fewer than half of the people who live in Colorado's Front Range were born there. The majority—including us—are transplants. Many of us come from the East, but no matter where we come from, we're all drawn here for similar reasons . . . the mountains, the outdoor lifestyle, the quality of life. One thing we all also share is that we've left our families behind, thousands of miles away. Our friends here become our "other" family. They're our Colorado family. And for holidays when we all aren't traveling across the country to see our "real" relatives, we celebrate together. Often, that means that we host a Thanksgiving dinner at our home in Boulder, and no Thanksgiving would be complete without the turkey. Recently, in 2008, we began brining our turkey. It made a real difference, resulting in a juicier bird—that's not always easy to do in arid Colorado, where we consider 25 percent humidity to be a "wet" day, and even our turkey needs moisturizer. Serve with Corn Bread Stuffing (page 102), Cranberry Relish (page 102), Mashed Potatoes (page 104), and gravy.

Brine

About 1 gallon cold water

1 cup kosher salt

$\frac{1}{2}$ cup light brown sugar

1 tablespoon garlic powder

1 tablespoon dried sage

1 tablespoon dried thyme

Turkey

One 14- to 16-pound turkey, fresh if possible, or thawed if frozen

8 tablespoons (1 stick) salted butter, melted

$\frac{1}{2}$ apple, cored and cut into pieces

$\frac{1}{2}$ onion, cut into pieces

1 carrot, peeled and cut into segments

1 celery stalk, cut into segments

2 sprigs fresh thyme

5 fresh sage leaves

1 cup dry white wine

Gravy

2 tablespoons Artisan GF Flour Mix (page 15)

$\frac{1}{3}$ cup water

Salt and pepper

1. To make the brine: Combine 1 quart of water with the salt, brown sugar, garlic powder, sage, and thyme in a saucepan. Heat over medium-high heat, stirring, until the sugar and salt are dissolved.

2. Pour the mixture into a 5-gallon bucket. Add an additional 2 quarts of very icy water to cool the mixture off. When the brine is cold, add the bird to the bucket. Add additional icy water to cover the entire turkey (about 1 gallon of water total, but add as much as needed). Soak for 12 to 24 hours in the refrigerator.

3. Preheat the oven to 350°F.

4. Remove the bird from the water and rinse well, inside and out. Pat dry with paper towels.

5. Rub the turkey with the melted butter, inside and out. (Because the turkey is cold the butter will harden into little bits. Don't worry about that. It will melt in the oven.) Place the turkey breast-side down on a roasting rack in a large roasting pan. Put the apple, onion, carrot, celery, thyme, and sage in the cavity of the turkey. Pour the wine into the roasting pan.

6. Put the pan on the lowest rack in the oven and roast, uncovered, for 2 hours. Carefully turn the turkey over and baste with the juices in the bottom of the pan. Roast for about 90 minutes longer, or until the juices from the turkey run clear, or an instant-read thermometer registers 150°F when inserted deeply into a thigh (the temperature should rise 10°F "carryover" after you remove the turkey from the oven). Let the turkey rest for 15 minutes before carving.

7. To make the gravy: Set with the roasting pan (which should have lots of good drippings) over medium heat on the stovetop. Mix some flour and cold water together in a small bowl (you can scale the quantity up or down from the ingredients list in proportion to how much pan juices/drippings you have, and how much you want to thicken the gravy). Add to the pan and cook over medium heat, stirring, until it begins to thicken. Season to taste with salt and pepper.

turkey tacos

[MAKES 8 TACOS, 3 OR 4 SERVINGS]

We used to season our tacos using packets of store-bought taco seasoning spices. They were gluten-free, offered in a low-sodium version, and frankly, we thought they were pretty tasty. But even the low-sodium versions had a ton of salt, and the ingredient list—13 ingredients or more!—sounded more like a stuff from a chemistry kit than something we wanted to put into our bodies (the list often included MSG). Convinced that there was a better way, we created our own taco seasoning spice mix. It uses just four spices, tastes better, and we'll never go back to the taco seasoning packets!

½ pound lean ground turkey (you can also use ground beef, if you prefer)

⅓ cup water

1 teaspoon ground cumin

1 teaspoon chili powder

4 shakes of GF hot sauce (we like Frank's RedHot Original)

Salt and pepper (dash of each—about ½ teaspoon total)

8 (½ recipe) Fresh Corn Tortillas (page 145)

Toppings

Shredded lettuce

Fresh Tomato-Cilantro Salsa (page 46)

Shredded Cheddar or Queso Quesadilla cheese

Sour cream

1. Heat a skillet over medium-high heat. Add the turkey and cook, stirring, until browned and cooked through. Add the water, cumin, chili powder, hot sauce, salt, and pepper and stir to evenly season the meat. Simmer for 5 minutes, or until the water has reduced.

2. Assemble the tacos by spooning the meat mixture into the tortillas and adding your choice of toppings.

curry-glazed pork tenderloin

[MAKES 3 TO 4 SERVINGS]

The beginnings of this recipe date back not to pork, but to salmon, when our friends Tom and Amy had us over for dinner in Denver and Tom grilled a curry-glazed salmon fillet. The next day, Kelli was so inspired that she spent her lunch hour scouring the Internet for curry-glaze recipe ideas. From those first beginnings, the dish slowly morphed into this curry-glazed tenderloin, which has become one of our all-time favorites. Even if you don't like curry, we think you'll love this dish. It doesn't taste much like curry—instead, the curry simply adds a little heat to the glaze.

¼ cup honey
2 tablespoons red curry paste
2 tablespoons tamari wheat-free soy sauce
2 tablespoons olive oil
3 garlic cloves, minced
One 1½- to 2-pound pork tenderloin

1. Combine the honey, curry paste, soy sauce, olive oil, and garlic in a medium bowl. Mix until well combined. Add the pork tenderloin, turning to coat. Cover and marinate for at least 30 minutes.

2. Preheat a grill to medium-high.

3. Grill the pork, turning, until the middle of the thickest section is no longer pink, about 20 to 25 minutes. (For larger or thicker tenderloins, reduce the grill heat to medium to avoid burning or over-caramelizing the outside of the pork before the meat cooks through.) Brush the pork with the glaze until 5 minutes before it is cooked through. (A brush with silicone bristles works very well for this, and is easily cleaned and disinfected afterward.) Let rest for 10 minutes before slicing and serving.

IN PRACTICE, WE rarely, if ever, check the internal temperature of the pork tenderloin when grilling (which, for the record, should be 150°F when it comes off the grill). Instead, we'll grill it—rotating it onto each of its four sides—until the curry-glaze begins to caramelize. A poke with a finger or grilling tongs will let you gauge how cooked the meat is, depending on how soft the tenderloin is when pressed. If in doubt, you can always cut into the pork to check that it no longer has any pink to its color. This will ensure a properly cooked, moist, and flavorful pork.

mexican spice-rubbed
pork tenderloin

[MAKES 3 TO 4 SERVINGS]

Between the two of us, we've traveled to Mexico on many occasions, both separately and together. One of the things we love best about the country is Mexican cuisine. With its emphasis on corn, fresh vegetables, and seasoned meats, it's especially easy to leave the gluten behind. It was a trip to Telluride, Colorado, though, that inspired this dish. We stopped in for dinner one night at Las Montañas, a restaurant on Telluride's historic main drag. As our luck would have it, the restaurant had recently hired a new executive chef, Alejandro Barreda. He's a native of Mexico City, and is celebrated as one of North America's best Mexican chefs. Barreda was on board at Las Montañas for only one year, with his goal to completely overhaul the menu and then move on. His fajitas were so good, we just had to make our own version at home, and we think this spice-rubbed pork tenderloin would make Barreda proud. The cumin and chili powder give the rub a nice punch of spice without being too hot, and impart a wonderful deep orange color to the outside of the cooked tenderloin. Serve with Fire-Roasted Corn Salsa (page 45) and Mexican Rice (page 88).

2 teaspoons ground cumin

2 teaspoons chili powder

1 teaspoon garlic powder

1/2 teaspoon ground pepper

1/2 teaspoon salt

2 tablespoons olive oil

One 2-pound pork tenderloin (or two 1-pound tenderloins)

1. Mix all the spices together in a bowl. Add the olive oil to make a paste. Rub the pork with the spice mixture to coat the entire tenderloin on all sides.

2. Heat a grill to medium-high.

3. Grill the pork, turning, until the middle of the thickest section of the tenderloin is no longer pink, about 20 to 25 minutes. (See the box on page 171 for notes on how to know when your grilled tenderloin is done.)

barbecue pulled pork

[MAKES 6 SERVINGS]

Pulled pork has been a Pete favorite forever (or thereabouts). Knowing this, when Kelli's sister Karla planned the baby shower for our daughter, she took the pulled pork under her wing. She's also a Texan, so we knew the pulled pork was in good hands. Some say that everything's bigger in Texas, and that's certainly true of Karla's menu planning! She spent three full days leading up to the baby shower smoking more than twenty pounds of pork butts. When it came time for the party, Pete was in hog heaven (forgive the pun, we couldn't resist!). This slow-cooker version of pulled pork is much more manageable, great tasting, and easy to make . . . especially since most of the "work" happens in the slow cooker while you're off doing something else.

1 cup water, or more if needed

1 medium onion, chopped

1/4 cup apple cider vinegar

1/4 cup ketchup

2 tablespoons molasses

2 tablespoons brown sugar

1 tablespoon paprika

1 tablespoon brown mustard

1 tablespoon Worcestershire sauce

1/2 teaspoon ground cayenne pepper

1/2 teaspoon salt

1/2 teaspoon ground pepper

2 pounds pork loin (we like to use a lean cut of pork), cut into large pieces

1. Combine 1 cup water, the onion, vinegar, ketchup, molasses, brown sugar, paprika, mustard, Worcestershire, cayenne, salt, and pepper in a slow cooker and stir to mix.

2. Add the pork, making sure all pieces are completely covered. If they are not, add additional water to cover.

3. Cook on low for 8 to 10 hours.

4. Remove the pork and shred using two forks, discarding any bits of fat (because who wants to bite a piece of gristle?). Put the shredded pork back into the sauce in the slow cooker and serve.

scalloped potatoes and ham

[MAKES 4 SERVINGS]

This dish is a Terry family favorite (Terry is Kelli's maiden name), especially the day after they've had a ham roast. It's a great way to use any leftover meat to create a new meal that's as delicious as the ham was on Day One. Plus, it's nearly a one-pot wonder (technically, a one–casserole dish wonder).

2 tablespoons salted butter

1 medium onion, chopped

1 garlic clove, minced

2 tablespoons Artisan GF Flour Mix (page 15)

2 to 2½ cups milk

¼ teaspoon ground nutmeg

½ teaspoon salt

½ teaspoon ground pepper

3 medium Yukon Gold potatoes, thinly sliced

1½ cups cooked GF ham, cut into bite-sized pieces (the actual quantity is pretty flexible—just make the dish as "hammy" as you'd like; don't be shy about putting more ham in there . . . we're not)

1. Preheat the oven to 350°F. Grease a 2-quart casserole dish.

2. Melt the butter in a saucepan over medium heat. Add the onion and garlic and sauté until soft. Add the flour and cook, stirring constantly, for 2 minutes. Add 2 cups of the milk, plus the nutmeg, salt, and pepper. Cook over medium heat until thickened, about 5 minutes.

3. Arrange half of the potatoes and 1 cup of the ham in the bottom of the prepared casserole, covering the bottom in a layer. Pour half of the milk mixture over the potatoes and ham. Repeat with the remaining potatoes, ham, and milk mixture. You can create more layers if you have a deeper casserole dish. If the potatoes are not completely covered by liquid, add additional milk as needed.

4. Bake for 1 hour, or until the potatoes are tender and browned on top.

bratwurst

[MAKES 6 SERVINGS]

We can count on bratwurst (and sausage and kielbasa, for that matter) appearing on our menu at least once a year, when we host our annual Oktoberfest. It is boiled in gluten-free beer then grilled. try the bratwurst with German Potato Salad (page 77), Applesauce (page 98), and Sauerkraut (page 99).

Two 12-ounce bottles GF beer (we recommend Redbridge)
1 onion, sliced
1 tablespoon peppercorns
6 GF bratwurst

1. Preheat a grill to medium-high.
2. Pour the beer into a pot large enough to fit the bratwurst. Add the onion and peppercorns and bring to a simmer over medium-high heat. Add the bratwurst. (If they aren't completely submerged, add more beer.) Simmer for about 15 minutes.
3. Remove the bratwurst from the beer, reserving the onion and discarding the beer and peppercorns. Grill the bratwurst until browned, about 7 minutes. Serve with the reserved onion.

Variations

- **Italian Sausage with Peppers and Onions:** For a slightly different variation on the bratwurst in beer theme, heat 1 tablespoon olive oil in a sauté pan and brown 4 Italian sausages until they're almost done. Remove the sausage from the pan, add another tablespoon of olive oil, plus sliced green and red bell peppers and sliced onion. When the veggies start to turn soft, add ¼ cup GF beer. Return the sausage to the pan and simmer for 10 to 15 minutes, until the peppers and onions are very soft and the sausage is fully cooked. (For a version without the beer but with more "char," take the Italian sausage, peppers, and onions straight to a preheated grill.)
- **Kielbasa:** For a little Polish fare, try kielbasa in lieu of (or in addition to) bratwurst. First, score the kielbasa with a sharp knife. Then cook the kielbasa over a preheated grill. Note: Kielbasa is inherently fatty and oily. Those drippings tend to flare up on a grill, causing lots of smoke and fire. Monitor your kielbasa closely, and keep it out of any direct flames (unless you want charred, blackened kielbasa . . .).

FOR MORE INFO about gluten-free beers, check out the box that accompanies the Carbonnade recipe on page 000. Here, we suggest using Redbridge, since it's the most widely available gluten-free beer nationally and its 100 percent sorghum flavor works great in cooking. However, if you can get your hands on some Green's gluten-free beer, by all means, do so! It's our favorite, though you may enjoy drinking it so much that you'll be reluctant to use it for cooking.

beef tenderloin with red wine reduction

[MAKES 4 SERVINGS]

Back in the days when Kelli worked in New York City, her days tended to be long. Pete worked from home then, as he does now, which gave him the flexibility to close up shop early and make a special dinner. Which is exactly what he did for Kelli's birthday one December, when he made this beef in a red wine sauce. We recommend making the sauce with a wine you'd enjoy drinking with dinner, and serve the remainder of the bottle at the table. Add a side of Garlic Mashed Potatoes (Variation, page 104).

Four 4-ounce beef tenderloin steaks
Salt and pepper
1 to 2 tablespoons olive oil
1 tablespoon salted butter
1 shallot, minced
1 tablespoon Artisan GF Flour Mix (page 15)
½ cup red wine
½ cup GF beef broth
4 fresh sage leaves
2 sprigs fresh rosemary
¼ teaspoon dried thyme
Salt and pepper

1. Season each steak with salt and pepper on both sides.
2. Heat the olive oil in a sauté pan over medium-high heat. Add the beef and sear for 3 to 5 minutes on each side (adjust the cooking time up or down, depending on how thick the beef is and your desired level of doneness). Remove the beef and set aside.
3. Melt the butter in the same pan used for the beef. Add the shallot and cook until soft and lightly browned. Stir in the flour and cook for an additional minute. Add the wine, broth, sage, rosemary, and thyme and cook until the sauce thickens, about 2 minutes. Add salt and pepper to taste. Discard the rosemary and sage.
4. Serve the sauce over the steaks.

garlic-lime skirt steak with cuban mojo

[MAKES 2 TO 4 SERVINGS]

Much credit for our love of Cuban cuisine, and this skirt steak, belongs to our brother-in-law, Peter, who is married to Kelli's sister Karen. Peter and his Cuban background are almost single-handedly responsible for turning us into Cuban cuisine fanatics. When we double-dated with Karen and Peter (they lived just a few miles from us in New Jersey), we'd often go out to Zafra in Hoboken, one of the best Cuban restaurants around (a bold claim, we know). It's small, but undeniably authentic. For dinner, what to order was never a question: we each got a skirt steak. We frequented Zafra often enough that, even after moving to Colorado, the owners recognized us when we returned for dinner years later. The mojo for this skirt steak comes straight from Peter's mother, Migdalia. She hails directly from Cuba, and taught Kelli how to make the recipe. This is the real deal, straight from the source. We recommend serving it with sides of Yuca (page 96) and Tostones (page 97).

Skirt Steak
> 10 garlic cloves, peeled
> ½ teaspoon black peppercorns
> 1 teaspoon salt
> 1 lime, juiced
> ½ cup water
> ¼ cup olive oil
> 1 pound skirt steak

Mojo
> 2 garlic cloves, minced
> 2 tablespoons minced green bell pepper
> 1 teaspoon salt
> ½ bunch fresh cilantro, chopped
> ⅓ cup olive oil

1. To marinate the steak: Blend the garlic, peppercorns, and salt in a food processor to form a paste. Drizzle in the lime juice, water, and olive oil to form a marinade. Place the marinade in a shallow dish and add the steak, turning to coat. Cover and marinate for at least 1 hour, or up to 24 hours in the refrigerator.

2. To make the mojo: Combine the garlic, bell pepper, and salt in a mortar and grind with a pestle until smooth. Add the cilantro a little at a time and grind until the cilantro leaves are broken down. Stir in the olive oil.

3. Heat a grill to high.

4. Grill the steak to your desired level of doneness (we recommend medium-rare or medium, about 5 minutes on the first side and 3 to 5 minutes on the second side . . . any more than that and delicious skirt steak can quickly turn into shoe leather).

5. Serve the steak topped with the mojo.

meat loaf

[MAKES 6 SERVINGS]

Meat loaf must surely be one of the all-time great American comfort foods. It certainly is for Kelli's sister Kim and her husband, Steve. Kim called us for this recipe shortly after she and Steve got married. Now, they enjoy it so much that they make the meat loaf every week!

2 pounds ground turkey (or a blend of ground meats)

2 cups GF bread crumbs (see box, page 57)

1/2 medium onion, chopped

2 eggs

1 teaspoon garlic powder

1 1/2 teaspoons dried oregano

2 teaspoons dried basil

1 1/2 teaspoons salt

1 teaspoon ground pepper

1 teaspoon ground cumin

1 teaspoon paprika

1. Preheat the oven to 350°F.
2. Mix all of the ingredients together, using your hands, in a large bowl. Form into a loaf and place on a rimmed baking sheet.
3. Bake for about 60 minutes, or until an instant-read thermometer registers 155°F when inserted in the center.
4. Let the meat loaf rest for 10 minutes. Slice and serve.

You'll notice that the temperature of meat will continue to rise, even after it's been removed from the oven. This is known as carry-over cooking, or the carry-over temperature, and typically you can count on 5° to 15°F of carry-over. Food safety guidelines recommend cooking ground meat to a temperature of 160° to 165°F. Hence, for this recipe, we recommend taking the meat loaf out of the oven when the loaf's internal temperature is about 155°F. With carry-over, this will put you confidently into the safe zone without overcooking, drying out, or burning the loaf.

carbonnade

[MAKES 6 SERVINGS]

Also known as a Flemish beer roast, this carbonnade recipe has been passed down to us from Pete's Belgian side of the family. During the lean times of World War II in occupied Belgium, his grandmother smuggled meat on the black market so that her family could make dishes like this one, or to even have anything to eat at all. She would put the roast under her dress to look pregnant, and even had Nazi officers help her on and off trains, unaware of her contraband. These days, we obviously make the dish with much less peril to our lives, but with no less love.

4 slices GF bacon

2 pounds beef roast (bottom round, rump, or brisket)

2 large onions, thinly sliced

1 teaspoon sugar

$1/4$ teaspoon thyme

One 12-ounce bottle GF beer

Water

2 tablespoons cornstarch

1. Cook the bacon in a large skillet until crisp. Remove the bacon, crumble, and set aside.
2. Add the beef roast to the bacon drippings and brown on all sides.
3. Put the beef, reserved bacon, onions, sugar, and thyme in a slow cooker. Pour the beer over all the ingredients. Add just enough water to cover the ingredients, about 1 cup. Cook on low for 8 to 10 hours.
4. Remove the meat from the liquid. Place a strainer over a saucepan and strain the cooking liquid into the pan. Discard the onion and bacon.
5. Mix together the cornstarch with 2 tablespoons cold water in a small bowl. Add to the liquid. Cook over medium heat, stirring, until the liquid is thickened, to create a gravy.
6. Slice the meat and serve with the gravy.

TRADITIONAL BEER, WHICH is made from barley, and often with wheat as well, is not gluten-free. However, an increasing number of companies are offering gluten-free beers. Typically, GF beers are made from sorghum, rice, corn, buckwheat, or some combination thereof. Many micro and craft breweries have local or regional GF beers. The most widely distributed GF beers nationally, however, include Redbridge (from Anheuser-Busch), Bard's (from the Bard's Tale Beer Co.), New Grist (from Lakefront Brewery), and Green's (imported from Belgium). In taste tests we've hosted with both gluten-free and non-GF beer drinkers, Green's rated the highest for taste, followed by Redbridge, then Bard's, and lastly, New Grist.

new york strip steak in a peter luger–inspired sauce

[MAKES 4 SERVINGS]

The Peter Luger Steakhouse in Brooklyn has a reputation for simultaneously being one of the best in New York, and one of the most overrated and overpriced (aren't many steakhouses?). We suppose that a little of the good and the bad are almost inevitable for a restaurant that's been around for more than 120 years. We had our own Peter Luger experience when the family came together to celebrate Kelli's dad's birthday. There was steak, of course, and potatoes and a host of other sides we've since forgotten. But we haven't forgotten the Peter Luger Old Fashioned Steak Sauce. We think our Luger-inspired sauce is just as good as the original. Plus, it's free of all the pretense and doesn't come with a rude server (long a trademark of Luger's waitstaff). Serve with Grilled Asparagus (page 92), grilled sweet onions (using the same marinade as for the steak), and Jasmine Rice (page 86) or Brown Rice (page 89).

3 tablespoons red wine vinegar

3 tablespoons ketchup

2 tablespoons olive oil

2 tablespoons brown sugar

1 tablespoon Worcestershire sauce

$3/4$ cup canned no-salt-added diced tomatoes (about half of a 14.5-ounce can)

2 teaspoons fresh horseradish

$1/2$ teaspoon ground pepper

One 16-ounce New York strip steak

1. Combine the vinegar, ketchup, olive oil, brown sugar, and Worcestershire sauce in a medium bowl and whisk until all the sugar is dissolved. Puree the tomatoes using a handheld immersion blender. Add to the bowl. Add the horseradish and ground pepper, and whisk to thoroughly mix the steak sauce. It makes almost $1^{1}/_{2}$ cups sauce.

2. Reserve $1/2$ cup of steak sauce for the table. Place the remaining 1 cup or so sauce in a shallow dish. Add the steak and turn to coat. Cover and marinate 30 minutes.

3. Preheat a grill to medium-high.

4. Grill the steak to your desired level of doneness. Baste with the marinade while grilling until 5 minutes before done.

5. Let the steak rest for 5 to 10 minutes before serving.

DESSERTS

chocolate chip cookies

[MAKES 40 COOKIES]

Sometime around age eight or so, Pete won a blue ribbon at a county fair for his chocolate chip cookies. The true baker in the family, though, is Kelli. When we moved to Colorado in 2004, it became her mission to successfully make high-altitude chocolate chip cookies. She labored through many iterations, and just as she finally got the recipe right, Pete's doctor switched him to a gluten-free diet. Now, more than two and a half years later, the chocolate chip cookies are finally re-mastered. They're gluten-free, of course, and field-tested at a range of altitudes.

$1/2$ pound (2 sticks) salted butter, softened

$3/4$ cup packed light brown sugar

$3/4$ cup granulated sugar

1 teaspoon GF vanilla extract

2 eggs

$2^3/4$ cups Artisan GF Flour Mix (page 15)

$2^3/4$ teaspoons xanthan gum

1 teaspoon baking soda

$1/2$ teaspoon salt

6 ounces chocolate chips

1. Preheat the oven to 375°F.
2. Cream together the butter, brown sugar, granulated sugar, and vanilla in a mixer, about 2 minutes. Add the eggs one at a time, mixing until incorporated.
3. Add the flour, xanthan gum, baking soda, and salt. Mix until well blended. Mix in the chocolate chips.
4. Using a cookie scoop or a teaspoon, drop dough balls 2 inches apart onto ungreased cookie sheets (or in batches, if using only one cookie sheet).
5. Bake for 8 to 10 minutes, until lightly golden on top. Let the cookies rest for 5 minutes on the cookie sheets. Transfer to a wire rack to cool.

molasses cookies

[MAKES 36 COOKIES]

Molasses cookies can be either chewy or crunchy. We prefer ours chewy. When we were originally testing this recipe, Pete's brother, Mike, and his girlfriend, Rebecca, were visiting us from New York. They wanted to get out into the mountains for a long day, and so we set our sights on an ascent of Torreys Peak, one of the state's 14,000-foot-plus mountains. A backpack full of these cookies helped to sustain us en route to the top!

1 cup packed brown sugar

³/₄ cup (1¹/₂ sticks) salted butter, softened

¹/₄ cup molasses

1 egg

1 teaspoon baking soda

1¹/₂ teaspoons ground cinnamon

1 teaspoon ground ginger

¹/₂ teaspoon ground cloves

2¹/₄ cups Artisan GF Flour Mix (page 15)

2¹/₄ teaspoons xanthan gum

¹/₄ cup granulated sugar

1. Preheat the oven to 375°F.
2. Cream together the brown sugar and butter in a mixer. Add the molasses, egg, baking soda, cinnamon, ginger, and cloves.
3. Stir in the flour and xanthan gum.
4. Put the granulated sugar in a small bowl. Shape the cookie dough into 1-inch balls and roll them in the sugar to coat. Place on ungreased cookie sheets about 2 inches apart.
5. Bake for 8 to 10 minutes, until the edges just become crispy. Let the cookies rest for 5 minutes. Transfer to a wire rack to cool.

frosted sugar cookies

[MAKES 45 COOKIES]

Kelli's family used to make dozens of batches of sugar cookies for most holidays. It was a monumental endeavor that required each person to be assigned a task in the assembly line—make the dough, cut out the cookies, bake the cookies, frost and decorate, etc. By the end of the day, everyone had a serious case of burnout, but the effort was worth the result.

Cookies

1 1/2 cups confectioners' sugar

1/2 pound (2 sticks) salted butter, softened

1 egg

1 teaspoon GF vanilla extract

1/2 teaspoon GF almond extract

2 3/4 cups Artisan GF Flour Mix (page 15)

1 tablespoon xanthan gum

1 teaspoon baking soda

1 teaspoon cream of tartar

Frosting

1 1/2 cups confectioners' sugar

2 1/2 tablespoons salted butter, softened

1 1/2 tablespoons heavy cream

3/4 teaspoon GF vanilla extract

1. To make the cookies: Preheat the oven to 375°F.

2. Cream together the confectioners' sugar and butter in a mixer until light and fluffy. Add the egg, vanilla, and almond extract.

3. Stir in the flour, xanthan gum, baking soda, and cream of tartar.

4. There are two options to shape the cookies: easy, and standard.

   - **Easy option:** Scoop rounded teaspoons of dough and drop on ungreased cookie sheets 2 inches apart. Gently flatten the cookies slightly with the palm of your hand.

   - **Standard option:** Refrigerate the dough for 3 hours (this chilling period allows the dough to "firm up," making it easier to work with when rolling out and cutting various shapes). Carefully roll the dough out into a 1/4-inch-thick sheet between two pieces of plastic wrap. Use cookie cutters to cut out desired shapes. Carefully remove the cookies from the plastic wrap and place on ungreased cookie sheets.

5. Bake the cookies for 7 to 8 minutes, until the edges are lightly brown. Let the cookies rest for 5 minutes. Transfer to a wire rack to cool.

6. To make the frosting: Cream together all ingredients until smooth.

7. When the cookies are completely cooled, ice them with the frosting.

snickerdoodles

[MAKES 45 COOKIES]

The snickerdoodle, a cookie coated in cinnamon sugar, is easily a favorite of Kelli's sister Karen. She asks Kelli to make these cookies every time we all get together. We can't blame Karen, though. The cookies are devilishly good.

1½ cups + 2 tablespoons sugar

½ pound (2 sticks) salted butter, softened

2 eggs

3 cups Artisan GF Flour Mix (page 15)

1 tablespoon xanthan gum

2 teaspoons cream of tartar

1 teaspoon baking soda

¼ teaspoon salt

2 teaspoons ground cinnamon

1. Preheat the oven to 400°F.
2. Cream together 1½ cups of the sugar and the butter in a mixer until light and fluffy. Stir in the eggs one at a time to incorporate.
3. Stir in the flour, xanthan gum, cream of tartar, baking soda, and salt.
4. Mix together the remaining 2 tablespoons sugar and the cinnamon in a small bowl.
5. Using a cookie scoop or a teaspoon, scoop the dough and roll it in your palms into a ball. Roll the dough balls in the cinnamon sugar and place on ungreased cookie sheets 2 inches apart.
6. Bake for 8 to 10 minutes, until slightly brown at the edges. Let rest on the cookie sheets for 5 minutes. Transfer to a wire rack to cool.

peanut butter cookies

[MAKES 36 COOKIES]

Growing up, Kelli spent her summers at a family lake house on Cayuga Lake in New York's Finger Lakes region. It was often a packed house, filled with aunts and uncles and cousins in addition to the immediate family. To keep all those people well-fed, Kelli's grandmother always had certain treats on hand and at the ready— peanut butter cookies were one of them. We offer up our standard peanut butter version here, but we've also made the same recipe with cashew and almond butter. They turn out equally well, and the flavor is simply a matter of preference.

8 tablespoons (1 stick) salted butter

1/2 cup peanut butter

1/2 cup granulated sugar, plus more for rolling the dough balls

1/2 cup packed brown sugar

1 teaspoon GF vanilla extract

1 egg

1 1/2 cups Artisan GF Flour Mix (page 15)

1 1/2 teaspoons xanthan gum

1/2 teaspoon baking soda

1/2 teaspoon GF baking powder

1. Preheat the oven to 375°F.
2. Cream together the butter, peanut butter, granulated sugar, brown sugar, and vanilla in a mixer. Add the egg and mix until combined.
3. Add the flour, xanthan gum, baking soda, and baking powder and mix to incorporate.
4. Shape the dough into 1-inch balls and roll them in granulated sugar. Place the cookies on ungreased cookie sheets 2 inches apart and flatten with a fork, making crisscross marks.
5. Bake for 7 to 9 minutes, until lightly browned. Let rest on the cookie sheets for 5 minutes. Transfer to a wire rack to cool.

chocolate cookies

[**MAKES 18 COOKIES**]

We'll be honest—while we like chocolate cookies, the real reason we developed this cookie recipe was so that we could take the finished cookies, crumble them, and use them as a layer of chocolate crunchies in a vanilla-chocolate frozen yogurt cake (page 208). Even so, the cookies are great on their own as an actual cookie. A few years ago, one of Kelli's coworkers enjoyed the cookies so much that she asked for the recipe. Kelli told her no, because "one day I'm going to write a cookbook." That was back in Kelli's self-described "proprietary days," when she kept her recipes under lock and key. These days, thankfully, our shared perspective is one of sharing, and so we happily say, "Here's the recipe."

8 tablespoons (1 stick) salted butter, softened

$1/2$ cup packed light brown sugar

$1/4$ cup granulated sugar

$1/2$ teaspoon GF vanilla extract

1 egg

1 cup Artisan GF Flour Mix (page 15)

$1^1/2$ teaspoons xanthan gum

$1/2$ teaspoon baking soda

$1/2$ cup cocoa powder

$1/4$ teaspoon salt

1. Preheat the oven to 375°F.
2. Cream together the butter, brown sugar, granulated sugar, and vanilla in a mixer. Add the egg, mixing until incorporated.
3. Add the flour, xanthan gum, baking soda, cocoa powder, and salt and mix until well blended.
4. Using a cookie scoop or a spoon, drop dough balls onto a cookie sheet 2 inches apart.
5. Bake for 10 minutes, until the edges are crispy. Let the cookies rest for 5 minutes. Transfer to a wire rack to cool.

blondie cookies

[MAKES 20 COOKIES]

Sure, we love a blondie cookie for its own sake. But as with the Chocolate Cookies (page 187), we had ulterior motives for developing this recipe. When developing gluten-free versions of pies and cakes with a graham cracker crust (for example, our Cheesecake, page 196, Peanut Butter Chocolate Bars, page 226, and Magic Bars, page 227), we needed something to use in lieu of graham crackers. There was no immediate gluten-free analogue, but we soon found that the taste and texture of this cookie worked great for crusts, and it has since become our go-to cookie for making a crumb crust. That makes it a double threat: both as a cookie and as a crust. And although on paper the recipe looks like one for butterscotch cookies (without butterscotch chips), it doesn't taste like butterscotch, and we prefer to think of it as a chocolate chip cookie . . . without the chocolate chips.

8 tablespoons (1 stick) salted butter, softened

$1/4$ cup + 2 tablespoons granulated sugar

$1/4$ cup + 2 tablespoons packed brown sugar

$1/2$ teaspoon GF vanilla extract

1 egg

$1^1/4$ cups + 2 tablespoons Artisan GF Flour Mix (page 15)

$1^1/4$ teaspoons xanthan gum

$1/2$ teaspoon baking soda

$1/4$ teaspoon salt

1. Preheat the oven to 375°F.
2. Cream together the butter, granulated sugar, brown sugar, and vanilla in a mixer, about 2 minutes. Add the egg, mixing until incorporated.
3. Add the flour, xanthan gum, baking soda, and salt and mix until well blended.
4. Using a cookie scoop or a teaspoon, drop dough balls onto a cookie sheet 2 inches apart.
5. Bake for 10 to 15 minutes, until golden brown. Let the cookies rest for 5 minutes on the cookie sheet. Transfer to a wire rack to cool.

Variation

These cookies can be made into blondie bars by spreading the batter into an ungreased 9 x 9-inch pan and baking for 15 to 20 minutes, until golden brown on top.

speculaas cookies

[**MAKES 60 COOKIES**]

Speculaas are traditional Belgian cookies best described as thin, crunchy gingerbread. This recipe dates back five generations, to Pete's great-great-grandmother, Sofie Marie Goetjaer-Beke, who was born in 1879. Our version is largely unaltered from her original, save for modifying it to make it gluten-free.

3 cups Artisan GF Flour Mix (page 15)

2 teaspoons xanthan gum

1/2 teaspoon GF baking powder

2 teaspoons ground ginger

2 teaspoons ground cinnamon

1 teaspoon ground nutmeg

1 teaspoon ground cloves

1/4 teaspoon salt

1/2 pound (2 sticks) salted butter, softened

1 cup packed dark brown sugar

1 teaspoon GF almond extract

2 tablespoons rum or cognac

1. Sift together the flour, xanthan gum, baking powder, ginger, cinnamon, nutmeg, cloves, and salt and set aside.

2. Cream the butter and brown sugar in a mixer until fluffy. Add the almond extract.

3. Add the dry ingredients and mix until incorporated. The batter will be very crumbly.

4. Add the rum to form a paste-like dough. Shape the dough into a log 2 1/2 inches in diameter. Wrap in plastic wrap and refrigerate for 3 hours.

5. Preheat the oven to 350°F. Butter cookie sheets.

6. Slice the chilled dough into 1/4-inch-thick slices and place on the prepared cookie sheets 1 inch apart.

7. Bake for 10 to 12 minutes, until the edges start to brown. Let rest on the cookie sheets for 5 minutes. Transfer to a wire rack to cool.

IN BELGIUM, SPECULAAS cookies were traditionally made for St. Nicholas Day, December 6, which is celebrated as the Belgian Christmas. More recently, the cookies are available year-round. They're often stamped or pressed into wooden molds that leave a bas-relief of scenes from daily life—a windmill, say, or the façade of a building. Whether they are simple or ornate, store your speculaas in an airtight container. We think the cookies are best a few days after baking, when the flavor has had time to "ripen."

coconut macaroons

[MAKES 24 COOKIES]

Coconut macaroons are a naturally gluten-free treat. Our version is light, airy, and delicate, compared to other macaroons that can be dense and chewy. We'll sometimes take these as a snack while on a road trip, or while hiking or backpacking, though they tend not to last long in the car or on the trail. Our self-restraint is weak.

2 egg whites
1 teaspoon GF vanilla extract
2/3 cup sugar
1 to 2 cups flaked, sweetened coconut

1. Preheat the oven to 325°F.
2. Whip the egg whites and vanilla in a mixer until soft peaks form. Add the sugar—1 tablespoon at a time—while continuing to whip until stiff peaks form.
3. Fold the coconut into the stiff egg whites (use more coconut if you like it, use less if you want more meringue).
4. Drop rounded teaspoons of dough onto a pair of cookie sheets 1 inch apart (or bake in batches on a single cookie sheet). Bake for 20 minutes, or until the tops are lightly brown.

pie dough

[MAKES ENOUGH DOUGH FOR TWO 9-INCH PIECRUSTS]

This recipe is based on one from Kelli's grandmother, who never had official measurements for the recipe. Kelli fondly remembers those days spent in the kitchen baking with Grandma Bonham when she watched her make this recipe hundreds of times. But when it came time to write the recipe down and make it gluten-free, Kelli realized she'd have to figure it out nearly from scratch. Much trial and error later, and success. We use this pie dough with our recipes for Apple Pie with Streusel Topping (page 194), Pumpkin Pie (page 195), and Blueberry Pie (page 193).

2¼ cups Artisan GF Flour Mix (page 15)
1 teaspoon salt
8 tablespoons (1 stick) cold salted butter
1 egg
⅓ cup cold water
2 teaspoons apple cider vinegar

1. Mix together the flour and salt. Cut the butter into the flour using a pastry blender, two knives, or your hands until it resembles fine crumbs.

2. Mix together the egg, water, and vinegar. Make a well in the flour mixture and pour the wet ingredients inside. Mix together by hand until a dough forms.

3. Divide the dough into two pieces. Wrap in plastic wrap and refrigerate for 30 minutes. Note: If you are not using the dough right away, freeze it to use at a later time. It will keep frozen for 1 month.

4. Roll each piece of dough out between two pieces of plastic wrap, aiming for a circular piecrust that will fit your pie plate. Use one dough half to line a 9-inch pie plate (the other can be used for a top crust or a second pie).

5. To bake the crust without any filling, preheat the oven to 350°F.

6. Dock the dough with a fork and crimp the edges.

7. Bake for 15 minutes, or until light golden brown.

8. Or, use and bake the dough as per the particular pie recipe's instructions.

IN TRADITIONAL BAKING with gluten, dough can be overworked. This is because gluten gives dough elasticity and tension, and kneading or working a dough too much can build up excessive tension. In these cases, you must let the dough rest in order for the gluten to relax before continuing to work with the dough. Since gluten-free doughs don't have gluten, strictly speaking they don't need to rest. You can work with them right away, without a "resting time." However, we do find that popping the dough in the refrigerator briefly to chill the dough makes it easier to work with.

sweet pastry dough

[MAKES ENOUGH DOUGH FOR TWO 9-INCH TART CRUSTS]

Kelli first made sweet pastry dough in college, when she began making fruit tarts. This gluten-free version has been adapted from a shortbread cookie recipe. We've used it with phenomenal results.

6 tablespoons salted butter, softened
1/2 cup + 2 tablespoons confectioners' sugar
3 egg yolks
1 egg
1 1/2 cups Artisan GF Flour Mix (page 15)
1 teaspoon xanthan gum

1. Cream together the butter and confectioners' sugar in a mixer. Add the yolks and egg and beat until the batter is smooth. Scrape down the side of the bowl to make sure everything is well mixed.

2. Slowly add the flour and xanthan gum, mixing only to incorporate. The dough will be the consistency of firm cookie dough.

3. Divide the dough in half and wrap each piece in plastic. Refrigerate for 30 minutes. Note: If you are not using the dough right away, you can freeze the dough to use at a later time. It will keep frozen for 1 month.

4. To bake a crust, preheat the oven to 350°F.

5. Press one half of the dough into a 9-inch tart pan. Line the dough with parchment paper or greased aluminum foil, pressing into the side and leaving enough paper/foil to extend beyond the pan. Fill with dried beans, rice, or baking weights to weigh the dough down and prevent it from shrinking.

6. Bake the weighted crust for 15 minutes. Remove the pan from the oven and take out the lining and weights. Return the pan to the oven and bake for an additional 5 minutes, or until the crust is golden brown.

7. Let the crust cool completely.

*B*LIND BAKING REFERS to baking a pie shell without any fillings. Often, as in this recipe, the shell is lined and filled with some form of weights that help the crust hold its shape while baking. Blind baking is used for several types of pies—for pies that have a chilled filling, for piecrusts that have a longer baking time than their filling, or for crusts that would become too soggy if baked for the full time with their filling.

blueberry pie

[MAKES 12 SERVINGS]

Blueberry is easily one of Pete's favorite kinds of pie. Kelli thinks he's convinced that blueberries are in season year-round, and hence, this pie can be made all year as well. Pete argues that, thanks to the modern marvel of the freezer, you can bake with blueberries in all seasons! Regardless of when you make it, this pie is a sweet classic whose flavor is brightened by fresh lemon juice.

Pie Dough (page 191), prepared through step 3
3/4 cup sugar
1/3 cup Artisan GF Flour Mix (page 15)
Dash salt
6 cups fresh or frozen blueberries
1/2 lemon, juiced

Note: if using frozen blueberries, use 1/2 cup Artisan GF Flour Mix and bake for an extra 15 to 25 minutes.

1. Preheat the oven to 375°F.
2. Roll out one piece of dough and use to line a 9-inch pie plate. Roll out the second dough half and set aside.
3. Mix together the sugar, flour, and salt. Add the blueberries and toss to coat.
4. Put the fruit in the pie shell and sprinkle the lemon juice over the filling. Place the second dough round over the fruit. Crimp the edge to seal in the fruit. Cut a few slits in the top of the pie to let the steam escape.
5. Bake the pie for 50 minutes, or until the fruit is bubbling through the crust.
6. Let the pie rest for 1 hour before slicing. This will allow the fruit to set up and not be too runny.

apple pie with streusel topping

[MAKES 12 SERVINGS]

No matter when Kelli and her family visited her Grandma Bonham's house, there was always a freshly baked apple pie waiting. (Grandmas always seem to make the best apple pies, don't they?) Pete's Grandma Spirio was much the same. In fact, she knew that Pete liked apple pie so much that for family parties and holidays, she'd bake a large apple pie for dessert, and also bake a second, smaller personal pie just for Pete. Talk about spoiled. But that was then, and this is now—when we spoil ourselves with this GF apple pie.

Pie

 1/2 cup granulated sugar

 2 tablespoons Artisan GF Flour Mix (page 15)

 1 teaspoon ground cinnamon

 1/4 teaspoon ground nutmeg

 4 to 5 apples, cored, peeled, and sliced

 1/2 recipe Pie Dough (page 191), prepared through step 4 (unbaked pie shell)

Streusel Topping

 1/2 cup Artisan GF Flour Mix (page 15)

 1/2 cup packed brown sugar

 1 teaspoon ground cinnamon

 4 tablespoons (1/2 stick) cold salted butter

1. Preheat the oven to 375°F.
2. To make the pie: Mix the granulated sugar, flour, ground cinnamon, and nutmeg in a large bowl. Toss the apples in the flour mixture to coat. Put the apples in the prepared pie shell.
3. To make the streusel topping: Mix together the flour, brown sugar, and cinnamon. With your hands, mix in the butter until crumbles form. Sprinkle the streusel topping over the apples.
4. Bake the pie for 50 minutes, or until the apples are juicy and the topping is browned.

pumpkin pie

[**MAKES 12 SERVINGS**]

To us, pumpkin pie is a fall thing, plain and simple. Starbucks may have its seasonal pumpkin spice latte, but that's no substitute for this pie. It's silky smooth, and the blend of spices give the pumpkin great depth of flavor.

15 ounces pumpkin puree (homemade or canned)

One 14-ounce can sweetened condensed milk

2 eggs

1½ teaspoons ground cinnamon

½ teaspoon ground nutmeg

¼ teaspoon ground cloves

½ recipe Pie Dough (page 191), prepared through step 4 (unbaked pie shell)

1. Preheat the oven to 375°F.
2. Mix together the pumpkin, condensed milk, eggs, cinnamon, nutmeg, and cloves in a large bowl until smooth and well combined.

3. Pour the filling into the prepared pie shell.
4. Bake the pie for 50 to 55 minutes, until the filling sets on the edges but still jiggles in the middle.

cheesecake

Friends have called this "a light cheesecake that doesn't feel heavy while you're eating it." Our buddy Rob—who's single and thin as a rail—wasn't shy about taking more than half an entire cheesecake home with him for leftovers. Both examples are testaments, we think, to the fact that this GF cheesecake is as good as "the real thing."

Crust
Blondie Cookies (page 188)
4 tablespoons (1/2 stick) salted butter, melted

Filling
32 ounces full-fat cream cheese (no light, low-fat, or other versions!), softened
1 2/3 cups sugar
4 eggs
1 cup full-fat sour cream (again, no cheating with light or low-fat versions)
3/4 cup whole milk
1/4 cup Artisan GF Flour Mix (page 15)
1 tablespoon GF vanilla extract
1 teaspoon lemon juice

1. To make the crust: Preheat the oven to 350°F.
2. Using a food processor or a zip-top bag and rolling pin, crush the blondie cookies until they are fine crumbs. (If crushing by hand, it is best if the cookies are one day old.) Mix in the butter to form moist crumbs. Press the crumb mixture firmly in the bottom and halfway up the side of a 10-inch springform pan.
3. Blind bake the crust for 10 to 15 minutes, until slightly golden brown. Let cool.
4. To make the filling: Combine the cream cheese and sugar in a mixer and blend until smooth. Add the eggs one at a time, stirring just to incorporate. Add the sour cream, milk, flour, vanilla, and lemon juice and mix just until smooth. Do not overmix.
5. Pour the filling into the baked crust. Bake for 60 minutes. Turn the oven off, but leave the cheesecake inside with the oven door closed and let set for 2 hours.
6. Refrigerate until serving, at least 2 hours.
7. To serve, run a knife around the edge of the pan, then release the side of the pan and remove, leaving the bottom in place.

For both this cheesecake and for the pumpkin cheesecake that follows on page 197 be sure to plan ahead and allow enough time to make the recipe before you want to serve it. If starting completely from scratch, you'll first need to make the cookies for the crumb crust, and then allow for the cheesecake to bake (about 1 hour), additional time in the oven (2 hours), and additional time in the fridge (another 2 hours). Budget your time accordingly.

pumpkin cheesecake

[MAKES 12 SERVINGS]

Kelli made this for "our" first Oktoberfest (we hosted the event together, though we weren't officially dating at the time). Kelli forgot about Pete's lactose intolerance when she planned a pumpkin cheesecake. Fortunately, he had some emergency lactase pills on hand, and the pumpkin cheesecake was enjoyed by all.

Crust
- 2½ cups crumbs from Molasses Cookies (page 183)
- 1 cup walnuts
- 5 tablespoons salted butter, melted

Filling
- 16 ounces full-fat cream cheese, softened
- ¾ cup packed brown sugar
- 3 eggs
- 30 ounces pumpkin puree (homemade or canned)
- ½ cup heavy cream
- 1 teaspoon GF vanilla extract
- 1 teaspoon ground cinnamon
- ½ teaspoon ground ginger
- ½ teaspoon ground nutmeg

1. Preheat the oven to 325°F.
2. To make the crust: Blend the cookie crumbs and walnuts in a food processor until they are fine crumbs. Pour in the butter while mixing to form moist crumb mixture. Press the crumb mixture in the bottom and up the side of a 9-inch spring-form pan.
3. Bake the crust for 10 to 15 minutes, until slightly golden brown. Let cool.
4. To make the filling: Combine the cream cheese and brown sugar in a mixer and blend until smooth. Add the eggs one at a time, stirring just to incorporate. Add the pumpkin, cream, vanilla, cinnamon, ginger, and nutmeg and mix just until smooth. Do not overmix.
5. Pour the filling into the baked crust. Bake for 50 minutes. Turn the oven off, but leave the cheese-cake inside with the oven door closed and let set for 2 hours.
6. Refrigerate until serving, at least 2 hours.
7. To serve, run a knife around the edge of the pan, then release the side of the pan and remove, leaving the bottom in place.

chocolate cake with vanilla frosting

[MAKES 12 TO 16 SERVINGS]

Kelli's grandmother was a big influence behind Kelli's huge love of baking. Kelli remembers making this recipe at age four with Grandma Bonham. When she told Kelli to add an egg to the cake batter, young Kelli obliged . . . shell and all! Aside from being modified to make it gluten-free, the recipe is largely unaltered from Kelli's grandmother's version. It's moist and bursting with chocolate flavor.

Cake

- 1/2 pound (2 sticks) salted butter
- 1 cup water
- 1/2 cup cocoa powder
- 2 cups sugar
- 2 eggs
- 1 cup sour cream
- 2 1/2 cups Artisan GF Flour Mix (page 15)
- 1 1/2 teaspoons xanthan gum
- 1 teaspoon baking soda
- 1 teaspoon GF vanilla extract
- 1/2 teaspoon salt

Frosting

- 8 tablespoons (1 stick) salted butter, softened
- 4 cups confectioners' sugar
- 1/2 cup heavy cream
- 2 teaspoons GF vanilla extract

1. Preheat the oven to 350°F. Grease two 8-or 9-inch cake pans (round or square). Sprinkle cocoa powder into the greased pans and coat the bottoms and sides by tipping the pans to distribute the cocoa. Shake out any excess cocoa.

2. To make the cake: Melt the butter in a saucepan over low heat. Add the water and cocoa and bring to a boil.

3. Combine the cocoa mixture and the sugar in a mixer and mix to dissolve the sugar. Mix in the eggs, sour cream, flour, xanthan gum, baking soda, vanilla, and salt on slow speed using the paddle attachment. Scrape down the side of the bowl. Mix for 30 seconds at medium speed.

4. Divide the batter between the two prepared pans. Gently tap the pans on a solid surface (i.e., the countertop) to release any air bubbles in the batter.

5. Bake the cakes for 30 to 35 minutes, until a wooden toothpick inserted into the center comes out clean. Cool fully in the pan, then carefully transfer the cakes to a wire rack.

6. To make the frosting, cream all ingredients together until smooth. For thicker frosting, add more powdered sugar.

7. Put the first cake layer on a cake plate and frost with a thin layer of frosting. Place the second cake layer directly on top and cover the entire cake with frosting.

fruit tart

[MAKES 12 TO 14 SERVINGS]

Every bakery, it seems, offers a fruit tart. They look like a million bucks, but here's a secret: they're not difficult to make. You can easily make phenomenal fruit tarts at home, and the cream filling and fresh fruit make for a tart that tastes as good as it looks.

Pastry Cream
- 1/4 cup sugar
- 1 tablespoon cornstarch
- 2 egg yolks
- 1 cup whole milk
- 1/2 tablespoon salted butter
- 1 teaspoon GF vanilla extract
- 1/2 cup heavy cream

Crust and Fruit Topping
- 1 baked and cooled 9-inch tart shell (1/2 recipe Sweet Pastry Dough, page 192)
- Strawberries, sliced
- Mandarin orange segments
- Kiwis, peeled and sliced
- 2 tablespoons apple jelly

1. To make the pastry cream: Mix the sugar and cornstarch together in a bowl. Whisk in the egg yolks, beating until light in color.

2. Heat the milk in a small saucepan over high heat to bring to a boil. Temper the egg mixture by slowly pouring about half of the hot milk into the eggs while whisking. Pour the tempered eggs back into the remaining milk in the saucepan while whisking and return to the heat.

3. Bring the mixture to a boil and cook, whisking, for 1 minute. Remove from the heat and stir in the butter and vanilla. Immediately transfer the pastry cream to a container and place a piece of plastic wrap directly on the surface of the pastry cream. This prevents a skin from forming. Cover and refrigerate until cool.

4. Chill a small bowl and whisk (or a handheld mixer's beaters) in the freezer for about 5 minutes. Pour the cream into the bowl. Whisk/beat until the cream is thick and stiff peaks form. Fold the whipped heavy cream into the cool pastry cream.

5. To assemble the tart: Pour the pastry cream into the cooked tart shell. Arrange the strawberries, oranges, and kiwis on top in a decorative design.

6. Melt the apple jelly on the stovetop (or in a microwave) until it is warm and thin/runny. If necessary, add a small amount of water. Glaze the fruit with the jelly using a pastry brush.

7. Refrigerate the tart for at least 2 hours, or until set. Carefully remove the side of the tart pan (leave the bottom round in place beneath the tart) and place the tart on a serving plate.

angel food cake with strawberries and homemade whipped cream

[MAKES 12 TO 16 SERVINGS]

Most people we know buy their angel food cakes from the bakery or supermarket. That's not an option if you're gluten-free (we've never personally seen a GF angel food cake for sale anywhere). But that's also not a loss. This GF angel food cake is as good as any we've had, gluten-free or otherwise. It's light and fluffy and, as great angel food cakes are, very sweet.

Angel Food Cake

1 1/2 cups egg whites at room temperature (10 to 12 eggs)

2 teaspoons GF vanilla extract

1/2 teaspoon GF almond extract

1 1/2 teaspoons cream of tartar

1/4 teaspoon salt

1/2 cup granulated sugar

1 1/2 cups sifted confectioners' sugar

1 cup sifted Artisan GF Flour Mix (page 15)

1 1/2 teaspoons xanthan gum

Homemade Whipped Cream

1/2 pint (1 cup) heavy cream

1 to 2 tablespoons confectioners' sugar, depending upon taste for sweetness

1 teaspoon GF vanilla extract

1 quart strawberries, sliced

1. To make the cake: Preheat the oven to 350°F.
2. Whip the egg whites, vanilla, almond extract, cream of tartar, and salt in a mixer using the whisk attachment until soft peaks form. Add the granulated sugar a little at a time, beating until stiff peaks form. Do not under-mix (make sure your peaks are stiff!).
3. Sift together the confectioners' sugar, flour, and xanthan gum. Carefully fold the flour mixture into the egg whites just until all the flour is mixed in.
4. Pour the batter into a 10-inch angel food cake pan. Bake for 40 to 45 minutes on the lowest rack in the oven, until browned and dry in the cracks that form on top. Immediately invert the cake to cool thoroughly upside down.
5. To make the whipped cream: Chill a mixing bowl and a whisk or egg beaters in the freezer for 5 minutes. Pour the cream into the cold bowl. Whip the cream until it starts to thicken. Add the confectioners' sugar and vanilla and whip until soft peaks form.
6. Once cooled, loosen the cake from the sides and bottom of the pan and remove it to a serving plate. Serve with fresh strawberries and whipped cream.

*T*HIS IS ONE of the only cakes that is baked in an un-prepped (ungreased) pan. There's an important reason for that. Angel food cakes are allowed to cool upside down, which enables the cake to maintain its "loft" until it is fully cooled. The ungreased pan allows the angel food cake to stick to the sides and bottom of the pan so that it doesn't fall out (as it would with a greased pan) when you invert the cake to cool. Also, this recipe calls specifically for an angel food cake pan, which is a type of tube pan. Tube pans are typically circular, with a "tube" in the middle that results in the finished cake having the shape of a donut, with a hole in the middle. Some, such as Bundt pans, are 1-piece tube pans, and often have fluting or other decoration. Others, such as the angel food cake pan, are two-piece tube pans, which allow you to cut the cake away from the sides of the pan first, then remove the outside of the pan, and finish cutting the cake away from the base of the pan.

strawberry shortcake

[MAKES 6 SERVINGS]

This strawberry shortcake recipe was one of the first desserts that we adapted to be gluten-free as we developed and tested our gluten-free flour mix. It's always been a crowd-pleaser, and this early success motivated us to keep pushing forward with GF baking, despite some occasional challenges and setbacks along the way.

Shortcake
- 2 cups Artisan GF Flour Mix (page 15)
- 2 teaspoons GF baking powder
- 1/4 cup sugar
- 8 tablespoons (1 stick) salted butter
- 1 egg, beaten
- 2/3 cup milk

Topping
- 1 quart strawberries
- 1/4 cup sugar
- Homemade Whipped Cream (page 200)

1. To make the shortcake: Preheat the oven to 450°F. Grease an 8-inch round baking pan.
2. Stir together the flour, sugar, and baking powder in a bowl. Cut in the butter until the mixture resembles coarse crumbs.
3. Combine the egg and milk, and add to the dry ingredients. Stir to form a thick batter.
4. Spread the batter into the prepared pan. Bake for 20 minutes, or until a wooden toothpick inserted in the center comes out clean.
5. To top the cake: Combine the strawberries and sugar in a bowl, and let sit for at least 15 minutes to allow the juices to run.
6. Cut the shortcake into 6 pieces. Top each piece with the strawberries and whipped cream.

yellow cake with chocolate fudge frosting

[MAKES 12 TO 16 SERVINGS]

This is a simple classic that can easily be multiplied to make a larger sheet cake for feeding lots of people at a party.

Yellow Cake
1³/₄ cups sugar
³/₄ cup (1¹/₂ sticks) salted butter, softened
2 teaspoons GF vanilla extract
2 eggs
3 cups Artisan GF Flour Mix (page 15)
2 teaspoons xanthan gum
2¹/₂ teaspoons GF baking powder
¹/₂ teaspoon salt
1¹/₄ cups milk

Chocolate Fudge Frosting
4 cups confectioners' sugar
¹/₂ pound (2 sticks) salted butter, softened
4 ounces unsweetened chocolate, melted
3 tablespoons milk, plus more if needed
1¹/₂ teaspoons GF vanilla extract

1. To make the cake: Preheat the oven to 350°F. Generously grease two 8- or 9-inch cake pans (round or square). Sprinkle flour into the greased pans and coat by tipping the pan. Shake out any excess.

2. Cream together the sugar, butter, and vanilla in a mixer, beating about 1 minute on high speed. Scrape down the side of the bowl to make sure everything is incorporated. Add the egg and mix to incorporate.

3. Combine the flour, xanthan gum, baking powder, and salt in a separate bowl.

4. Add some of the flour, and then some of the milk, to the creamed butter and sugar and mix. Repeat until all the flour and milk are incorporated into the butter and sugar.

5. Divide the batter between the two prepared pans. Bake the cake for 30 to 35 minutes, until a wooden toothpick inserted in centers comes out clean. Cool fully in the pans, then carefully transfer the cakes to wire racks.

6. To make the frosting: Beat all ingredients together in a mixer until smooth. Add additional milk, 1 teaspoon at a time, if the consistency is too thick.

7. Put the first cake layer on a cake plate and frost with a thin layer of frosting. Place the second cake layer directly on top and cover the entire cake with frosting.

mock cake

[MAKES ABOUT 16 SERVINGS]

Mock cake is a traditional Polish sweet bread with a poppy seed filling. The name is an Americanized version of the proper Polish name for the cake: makowiec. *We traditionally serve it for holidays such as Christmas and Easter, a practice we've inherited from Pete's Polish side of the family (his paternal great-grandparents immigrated from Warsaw). Admittedly, when introducing friends to mock cake, they tend to love it or hate it (because of the unique flavor of the poppy seed filling). We can't get enough of it, and hope you can't, either.*

3/4 cup milk

1/2 cup sugar

8 tablespoons (1 stick) salted butter

1 1/2 teaspoons salt

1/3 cup warm water (about 110°F)

4 1/2 teaspoons (2 packages) active dry yeast

3 eggs

4 1/2 to 5 cups Artisan GF Flour Mix (page 15)

2 teaspoons xanthan gum

One 12.5-ounce can poppy seed filling (we recommend the Solo brand)

1. Heat the milk in a saucepan over medium heat until bubbles form around the edge of the pan (scald the milk). Stir in the sugar, butter, and salt. Cool until lukewarm (about 115°F).

2. Combine the warm water and yeast in a bowl and let stand until the mixture bubbles, about 5 minutes. The bubbles mean your yeast is alive and ready to go.

3. Add the lukewarm milk mixture and the eggs to the yeast mixture and stir to combine.

4. Mix together 4 1/2 cups flour and the xanthan gum in a separate bowl. Stir into the milk-egg mixture. Add more flour if needed to make the dough soft and smooth, but not tacky. Form the dough into a ball.

5. Roll out the dough between two large sheets of plastic wrap to form a rectangle that is 18 x 10 inches. (You can create large sheets of plastic by slightly overlapping the long edges of two sheets of plastic wrap.) Remove the top layer of plastic wrap.

6. Spread the poppy seed filling over the dough, leaving one inch bare on all but one long edge.

7. Starting with the edge without a bare border, carefully roll the dough "jelly-roll style" into a large log using the plastic wrap on the bottom of the dough to lift and roll the dough.

8. Place the dough roll on an ungreased cookie sheet (you may have to create a U-shape with the log in order for it to fit on the sheet). Cover and set in a warm location free from drafts and let rise for 30 minutes.

9. Preheat the oven to 350°F.

10. Bake the mock cake for 25 minutes, or until it is golden brown. Keep an eye on the cake while it bakes. If it is browning too much on top, put a piece of tinfoil over the cake to prevent over-browning while the inside cooks through.

flourless chocolate cake
with chocolate ganache

[MAKES 12 TO 16 SERVINGS]

Flourless chocolate cake is almost always a naturally gluten-free dessert. As a result, many restaurants feature it on their dessert menu as an easy gluten-free option. If you like chocolate, you'll like this cake . . . whether you're gluten-free or not. Admittedly, this is a very rich cake, partly by design. We recommend serving small portions that are more deeply satisfying than a larger portion of a blander cake. Even so, we make this only for special occasions, or when we really need to indulge a craving . . . and nothing else will do. If desired, serve the cake with Homemade Whipped Cream (page 200) and berries, or Raspberry Sauce (page 214).

Cake

    14 ounces dark chocolate
    1 pound salted butter
    1¼ cups sugar
    1 cup half-and-half
    1 tablespoon GF vanilla extract
    ½ teaspoon salt
    8 eggs

Chocolate Ganache

    6 ounces heavy cream
    6 ounces semisweet chocolate, cut into small pieces

1. To make the cake: Preheat the oven to 350°F. Grease a 10-inch springform pan.

2. Melt the chocolate and butter in a heavy saucepan over low heat. Remove from the heat and add the sugar, stirring to dissolve. Stir in the half-and-half, vanilla, and salt.

3. Whisk the eggs in a separate bowl. Slowly mix the chocolate mixture into the eggs, mixing constantly until well blended.

4. Pour the batter into the prepared pan. Bake for 45 minutes, or until it is almost set. Let cool completely.

5. Remove the side of the pan and refrigerate the cake until chilled. (Leave the base of the springform pan beneath the cake.)

6. To make the ganache: Heat the heavy cream in a heavy saucepan over medium heat. Remove from the heat and whisk in the chocolate, stirring until the chocolate is completely melted and the ganache is shiny and smooth.

7. Place the chilled cake on a wire rack with waxed paper underneath. Pour the ganache over the cake and spread to cover, allowing any excess to drip off onto the waxed paper. Place the cake on a serving plate (remember: the base of the springform pan should still be beneath the cake).

zucchini cake with cream cheese frosting and fresh fruit

[MAKES 16 SERVINGS]

This recipe was unabashedly inspired by The Market, a deli and bakery in Larimer Square, in Denver's LoDo District. The Market's version is called the Spring Fling Cake. Kelli's sister Karla has dubbed this our Sunshine Cake. We call it a great way to use zucchini. When our friends Jess and Dave had an overwhelming surplus of zucchini from their community garden plot, we were happy to put some of that zucchini to good use and make one of these cakes!

Zucchini Cake

2 cups shredded unpeeled zucchini (about 2 medium zucchini)

$1^3/_4$ cups sugar

1 cup vegetable oil

3 eggs

1 tablespoon GF vanilla extract

$2^1/_2$ cups Artisan GF Flour Mix (page 15)

2 teaspoons xanthan gum

2 teaspoons baking soda

2 teaspoons GF baking powder

$^1/_2$ teaspoon salt

Cream Cheese Frosting

8 ounces cream cheese, softened

8 tablespoons (1 stick) salted butter, softened

3 cups confectioners' sugar

1 teaspoon GF vanilla extract

Sliced Fruit

1 mango, peeled, pitted, and sliced

1 pint strawberries, sliced

2 kiwis, peeled and sliced

1. To make the cake: Preheat the oven to 350°F. Grease two 8- or 9-inch cake pans (round or square). Sprinkle flour into the greased pans and coat the bottoms and sides fully by tipping the pans to distribute the flour. Shake out any excess flour.

2. Combine the zucchini, sugar, oil, eggs, and vanilla in a mixer. Add the flour, xanthan gum, baking soda, baking powder, and salt, stirring until combined. Scrape the side of the bowl and mix at medium speed for 30 seconds.

3. Divide the batter between the two prepared pans and gentle tap the filled pans on a solid surface (i.e., the kitchen counter) to release any air bubbles in the batter.

4. Bake the cakes for 45 to 50 minutes, until a wooden toothpick inserted in the centers comes out clean. Cool fully in the pans, then carefully transfer the cakes to wire racks.

5. To make the frosting: Cream together the cream cheese and butter until smooth. Mix in the confectioners' sugar and vanilla. Beat on high until the frosting is light and fluffy, about 5 minutes.

6. To assemble the cakes: Put the first cake layer on a cake plate and frost with a thin layer of frosting. Top with about one third of the sliced fresh fruit. Place the second cake layer directly on top and cover the entire cake with frosting. Arrange the remaining fruit decoratively on top.

HERE'S A SECRET for creating a professional-looking frosted cake: First frost the cake with a very thin layer of frosting. Then, pop the cake into the freezer for 10 minutes, or until the frosting sets firm. This traps any crumbs from the cake in the thin frosting layer. Then frost the entire cake with a beautiful layer of frosting free of any crumbs. Frosting is also a great way to cosmetically (and structurally, if your cake has really fallen off the deep end) fix any imperfections, such as dips, concavities, or other sources of "character" for your cake.

vanilla-chocolate frozen yogurt cake
with chocolate crunchies

[MAKES 12 TO 16 SERVINGS]

This is our version of the Carvel ice cream cake, which is layers of chocolate and vanilla ice cream with a thin layer of chocolate crunchies in between. It was Pete's birthday cake of choice for most of his thirty-plus years. Armed with a bottle of lactase pills (to counter his lactose intolerance), he'd devour his slice, as well as any remaining cake that was left after the rest of the party guests had their slices. As a frozen yogurt cake, this version circumvents the lactose problem for most people (including Pete), and the GF chocolate crunchies make the cake gluten-free to boot! For those of you without lactose issues, we also include vanilla and chocolate ice cream recipes (and of course you're not obligated to make the cake . . . you can always just enjoy the ice cream or fro yo all by itself!).

½ gallon (2 quarts) chocolate frozen yogurt or ice cream, store-bought or home-
    made (see pages 209–210)
½ gallon (2 quarts) vanilla frozen yogurt or ice cream, store-bought or homemade
    (see pages 209–210)
Chocolate Cookies (page 187)
½ cup heavy cream
GF piping gel, optional

1. Set the frozen yogurts on the kitchen counter and allow them to partially thaw, about 30 minutes. They should be a soft, workable consistency, but not melted or liquid.

2. Meanwhile, put the chocolate cookies in a large zip-top bag and crush them with a rolling pin to form small crunchies.

3. Press the chocolate frozen yogurt into a smooth layer in the bottom of a 10-inch springform pan using a spoon. Sprinkle the chocolate crunchies on top. Place the pan in the freezer for 10 minutes to start to allow the frozen yogurt to firm up.

4. Remove from the freezer and carefully press the vanilla frozen yogurt on top of the crunchies. Return to the freezer and chill for 1 hour.

5. Chill a small bowl and whisk (or a handheld mixer's beaters) in the freezer for about 5 minutes. Whip the cream in the chilled bowl with the chilled whisk to form stiff peaks.

6. Remove the outside ring of the springform pan. Cover the top and side of the cake with a thin layer of whipped cream. Work quickly because it will freeze as you spread it on the cake.

7. If desired, write on the top of the cake with piping gel.

As with the cheesecakes (pages 196 and 197), this is a recipe where it pays to plan well ahead of time. You'll need to make the chocolate cookies first (for the crunchies), then the frozen yogurt or ice cream, and then once you've made the cake, allow it time to set up in the freezer. Budget your time accordingly!

homemade frozen yogurt

[**MAKES 1 TO 1½ QUARTS**]

For Chocolate Frozen Yogurt

³/₄ cup cocoa powder

³/₄ cup sugar

1 teaspoon GF vanilla extract

2 cups plain yogurt

1 cup whole milk

For Vanilla Frozen Yogurt

³/₄ cup sugar

2 teaspoons GF vanilla extract

1½ cups plain yogurt

1½ cups whole milk

To make the chocolate or the vanilla frozen yogurt:
Whisk all ingredients together well and then add to
your ice cream maker and finish as per its instructions. Please note that the flavor of the yogurt you
use—and in particular its relative sweetness and tart-
ness/sourness—will carry through in the final flavor of
the frozen yogurt. We recommend using a yogurt
that is either slightly sweet, neutral, or slightly tart.
Very tart yogurts will leave a similarly tart aftertaste
in the frozen yogurt.

homemade ice cream

[MAKES 1 TO 1½ QUARTS]

For Chocolate Ice Cream
    ¾ **cup cocoa powder**
    ¾ **cup sugar**
    2 cups whole milk
    1 cup heavy cream

For Vanilla Ice Cream
    2 cups whole milk
    ⅔ **cup sugar**
    1 cup heavy cream
    1 teaspoon GF vanilla extract

To make chocolate ice cream: Combine the cocoa and sugar in a large bowl. Add the milk and cream and stir to combine. Add to your ice cream maker and finish as per its instructions.

To make vanilla ice cream: Combine the milk and sugar and mix until the sugar is dissolved. Add the cream and vanilla and stir to combine. Pour into your ice cream maker and finish as per its instructions.

Note: Many of the common ice cream makers (such as the Cuisinart ICE-20, which is the model we use) make about 1 to 1½ quarts of frozen yogurt or ice cream, so you'll need to make two batches of chocolate and two of vanilla for the frozen yogurt cake recipe. Alternatively, you can use store-bought half-gallons of frozen yogurt or ice cream as a shortcut.

carrot cake

[MAKES 12 TO 16 SERVINGS]

This is our brother-in-law Steve's favorite cake. Kelli originally learned how to make carrot cake using carrot baby food instead of fresh carrots. In the box below, we offer several ways . . . take your pick.

2³/₄ cups Artisan GF Flour Mix (page 15)

1¹/₂ teaspoons xanthan gum

2 teaspoons baking soda

2 cups sugar

2 teaspoons ground cinnamon

1 cup vegetable oil

3 eggs

1 tablespoon GF vanilla extract

2 cups finely grated or shredded carrots (about 4 medium carrots)

1 cup flaked, sweetened coconut

²/₃ cup crushed pineapple (fresh, or drained from an 8-ounce can)

Cream Cheese Frosting (page 206)

1. Preheat oven to 350°F. Grease two 8- or 9-inch cake pans. Sprinkle flour into the greased pans and coat the bottoms and sides by tipping the pan to distribute the flour. Shake out any excess.

2. Mix the flour, xanthan gum, baking soda, sugar, and cinnamon in a mixer. Add the oil, eggs, and vanilla and mix well, scraping down the side of the bowl. Beat at medium speed for 30 seconds.

3. Add the carrots, coconut, and pineapple. Stir to combine.

4. Divide the batter equally between the two prepared pans. Bake for 1 hour, or until a toothpick inserted into the centers comes out clean. Cool for 10 minutes in the pans, then carefully transfer the cakes to wire racks to cool completely.

5. To assemble the cake, put the first layer on a cake plate and frost the top. Set the second cake layer on top of the frosting and frost the entire cake.

For a carrot cake with a smoother texture, use pureed carrots instead of shredded carrots. To puree carrots, peel 4 medium carrots, cut them into 3- to 4-inch segments, and then steam them for 10 to 12 minutes. Transfer the carrots to a food processor and puree for up to 2 minutes, adding a small amount of water if needed to achieve a smooth consistency. Or, for a shortcut, use 5 ounces of carrot baby food.

almond cake

[MAKES 16 SERVINGS]

During the welcome toast at our wedding reception, Kelli's dad joked that she was born with a spatula in one hand and a bottle of almond extract in the other. She's always had a love of almond, it seems. This cake is intensely almond flavored thanks to the almond paste, which also creates a denser cake. More often than not, this is the cake that Pete will bake for Kelli's birthday. The recipe itself was inspired by a version from the Waldorf-Astoria, whose pastry chef shared the recipe with Kelli years ago. Serve with Raspberry Sauce (page 214) and Homemade Whipped Cream (page 200).

10 1/2 ounces almond paste

1 1/3 cups sugar

5 eggs, beaten

1 1/4 cups (2 1/2 sticks) salted butter, softened

3/4 cup + 2 tablespoons Artisan GF Flour Mix (page 15)

1. Preheat the oven to 350°F. Grease a 10-inch springform pan. Sprinkle flour into the greased pan and coat the bottom and side by tipping the pan to distribute the flour. Shake out any excess.

2. In a stand mixer, mix together the almond paste and sugar in a large bowl until uniformly mixed. Mix in half of the beaten eggs to make a paste. Mix in the softened butter a little at a time until all is incorporated. Mix in the remaining eggs.

3. Add the flour and mix well, but do not beat. Just mix to combine.

4. Transfer the batter to the prepared pan. Bake for 40 minutes, or until the cake is browned on top and looks a little soft in the middle.

5. Cool completely in the pan. Remove the side of the pan and wrap the cake well with plastic. Refrigerate at least 8 hours before serving.

cinnamon sugar tortillas

[MAKES 4 SERVINGS]

Call this the lazy man's crepe. It seemed an obvious (to us) way to use up leftover tortillas and make a super-quick, easy, and tasty dessert. As a hearty handful of our baking recipes are, this one is inspired by Kelli's grandmother, who would make a similar dessert using leftover piecrust dough.

4 leftover Fresh Corn Tortillas (page 145)
2 tablespoons salted butter, melted
2 tablespoons sugar
2 teaspoons ground cinnamon

1. Preheat the broiler in the oven or a toaster oven.
2. Brush each tortilla on one side with melted butter. Mix together the cinnamon and sugar, and sprinkle over the tortillas.
3. Place the tortillas on a cookie sheet or piece of aluminum foil. Heat under the broiler, watching closely, until the sugar is melted, but not burned.

dessert crepes with a trio of sauces

[MAKES 10 SERVINGS]

When Kelli's oldest sister, Sandy, moved back home after college, she would sometimes make dessert crepes—complete with ice cream and chocolate sauce—for her younger sisters. Later that year, when Kelli was in sixth grade, she had to demonstrate a step-by-step process for the class. Her chosen process: how to make dessert crepes. As so many good recipes do, these dessert crepes have ties that connect us to family and friends. The crepes in particular we modified to be gluten-free from a version that comes from Pete's friend Diane. The Irish Whiskey Brown Sugar Sauce also has ties to Diane—years ago she and Pete took a trip to Prince Edward Island, in Canada's Atlantic Maritime Provinces. Out for dinner one night in Charlottetown, the server tipped Pete off to the "chef's specialty" for dessert (crepes with an Irish whiskey brown sugar sauce), which wasn't on the menu. The Chocolate Sauce comes from our friend Maury's grandmother—Meemaw. Lastly, the Raspberry Sauce was inspired by a similar blueberry sauce recipe from Carol Throop, a family friend of Kelli's parents.

Crepes (page 33)
Ice cream
Raspberry Sauce, Chocolate Sauce, or Irish Whiskey Brown Sugar Sauce (below)

1. Lay a crepe flat on a plate. Put a few scoops of ice cream down the middle.
2. Fold over each side and turn the entire crepe over to have the seam on the bottom.
3. Drizzle (or drown) with the sauce of your choice.

raspberry sauce

[MAKES 2 CUPS]

2/3 cup sugar
1 tablespoon cornstarch
Dash salt
1/2 cup cold water
1 pint fresh raspberries, or one 12-ounce package frozen raspberries

Combine the sugar, cornstarch, and salt in a saucepan. Stir in the water. Add the berries and bring to a boil. Simmer until clear and thickened, about 4 minutes. Refrigerate until chilled.

chocolate sauce

[MAKES 2 CUPS]

1 cup sugar
$^1/_2$ cup cocoa powder
1 cup corn syrup
1 cup evaporated milk
$^1/_3$ cup ($^2/_3$ stick) salted butter
1 teaspoon GF vanilla extract
$^1/_4$ teaspoon salt

Whisk together the sugar and cocoa in a medium saucepan. Add the corn syrup, evaporated milk, butter, vanilla, and salt and cook over medium heat, stirring constantly.

Bring to a full boil (still over medium heat) and cook, stirring, for 5 minutes, until thick and glossy.

irish whiskey brown sugar sauce

[MAKES 1$^1/_2$ CUPS]

$^3/_4$ cup packed brown sugar
$^1/_2$ cup half-and-half
2 tablespoons salted butter
1 egg, beaten
2 tablespoons whiskey (see the box on page 235 for information about gluten-free distilled spirits)

1. Heat the brown sugar, half-and-half, and butter in a saucepan over low heat until the butter is fully melted and the sugar is dissolved.
2. Remove from the heat and temper the egg by adding a little of the hot mixture to the egg, whisking constantly, and then returning the egg to the mixture on the stove.
3. Whisk in the whiskey and bring to a boil over medium heat. Boil for 1 minute, until smooth. Refrigerate until chilled.

rice cereal treats

[MAKES 24 SQUARES]

If you spent even a fraction of your childhood in America, then we think there's a pretty good chance you've eaten—or at least heard of—Rice Krispie treats, the bar cookie made with rice cereal, marshmallows, and butter. Unfortunately, Rice Krispies themselves aren't gluten-free . . . they're made with malt flavoring, a source of gluten. Walking the grocery store aisles one day, though, we stumbled across a gluten-free toasted rice cereal (it's made by Erewhon, is organic, and has only three ingredients—we love it). Our first thought upon seeing the cereal was, "We can make treats!" Growing up, Pete's Polish grandmother, Lu (short for Leokadja), would make these often. Even in adulthood today, Pete has a hard time not eating his way through an entire tray. It's a great option for a child's birthday party. The treats are also durable and easy to travel with. We wrap them individually in plastic wrap and take them to the mountains for climbing trips.

4 tablespoons (½ stick) salted butter
One 10-ounce package regular marshmallows
6 cups GF toasted/crisp rice cereal

1. Melt the butter over low heat in a large saucepan. Add the marshmallows and stir until melted. Remove from the heat. Stir in the rice cereal.

2. Transfer to a buttered 13 x 9-inch pan and spread evenly. To effectively spread the "batter" in the pan, first loosely cover the entire pan with a sheet of plastic wrap, then use your hands to press the treats evenly into the pan. (This also prevents the sticky cereal from sticking to your hands!)

3. Remove the plastic wrap and let the treats cool. Cut into squares.

apple crisp

[MAKES 6 SERVINGS]

Apple Crisp was the first dessert Pete learned to make in his eighth-grade home economics class in middle school. This recipe is an oldie, but a goodie. Serve warm with vanilla frozen yogurt or ice cream (page 209 and page 210).

5 cups cored, peeled, and sliced apples (about 5 medium apples)
2 tablespoons granulated sugar
1/2 cup packed brown sugar
1/2 cup Artisan GF Flour Mix (page 15)
1 teaspoon ground cinnamon
4 tablespoons (1/2 stick) salted butter

1. Preheat the oven to 375°F. Grease a 9 x 9-inch baking pan.
2. Combine the apples and granulated sugar in the prepared pan and toss to mix.
3. Mix together the brown sugar, flour, and cinnamon in a bowl. Cut in the butter until the mixture resembles course crumbs. Sprinkle the mixture over the apples.
4. Bake the crisp for 30 to 35 minutes, until the apples are juicy and soft and the top is crispy and browned.

brownies

[MAKES 12 BROWNIES]

Why is it that, when it comes to brownies, many people's default seems to be to make a box mix? Brownies are so easy to make from scratch at home. And they're moist and rich in flavor to boot. We can't figure why you'd go another route. In fact, we enjoy this from-scratch gluten-free version better than the regular, gluten version of brownies we used to eat years ago!

9 tablespoons (1 stick + 1 tablespoon) salted butter

1 ounce unsweetened chocolate

3 tablespoons cocoa powder

2 eggs

$1/2$ cup granulated sugar

$1/4$ cup packed brown sugar

1 teaspoon GF vanilla extract

$3/4$ cup Artisan GF Flour Mix (page 15)

1. Preheat the oven to 350°F. Grease an 8 x 8-inch baking pan.
2. Melt the butter, chocolate, and cocoa in a saucepan. Remove from the heat, and stir in the eggs, sugar, and vanilla, mixing until smooth. Stir in the flour until combined.
3. Spread the batter in the prepared pan. Bake for 30 minutes, until the brownies are cooked through but still tender and moist.
4. Cool, cut, and serve.

*I*F YOU DON'T have the unsweetened chocolate, you can substitute 3 tablespoons additional cocoa powder and 1 tablespoon additional butter. Conversely, if you don't have the cocoa powder, you can substitute 1 additional ounce unsweetened chocolate and omit 1 tablespoon butter.

THE OVERWHELMING MAJORITY of brownie recipes around the world—including ours—are all based on the same set of ingredients: butter, chocolate, eggs, sugar, vanilla extract, and flour. (They also all start, more or less, with similar ratios of those ingredients that bakers then adjust to suit personal preferences. For that reason, a team of students in an Advanced Kitchen Chemistry course at MIT even did a study in optimizing the über-brownie recipe!) In this way, brownie recipes are a bit like DNA—despite the incredible variety of life coded by DNA, every strand is made up of the same four nucleotide bases (C, G, A, and T, if you were wondering). The differences all come down to the combinations and sequences. So it is with brownies and their apparent diversity, despite being based in the same small set of ingredients. Subtle variations in the combinations and ratios of ingredients give us a multitude of brownie recipes, including our gluten-free version. Ours, for its part, uses a blend of unsweetened chocolate and cocoa powder to impart a rich chocolate flavor and a moist, chewy texture. We also use a little less flour than most. That's because gluten-free flour is finer than wheat flour, and absorbs moisture more readily. If you made these brownies with a wheat-quantity equivalent of gluten-free flour, the GF flour would suck up the moisture, leaving you with a dry brownie. Instead, this recipe remains nice and moist.

sticky caramel popcorn

[MAKES 16 SERVINGS]

The inspiration for this recipe comes from Kelli's childhood friend Karina Jolles. The Jolles clan would make such a large batch of caramel popcorn at once that they'd have to mix it in their kitchen sink because no bowl or pan was near big enough! Although caramel popcorn is usually baked at the end for the caramel to "set up," we like to forgo the baking and leave it gooey.

2 cups packed brown sugar

$1/2$ pound (2 sticks) salted butter

$1/2$ cup light corn syrup

1 teaspoon salt

1 teaspoon baking soda

1 teaspoon GF vanilla extract

16 cups popped corn

1. Combine the sugar, butter, corn syrup, and salt in a medium saucepan and cook over medium heat, stirring constantly, until the mixture boils. Continue boiling without stirring for 5 minutes.

2. Remove from the heat and stir in the baking soda and vanilla. This creates the caramel.

3. Pour the caramel over the popped corn in a large bowl and stir until distributed evenly. Let cool.

4. Store in an airtight container.

Variations

- **Hard Caramel Popcorn:** Transfer the caramel corn into one or more large baking pans and bake in a 250°F oven, stirring occasionally, for 1 hour, or until the caramel is no longer tacky. Remove from the oven, let cool, and break into pieces.

- **Sugar Popcorn:** When Pete's cousins, Sarah and Sharon, visited the United States from Belgium in the mid-1990s, they introduced Pete to a Belgian version of caramel corn: Sugar Popcorn. Put enough oil in a large heavy saucepan to cover the bottom. Add $1/2$ cup unpopped corn kernels and place over medium-high heat. Before the kernels begin to pop, add $1/2$ cup sugar. Once the kernels begin to pop, shake the saucepan regularly until all the kernels have popped. If desired, sprinkle lightly with salt.

kolachkis

[MAKES 36 COOKIES]

Kolachkis are a traditional Eastern European treat that is also quite popular in the Binghamton region of New York, part of a greater area known as the Southern Tier. The area experienced a wave of immigrants from Eastern Europe during the late 19th and early 20th centuries, and they brought their beloved kolachkis *with them. Kelli's family has roots in Binghamton, and consequently, has inherited a love of* kolachkis. *Her family makes the treats every Christmas. They can be made with a variety of fillings—almond and apricot are two favorites. Call them cookies, or call them pastries, or just call them* kolachkis. *Whichever, they're great. This recipe turns out a little flaky, in a good pastry sort of way.*

1/2 pound (2 sticks) salted butter, softened
8 ounces cream cheese, softened
2 1/2 cups Artisan GF Flour Mix (page 15)
2 teaspoons xanthan gum
Confectioners' sugar
One 12-ounce can fruit or nut filling (apricot, raspberry, almond, cherry)

1. Preheat the oven to 350°F.
2. Combine the butter and cream cheese in a mixer and mix on medium speed until completely incorporated. Stir in the flour and xanthan gum. Wrap in plastic and refrigerate the dough overnight.
3. Roll out the dough in a generous amount of confectioners' sugar to less than 1/8-inch thick. Cut into 2 1/2-inch squares.
4. Put about 1 heaping teaspoon filling in the center of each square. Roll up the dough to enclose the filling, leaving the ends of the roll open. You can also fold them corner to corner. Place on un-greased cookie sheets. (When working with the dough, do not let it get to room temperature. If it begins to get too soft, put it back in the refrigerator for a few minutes. And don't let the prepared cookies set on the cookie sheets at room temperature for too long or they will melt too much in the oven.)
5. Bake for about 15 to 20 minutes, until the edges just turn golden brown.
6. Let rest for 5 minutes on the cookie sheets. Transfer to wire racks to cool completely and sprinkle with confectioners' sugar.

indian pudding

[**MAKES 8 SERVINGS**]

Kelli and Pete both first had Indian pudding separately as a dessert at The Antlers, a restaurant outside the town of Ithaca, New York. Neither one of us can remember what we ate for dinner, but we both remember the pudding fondly, inspiring us to develop this recipe years later. Serve warm with vanilla frozen yogurt or ice cream (page 209 and page 210).

4 cups milk

$^2/_3$ cup cornmeal

$^1/_2$ cup molasses

2 eggs

$^1/_4$ cup packed brown sugar

2 teaspoons ground cinnamon

1 teaspoon ground ginger

$^1/_4$ teaspoon ground nutmeg

$^1/_2$ teaspoon salt

3 tablespoons salted butter

1. Preheat the oven to 325°F. Grease a 2-quart baking dish.
2. Heat 3 cups of the milk in a large saucepan over medium-high heat until bubbles form around the edge of the pan (scald the milk).
3. Meanwhile, mix together the remaining 1 cup milk, the cornmeal, molasses, eggs, brown sugar, cinnamon, ginger, nutmeg, and salt in a bowl.
4. Slowly whisk the cornmeal mixture into the scalded milk. Cook over medium heat, stirring constantly, until the mixture begins to thicken, about 5 minutes. Remove from the heat and add the butter, stirring until melted.
5. Pour the mixture into the prepared baking dish and cover with aluminum foil. Set the baking dish inside a large roasting pan. Pour enough hot water into the roasting pan to come halfway up the sides of the baking dish.
6. Carefully place the roasting pan in the oven and bake for 1 hour. Remove the foil and bake for 1 hour longer (2 hours of total baking time), until it sets up.
7. Remove from the oven and remove the baking dish from the water bath. Cool for 30 minutes. Serve warm.

flan

[MAKES 8 SERVINGS]

This recipe for flan comes from straight from Migdalia, the mother of our brother-in-law Peter. It can be made either as one large dessert, or as many individually sized desserts (see variation below) Either way, with the caramel poured over the custard, it's a delightfully decadent and rich dessert.

½ cup granulated sugar
½ cup packed brown sugar
4 eggs
One 14-ounce can sweetened condensed milk
One 12-ounce can evaporated milk
2 teaspoons GF vanilla extract

1. Preheat the oven to 350°F.
2. Heat the granulated sugar and brown sugar in a heavy saucepan over low heat until melted. Do not stir (for example, with a spoon), but rather swirl the sugar in the pan while holding the handle. As soon as the sugar begins to caramelize (turn golden brown), remove from the heat and pour into the bottom of an 8- or 9-inch baking dish, tipping the dish to coat the bottom.
3. Whisk the eggs in a medium bowl. Stir in the condensed milk, evaporated milk, and vanilla.
4. Pour the mixture into the prepared baking dish and cover with aluminum foil. Set inside a large roasting pan. Pour enough hot water into the roasting pan to come halfway up the side of the baking dish.

5. Carefully place the roasting pan in the oven and bake for 1 hour, until it sets up (a knife inserted into the center comes out clean).
6. Remove from the oven and remove the baking dish from the water bath. Cool completely and refrigerate until serving.
7. Serve by inverting the baking dish over a serving plate to turn out the flan. The plate should have a lip in order to retain the caramelized sugar liquid that forms in the bottom of the pan. Slice and serve.

Variation

If making individual flans, use 6- to 8-ounce ramekins and bake for 30 to 45 minutes.

crème brûlée

Crème brûlée is a classic French dessert that is simple yet elegant. When we were married, our friend Jared, from college, gave us a hand torch as a wedding present, specifically so we could make this recipe!

2 cups heavy cream
¼ cup sugar, plus more for sprinkling
4 egg yolks
1 teaspoon GF vanilla extract

1. Heat the cream in a heavy saucepan over medium heat until it comes to a simmer. Whisk together the sugar, egg yolks, and vanilla in a small bowl until light in color. Slowly pour the cream into the egg mixture while whisking constantly.

2. Divide the mixture among 4 6- to 8-ounce ramekins. Place in a baking pan and fill the pan with enough very hot water to come halfway up the sides of the ramekins.

3. Bake for 40 to 45 minutes, until the edges are set but the center is still loose.

4. Remove from the oven and leave in the water bath until cooled. Remove the ramekins from the water bath and chill for at least 2 hours or up to 2 days before serving.

5. To serve, sprinkle a few teaspoons of sugar on top of each crème brûlée. (If water has accumulated on the surface, use a paper towel to absorb the liquid before sprinkling with sugar.) Melt the sugar with a handheld torch. If you do not have a torch, place under the broiler for a few minutes, watching carefully so the sugar does not burn!

fudge

[**MAKES 36 SQUARES**]

During one of our first dates—when Pete was living near Albany and Kelli was in northeast New Jersey—we took a daylong road trip to Bennington, Vermont, in the southern Green Mountains. While strolling through historic downtown, we popped into the Village Chocolate Shoppe, which had the most incredible fudge either of us had ever tried. We've tried a lot of fudge since that day, and nothing has measured up. We recently returned to the Shoppe in Bennington and confirmed that, for us, it's the Fudge Capital of the World. But this recipe is pretty darned good, too, and lets us satisfy the craving when we're home in Colorado.

1¾ cups sugar
4 ounces semisweet chocolate
⅔ cup half-and-half
2 tablespoons light corn syrup
2 tablespoons salted butter, cut into pieces
1 teaspoon GF vanilla extract

1. Line an 8 x 8-inch baking pan with tinfoil. Liberally grease the foil with butter.

2. Combine the sugar, chocolate, half-and-half, and corn syrup in a heavy saucepan. Heat over medium heat, stirring with a wooden spoon, until the sugar and chocolate have melted and the mixture has come to a boil.

3. Cover the saucepan and leave on the heat for 3 minutes to dissolve any sugar crystals that have formed on the side of the pan. Uncover and increase the heat to bring the mixture to a slow boil. Using a candy thermometer to accurately measure the temperature, bring the mixture to 234°F without stirring.

4. Remove from the heat and add the butter, but do not stir. Let the mixture cool until it reaches 110°F, 20 to 30 minutes depending upon the weight of your pot.

5. Stir in the vanilla. Beat the mixture with a wooden spoon or with an electric mixer until it has lost its shine. It will take about 5 minutes to get the fudge to be completely matte and creamy.

6. Spread the mixture in the prepared pan. Cool for at least 2 hours. When ready to cut the fudge into squares, lift the entire tray of fudge out of the pan using the tinfoil. This makes it easier to cut.

7. Store and serve at room temperature.

peanut butter chocolate bars

[MAKES 16 BARS]

Peanut butter and chocolate go together. They just do. It's a fact of life. As Kelli says, they're a "classic marriage of flavors." These no-bake peanut butter chocolate bars are like a homemade Reese's Peanut Butter Cup, but better.

Blondie Cookies (page 188)
1 cup + 2 tablespoons all-natural no-sugar-added peanut butter
1 cup + 2 tablespoons (2¼ sticks) salted butter, melted
2 cups confectioners' sugar
4 cups semisweet chocolate chips

1. Crush the blondie cookies using a food processor to make fine crumbs.
2. Mix together the cookie crumbs, 1 cup of the peanut butter, 1 cup of the melted butter, and the confectioners' sugar in a mixer until combined.
3. Press the mixture into a buttered 9 x 9-inch baking pan.
4. Melt the chocolate chips with the remaining 2 tablespoons peanut butter and the remaining 2 tablespoons butter in a small saucepan over very low heat, stirring constantly. Spread the chocolate mixture over the peanut butter layer. Refrigerate for 1 hour.
5. Cut the bars into squares and return to the refrigerator until serving.

magic bars

[MAKES 24 BARS]

These treats are known by many names—7-Layer Bars, Hello Dollies, Magic Bars. Our friend Jeff made them as a "cake" when he was on an expedition to climb Aconcagua, the highest peak in the Western hemisphere. He went around to the tent camps of other climbing teams, making friends with his Magic Bar offering. Our version is relatively simple, with chocolate and coconut. But you can jazz it up with as many toppings (such as chopped walnuts and butterscotch chips) as you'd like. Go ahead. Be crazy.

Blondie Cookies (page 188)
4 tablespoons (½ stick) salted butter
One 14-ounce can sweetened condensed milk
1½ cups chocolate chips
1 cup shredded, sweetened coconut

1. Preheat the oven to 350°F. Grease an 11 x 7-inch baking pan.

2. Crush the blondie cookies using a food processor (or a plastic zip-top bag and a rolling pin) to make fine crumbs. Stir in the butter to make wet crumbs.

3. Press the mixture into the bottom of the prepared pan. Pour the condensed milk over the pressed crust. Sprinkle the chocolate chips and coconut (or other toppings) on top.

4. Bake the bars for 30 minutes, or until golden brown at the edges. Let cool. Slice and serve.

DRINKS

red sangria

[MAKES 2 PITCHERS, 8 TO 10 SERVINGS]

Sangria, *which roughly translates as "bloody" (appetizing, isn't it?), is a wine punch popular in Spain and Portugal. Our version was inspired by Zafra, a Cuban restaurant in Hoboken, New Jersey. It's a BYO restaurant, so we'd stop at a nearby liquor store on our way to dinner, then hand over the bottle for the staff to work their magic. A pitcher of fresh sangria would be delivered to the table a few minutes later. We've had a lot of sangria since then, and we think ours is the best (better than Zafra's even!). The combination of flavors and fresh fruits is unmatched. If you like, refrigerate the pineapple cubes—they can almost serve as de facto ice cubes in the sangria.*

1 bottle (750 ml) red wine (merlot or rioja)
1/4 cup (2 ounces) brandy
1/4 cup Simple Syrup (see box, page 231)
Half 24-ounce jar mango in syrup, mango cubed and syrup reserved
1/2 fresh pineapple, peeled, cored, and cubed
1/2 orange, sliced
One 11.3-ounce can guava nectar
1/2 liter ginger ale
Ice

1. Mix the wine, brandy, and simple syrup together in a large punchbowl.
2. Add the mango and its syrup, the pineapple, orange slices, guava nectar, and ginger ale.
3. Add ice and serve.

ALL WINE IS naturally gluten-free (thank goodness). For this recipe, we recommend using either merlot, or rioja, a Spanish red wine. Our friend Ruben would always tell us: "Rioja is the best wine in the world!" It's pretty tasty, but Ruben is admittedly a heavily biased Spaniard who lives just outside of Barcelona. Most often, we'll use merlot, with spectacular results.

white sangria

Our friend Beth made this sangria when she hosted a get-together at her apartment in New York City. We'd never had a white sangria before, but we loved it, and came up with our own refreshing version.

1 bottle (750 ml) white wine (we recommend pinot grigio)
1/4 cup (2 ounces) peach schnapps
1/4 cup simple syrup (see box below)
2 peaches, peeled and sliced
1 Granny Smith apple, cored and sliced with skin on
1/2 liter ginger ale
Ice

1. Mix together the wine, schnapps, and simple syrup in a large punchbowl.
2. Add the peaches, apple, and ginger ale.
3. Add ice and serve.

To MAKE A simple syrup, heat equal parts sugar and water in a small saucepan on the stove, stirring until the sugar is fully dissolved. For example, 1/4 cup sugar plus 1/4 water will make nearly 1/2 cup simple syrup. We'll often make a large batch of syrup (more than we'll need for a given recipe), then measure off the appropriate amount and save the rest for later use.

lime rickey

[MAKES 1 PITCHER, 4 TO 6 HIGHBALL GLASSES]

Lime rickeys are a broad category of drinks—some alcoholic and some not—whose common denominator is lime juice. Our version uses gin, and it's a refreshing drink we associate with summertime.

2 cups (16 ounces) gin

1 cup freshly squeezed lime juice (about 5 limes)

1 cup Simple Syrup (see box, page 231)

2 liters seltzer water

Ice

Lime slices for garnish

1. Mix together the gin, lime juice, syrup, and seltzer in a large pitcher.

2. Serve over ice in highball glasses with slices of fresh lime.

mojito

[MAKES 4¹/₂ CUPS, 4 TO 6 SERVINGS]

A Mojito is a traditional Cuban drink comprised of five basic ingredients: rum, sugar, lime, mint, and carbonated water. Just the mere thought of a mojito makes us go "mmm." Pete's brother, Mike, makes a pretty mean mojito, as do our friends Jess and Andrew, who live in Longmont, Colorado. They have an abundance of mint growing in their yard—so much so that it often takes over the side of the driveway. Consequently, we'll spend many a summer evening enjoying mojitos at their house. Because really, what better way is there to use all that fresh mint?

1 cup freshly squeezed lime juice (about 5 limes)

1 cup + 1 tablespoon Simple Syrup (see box, page 231)

1¹/₂ cups (12 ounces) white rum

¹/₂ bunch fresh mint

1 cup seltzer water

Ice

Mint leaves and lime slices for garnish

1. Mix together the lime juice, 1 cup of the simple syrup, and the rum in a pitcher.

2. Muddle the mint in a mortar and pestle with the remaining 1 tablespoon simple syrup (when muddling, you simply want to bruise the mint leaves to release their oils). Add to the rum mixture.

3. Pour in the seltzer water.

4. Serve over ice and serve with a slice of lime and fresh mint leaves.

margarita

Margaritas are a classic drink made of tequila, triple sec, and lime juice (plus a little sugar for good measure). Often served alongside Mexican food, they may be the most popular tequila-based drink in the world. One of our local Mexican restaurants has a strict two-margarita per person limit, because the drinks are so stiff! This version, we think, has just the right balance of tequila, triple sec, and juice.

¾ cup (6 ounces) tequila
¾ cup freshly squeezed lime juice (from about 1 pound limes)
¾ cup Simple Syrup (see box, page 231)
⅓ cup (2⅔ ounces) triple sec
Ice
Salt, optional

1. Combine the tequila, lime juice, triple sec, and syrup in a pitcher.
2. For a margarita on the rocks, shake the margarita mix in a cocktail shaker, pour into a glass, and serve with ice.
3. For a frozen margarita, add the margarita mix to a blender, fill the blender with ice, and blend to the desired consistency.

4. For both versions, serve in margarita glasses, salt on the rim optional.

Variation

For an easy shortcut, you can substitute ¾ cup (6 ounces) frozen limeade mix for the fresh lime juice and simple syrup.

TEQUILA, WHICH IS made from the blue agave plant, is naturally gluten-free. And in general, all high-end, quality tequilas are gluten-free as a result. What's more, it's a distilled spirit, which would render it gluten-free anyway (for more info how distilling affects gluten in spirits, see the box on page 235). However, some low-end tequilas may have additives and colorings that are not gluten-free. Both the Jose Cuervo line of tequilas and the Sauza line (including Hornitos and Tres Generaciones) are gluten-free.

champagne citrus punch

[MAKES 6 CUPS, 6 TO 8 SERVINGS]

We like to host brunch for friends, and sometimes want to serve a drink in the spirit of, but different from, a mimosa. This champagne citrus punch is like a mimosa on steroids. Strictly speaking, we don't use champagne—we prefer cava, a Spanish sparkling white wine. But that's a minor technicality.

> 1 bottle (750 ml) sparkling wine
> 1 cup seltzer
> 2/3 cup orange juice
> 1/2 cup agave nectar
> 2 lemons, juiced
> 2 limes, juiced

Mix together all ingredients and serve chilled. For visual effect, you can garnish with sliced cross sections of oranges, lemons, and/or limes.

cupid's arrow

[MAKES 2 LARGE SERVINGS]

When we honeymooned in St. Lucia, the "official" drink of our trip was a local specialty called the Cupid's Arrow. We hadn't seen it ever before, and we haven't seen it since. An Internet search for "Cupid's Arrow" turns up about a dozen or more mixed drinks, none which even closely resemble the creamy, tropical delight we had in St. Lucia. Thankfully, the journal we kept while on the trip included a list of ingredients. From there, it was a matter of figuring out ratios until we had recreated the perfect Cupid's Arrow.

> 1/2 cup + 1 tablespoon whole milk
> 6 tablespoons (3 ounces) Amaretto di Saronno
> 3 tablespoons cream of coconut (not coconut milk)
> 1 teaspoon grenadine
> 1 1/2 trays ice cubes
> Nutmeg

1. Combine the milk, Amaretto, cream of coconut, grenadine, and ice in a blender and blend until smooth.
2. Pour into 2 large glasses. Sprinkle the top of each drink with ground nutmeg or freshly grated whole nutmeg.

Note: If you have a shot glass, you can use it to measure the ingredients. Since 3 tablespoons equals 1 shot (or 1.5 ounces), use 3 shots of milk, 2 shots of Amaretto, and 1 shot cream of coconut.

gin and tonic

Gin and tonic is one of Pete's favorite drinks, and just one example of many classic mixed drinks (such as the screwdriver, rum and Coke, and a very long list of others). We include it here as a representative example of gluten-free mixed drinks, not only because we love the drink but also for the sake of the information about distilled spirits in the box below.

Ice
1/4 cup (2 ounces) high-quality gin
Tonic water
1 lime wedge

1. Fill a highball glass with ice. Pour the gin over ice. Add tonic water to almost fill the glass.

2. Squeeze the lime wedge over the drink and drop the lime wedge in.

DISTILLED SPIRITS IS a class of alcohol that includes many of the harder liquors: vodka, gin, brandy, scotch, whiskey. When it comes to whether or not they contain gluten, the answer is usually "no," but sometimes is "it depends." Here's why: If the source grain for the alcohol is something like corn, potato or rice, then the source grain is gluten-free, and so the alcohol distilled from it should be, too. Even if the source grain contains gluten, such as wheat, that alcohol should, in theory, be gluten-free, too. That's because the process of distillation leaves the gluten behind (alcohol boils off first, becomes a gas, and is then condensed, while the gluten stays behind, resulting in a purified alcohol free of gluten). Even so, gluten sometimes does find its way into distilled spirits—either through cross-contamination in the facility, or via additives that are introduced to the alcohol after the distillation process, such as barley malt and certain flavorings or colorings. As for this gin and tonic, we recommend Tanqueray gin, which is gluten-free, though there are many other gluten-free gins out there.

piña colada

[MAKES 1 SERVING]

Piña coladas were our drink of choice during a trip to Curaçao, the "C" of the ABC islands of the Netherlands Antilles in the Caribbean. We explored the island from tip to tip, and from coast to coast, along the way sampling a wide variety of dishes, from grilled meats at roadside barbecue pits, to fresh seafood, to funchi, a local specialty served at a street market in Willemstad, Curaçao's capital city. Throughout it all, we washed the food down with piña coladas.

¼ cup (2 ounces) light rum
2 tablespoons (1 ounce) dark rum
¼ cup cream of coconut (not coconut milk)
Five 1-inch-plus cubes fresh pineapple
2 cups crushed ice

Combine all ingredients in a blender and blend until smooth.

Variation

If you don't have dark rum on hand, simply use 6 tablespoons (3 ounces, or 2 shots) of light rum.

juicy strawberry-banana smoothie

[MAKES 2 SERVINGS]

Full credit for this delicious smoothie belongs to our friend Greg. He and his wife, Emily, are part of our Monday night gang, a group of late-20 and early-30-somethings from our church, most of us married, many of us increasingly with kids, that gets together regularly. When Greg and Emily hosted recently, Greg dazzled us with his signature strawberry banana smoothies. Thankfully, he's shared his basic but excellent recipe with us, so that we in turn can share it with you.

1 banana, frozen
5 strawberries, frozen
1½ cups apple juice

Combine all the ingredients in a blender and blend until smooth. Add additional juice for a thinner smoothie.

Variation

Try substituting milk for the apple juice to create a creamy smoothie. Or try experimenting with other combinations of fresh and frozen fruit!

orange creamsicle smoothie

[MAKES 2 SERVINGS]

When a new Jamba Juice opened not far from our home, we couldn't help popping in for one of their straightforward, healthy, and often quite tasty, fresh fruit smoothies. We quickly became addicted, though, to one flavor in particular: the Orange Dream Machine. To us, it basically tasted like a blended orange Creamsicle, which is to say that it was awesome. Many people have concocted their own copycat versions of the Orange Dream Machine, and so have we. The only thing better than an Orange Dream Machine is an Orange Creamsicle Smoothie made at home.

1 scoop vanilla frozen yogurt or ice cream (pages 209–210)
1 generous scoop orange sherbet
$\frac{1}{2}$ cup milk
$\frac{1}{2}$ cup orange juice
$\frac{1}{2}$ tray ice

Combine all the ingredients in a blender and blend until smooth.

Variations

Add additional milk for a thinner smoothie. Add more orange sherbet to boost the balance of orange flavor, or more vanilla yogurt to boost the balance of cream flavor, to your liking.

limeade

[MAKES 1 SERVING]

There was once a time when we'd keep a few cans of frozen, concentrated drink mix in our freezer. More often than not, it was limeade. But we abandoned that practice long ago in favor of a refrigerator fruit bin full of limes. This from-scratch recipe makes for a much better limeade.

Ice
½ lime
Agave nectar
Seltzer water

1. Fill a highball glass halfway with ice. Squeeze the juice from the lime half into the glass. Add a good squeeze of agave nectar (a tablespoon or two).
2. Fill the glass up with seltzer water and stir. Add more agave if you would like a sweeter drink.

Variation

To make a pitcher of limeade all at once, juice 4 to 5 limes and add almost an equal volume of agave nectar. Fill the rest of the pitcher with seltzer water and ice, and stir.

AGAVE NECTAR COMES from a variety of agave species, including the agave salmiana plant, which grows wild and abundantly in the high desert of central Mexico, as well as the blue agave, which is also used to make tequila. Commercially, juice is expressed from the core of the agave (the piña), and that juice is then filtered and heated, converting the juice's carbohydrates into sugars. We use the Madhava brand of agave nectar, which follows a slightly different method of production: The agave nectar is harvested by local Mexican Indians on their own land, a nice, idealistic alternative to commercialized production, we think. The flower of the agave plant is removed, leaving a bowl-shaped cavity in the center of the live plant. That plant secretes its juice into the cavity, which is harvested up to twice a day for six to eight months. Once harvested, an enzyme is added to the juice, and excess water is evaporated, resulting in the same carbohydrate-to-sugar conversion as the heating method in commercialized production. Both methods of production are essentially parallel to the way maple sap is processed to make maple syrup.

APPENDIX

Product Recommendations— A Quick Reference Guide

This is a concise list of products we recommend or reference throughout the cookbook. Please note that this list only includes specialty gluten-free products, or ingredients whose gluten-free status may vary. As of this writing (July 2009), the following products are gluten-free and widely available in supermarkets nationally to the best of our knowledge. We use them ourselves regularly. However, product formulations or ingredients may change—always check labels to ensure that the product you're using is in fact gluten-free.

Almond extract: McCormick
Bacon: Hormel Black Label, Applegate Farms
Baking powder: Clabber Girl
Beer: Redbridge, Green's, Bard's, New Grist
Bread crumbs: Aleia's Gluten-Free Foods
Broth, chicken: Pacific Natural Foods
Cereal, crispy rice: Erewhon, Nature's Path Organics
Chili paste, ground fresh: Huy Fong Foods
Cookies: Mi-Del, Pamela's
Corn masa flour, instant: Maseca
Croutons: Aleia's Gluten-Free Foods
Curry paste, red: Thai Kitchen
Flours (sorghum, brown rice, etc.): Bob's Red Mill

Gin: Tanqueray
Ham: Boar's Head, Applegate Farms
Hot dogs: Applegate Farms, Coleman Natural
Hot sauce: Frank's RedHot Original
Molasses: Grandma's
Pasta: Tinkyáda Schar USA
Poppy seed filling: Solo
Rice noodles: A Taste of Thai
Soy sauce, tamari wheat-free: Eden Organic
Tequila: Jose Cuervo, Sauza
Vanilla extract: Rodelle
Yogurt, vanilla: Wallaby, Brown Cow, Stonyfield Farm, Fage

Note: If you have difficulty finding any of our product recommendations above, or are simply looking for alternatives, there are a number of resources you can look to. A basic Internet search for terms such as "gluten free store," "gluten free products list," and "gluten free grocery guide" will turn up numerous Web sites with gluten-free product listings. However, we especially recommend two printed guides to gluten-free supermarket shopping. One is Triumph Dining's *The Essential Gluten-Free Grocery Guide,* which includes over 30,000 products and is updated annually. The other is Cecelia's Marketplace's *Gluten-Free Grocery Shopping Guide,* which includes more than 25,000 products and is also updated annually. (For those readers with additional dietary restrictions, Cecelia's also offers additional grocery shopping guides that are gluten/casein-free, and gluten/casein/soy-free.

Gluten-Free Resources

GENERAL INFORMATION— ORGANIZATIONS, WEB SITES, AND SUPPORT GROUPS

The following organizations are excellent sources of further information about celiac disease, gluten intolerance, wheat allergy, the medical side of the gluten-free lifestyle, connecting with local support groups, and much more.

Celiac.com
www.celiac.com

Celiac Disease Awareness Campaign, National Institutes of Health
http://celiac.nih.gov

Celiac Disease Center, Columbia University
www.celiacdiseasecenter.org

Celiac Disease Foundation
www.celiac.org

Celiac Sprue Association
www.csaceliacs.org

Gluten-Free Living magazine
www.glutenfreeliving.com

Gluten-Free Restaurant Awareness Program
www.glutenfreerestaurants.org

Gluten Intolerance Group
www.gluten.net

Living Without magazine
www.livingwithout.com

National Foundation for Celiac Awareness
www.celiaccentral.org

Triumph Dining
www.triumphdining.com

CERTIFICATION AND LABELING STANDARDS

The following handful of Web sites offer great information about international and U.S. gluten-free labeling standards, as well as certification from the Gluten-Free Certification Organization.

Codex Alimentarius
www.codexalimentarius.net

Food Allergen Labeling and Consumer Protection Act of 2004, U.S. FDA
www.cfsan.fda.gov/~dms/alrgact.html

Gluten-Free Certification Organization
www.gfco.org

Q&A About the Proposed Gluten-Free Labeling Rule, U.S. FDA
tinyurl.com/nl2g7s

BLOGS

There are literally dozens of gluten-free blogs lurking out there on the Internet. We've selected a few of our favorites, the ones we read most often, to share with you. They're arranged alphabetically, so as not to give the impression of ranking one blog "higher" than another. They all contribute valuable perspective to living the gluten-free lifestyle!

Celiac Chicks
www.celiacchicks.com
Run by Kim and Kelly, two enthusiastic gluten-free women, with an emphasis on gluten-, corn-, and dairy-free recipes

Gluten-Free Easily
www.glutenfreeeasily.com
Run by Shirley, who leads a celiac/gluten intolerance support group in Virginia, with an emphasis on, you guessed it, living gluten-free easily

Gluten Free for Good
www.glutenfreeforgood.com
> Run by Melissa, a nutrition therapist with a degree in exercise science, with an emphasis on healthy living and the nutrition behind the diet

Gluten-Free Girl
http://glutenfreegirl.blogspot.com
> Run by Shauna, a writer, with an emphasis on memoir-style blog posts and recipes

Gluten Free Steve
http://glutenfreesteve.wordpress.com
> Run by Steve, who offers the rare male point of view in the world of gluten-free blogging, with an emphasis on living the gluten-free lifestyle

Hold the Gluten
http://holdthegluten.net
> Run by Maureen, a gluten-free mom, with a weekly podcast of wide-ranging gluten-free topics

Karina's Kitchen
http://glutenfreegoddess.blogspot.com
> Run by Karina, a visual artist with a flair for food photography, with an emphasis on seasonal, Mediterranean recipes

No Gluten, No Problem
http://noglutennoproblem.blogspot.com
> Run by us—Pete and Kelli—with an emphasis on recipes, product and restaurant reviews, travel, and the active gluten-free lifestyle

ACKNOWLEDGMENTS

AS WITH ANY book, *Artisanal Gluten-Free Cooking* was possible only because of the support of many people.

Our sincere thanks go out to our agent, Jenni Ferrari-Adler, for seeing the book's potential. And to our publisher, Matthew Lore, for believing in that potential, for helping us to refine and hone the book's concept, and for making the book a true collaboration between author and publisher.

Our deepest gratitude goes out to our Wednesday Night Dinner crew: Andrew and Jess, Josh and April, Chris and Laurel, Sara and Sam, and Jeff. The same gratitude also extends to our Monday Night Gang: Greg and Emily, Jess and Dave, Katie and Todd, Rob, and John. When hosting dinners, you eagerly and joyfully made those meals gluten-free to accommodate our needs. Thank you for welcoming us to the dinner table despite what must have been a steep learning curve for cooking gluten-free, and for not making us feel like dietary outcasts.

Thank you also to our family and friends: Kirk and Maury; Tom and Amy; Sarah and Jeff; Chris and Ilyse; Beth and Dave; Karla; Kim and Steve; Sandy; Karen and Peter; Scott and Sandy; Mike and Rebecca; Bob and Linda; Georgann; Connie and Mary; Joe Sr.; and Migdalia. You've been infinitely understanding and endlessly accommodating with our gluten-free dietary needs. You've offered loads of moral support and encouragement. And particularly as this book took shape, you tasted our recipes and offered feedback and constructive criticism when those recipes were in development, and you tested those recipes for us in different kitchens at different altitudes and in different climates.

We also want to say a big word of thanks to our community of fellow gluten-free bloggers, and especially: Steve at Gluten Free Steve, Melissa at Gluten Free for Good, Shirley at Gluten-Free Easily, and Maureen at Hold the Gluten. You constantly help to keep us humble and remind us that—as gluten-free bloggers, as cookbook authors, and as gluten-free foodies—we're part of something much bigger than ourselves . . . the gluten-free community and lifestyle.

And finally, our warmest thanks and deepest love go to our daughter, Marin. Though you'll be too young to even read these words when the book is published, we want you to know how much we appreciate your patience, flexibility, and joyous smile that lifted our spirits at all the right times. While we feverishly worked on recipe development and testing, and later, the manuscript itself, you entertained yourself on a play mat nearby, or sat happily cradled against Mom's chest in a carrier. Writing this book would not have been nearly the pleasure that it was if you weren't such an agreeable baby. Keep up the good work, thank you, and we love you!

INDEX

A

acorn squash, stuffed, 110
agave nectar, 238
ahi tuna, sesame-seared, 142
Aleia's Gluten-Free Foods, 57
almond cake, 212
Ancient Harvest quinoa, 79
angel food cake with strawberries, 200–201
appetizers and dips
  bacon-wrapped shrimp, 54
  bruschetta, 50
  caprese salad, 51
  chicken or beef sate with peanut dipping sauce, 58
  Chinese chicken-lettuce wraps, 62–63
  crab cakes, 52
  cucumber dip, 48
  fire-roasted corn salsa, 45
  guacamole, 47
  mango-pineapple salsa, 44
  mozzarella sticks, 56
  pigs in a blanket, 59
  red lentil dip with crudités, 49
  shrimp and vegetable tempura, 64–65
  shrimp cocktail with cocktail sauce, 55
  summer rolls with sweet and sour dipping sauce, 60–61
  tomato-cilantro salsa, fresh, 46
apple crisp, 217
apple pie with streusel topping, 194
apples, in stuffed squash, 110
apple salad and honey-mustard chicken, 76
applesauce, 98

artisanal cooking, definition of, 10
Asian-inspired cuisine
  beef or chicken sate with peanut dipping sauce, 58
  chicken pad Thai, 155
  Chinese chicken-lettuce wraps, 62–63
  coconut red curry stir-fry, 153
  honey-soy chicken with spicy sauce, 166
  noodle bowl, 130
  peanut sauce stir-fry, 154
  shrimp and vegetable tempura, 64–65
  summer rolls with sweet and sour dipping sauce, 60–61
asparagus, 92, 95
avocados, 47

B

bacon cider chicken, 165
bacon-wrapped shrimp, 54
balsamic vinegar, 81
banana nut muffins, 23
banana-strawberry smoothie, 236
barbecue pulled pork, 173
basil, in pesto pasta, 124
basil chiffonade, 119
basil pesto ravioli, 127
beef entrées
  garlic-lime skirt steak with Cuban mojo, 177
  New York strip steak, 180
  roast, for carbonnade, 179
  round roast, in chili, 116
  tenderloin with red wine reduction, 176
beef sate with peanut dipping sauce, 58

beer, gluten-free, 175, 179
beets, in Costa Rican slaw, 100
Belgium-inspired cuisine, 31, 189
bell peppers, stuffed, 111
biscuits, 30
black-eyed peas, 113
blenders, 12
blogs, 3, 240–41
blondie cookies, 188
blueberry muffins with streusel topping, 22
blueberry pie, 193
bourbon-pecan scones, 25
boy choy salad, 82
bratwurst, 175
bread, yeast, 26
bread crumbs, 57
breads
  cinnamon rolls, 36–37
  garlic naan, 29
  pigs in a blanket, 59
breads, quick
  biscuits, 30
  chocolate chip scones, 25
  corn bread, 28
  lemon poppy seed bread, 27
  muffins, 22–24
  pumpkin spice bread, 24
breakfasts
  Belgian waffles, 31
  chocolate chip scones, 25
  cinnamon rolls, 36–37
  crepes, 33
  French toast, 34
  French toast casserole, 35
  fruit salad with yogurt sauce, 38
  lemon poppy seed bread, 27
  muffins, 22–24

ABOUT THE AUTHORS

*H*USBAND AND WIFE team Kelli and Peter Bronski are also the coauthors of *Artisanal Gluten-Free Cupcakes* (The Experiment, 2011) and the cofounders of the acclaimed blog No Gluten, No Problem (http://noglutennoproblem.blogspot .com). *Easy Eats: The Magazine for Gluten-Free Living* named it one of the top three gluten-free blogs in a survey of more than 75 prominent gluten-free websites, and *The Kitchn* included it in a list of "10 Inspiring Blogs for Gluten-Free Food & Cooking," noting the couple's "thorough and lucid writing."

Kelli is a food and hospitality industry veteran, having graduated from Cornell University's prestigious School of Hotel Administration. She previously worked at the Waldorf-Astoria Hotel in New York City and spent nearly a decade with Hilton, where she earned their Circle of Excellence honor. Her passion for cooking and baking dates back to the early days of her childhood spent in the kitchen with her grandmother.

Pete is an award-winning writer (http://www.peter bronski.com) whose work has appeared in more than 75 magazines and other publications. He is the author of three books in addition to the couple's cookbooks. He has received a number of writing awards, including a first prize from the North American Travel Journalists Association and a gold prize from the Solas Awards for Best Travel Writing. Pete is a spokesperson for the National Foundation for Celiac Awareness.

Pete and Kelli (http://www.artisanglutenfree.com) have been gluten-free since January 2007, when Pete was diagnosed with celiac disease. (Their two young daughters also have suspected gluten sensitivities.) Together, Pete and Kelli have taught gluten-free cooking at venues such as Whole Foods and the Gluten-Free Culinary Summit. They have been featured in publications such as the *Daily Camera* and *Edible Front Range* magazine, appeared on Denver's NBC television affiliate, and been interviewed on National Public Radio's *The Splendid Table*.

The Bronskis live in New York's Hudson Valley with their daughters, Marin and Charlotte.